# WINNING FIXES

## EVERYTHING

# WINNING FIXES EVERYTHING

## HOW BASEBALL'S BRIGHTEST MINDS CREATED SPORTS' BIGGEST MESS

---

## EVAN DRELLICH

**HARPER**

*An Imprint of HarperCollinsPublishers*

HarperCollins books may be purchased for educational, business, or sales promotional use. For information, please email the Special Markets Department at SP-sales@harpercollins.com.

FIRST EDITION

Library of Congress Cataloging-in-Publication Data has been applied for.

ISBN 978-0-06-304904-8

23 24 25 26 27 LBC 5 4 3 2 1

FOR LINDA, MARY, AND STEVE

"What then is your responsibility?"

"To create conditions. To make happen what happens. I ain't in the
anthropomorphic business."

"Whatever business you in, where is your pity?"

"This ain't my commodity."

"IDIOTS FIRST," BERNARD MALAMUD

# CONTENTS

# INTRODUCTION

THERE WAS PROBABLY A BETTER USE OF MY TIME THAN TRUDGING UP AND down the long stairs of the converted schoolhouse I lived in for yet another cigarette in the Boston cold, but I needed to escape somewhere. It was February 2019, and I had just been fired. My reporting future was uncertain, my bank account was dwindling, and I was gaining weight rapidly. Every day, I was left to wonder whether I'd passed on the biggest story of my life.

A few months earlier, in October 2018, I was a Red Sox beat writer. In the penultimate round of the Major League Baseball postseason, the Sox were coincidentally playing the Houston Astros, a team I had once covered. The Astros at this point were the defending World Series champions, after winning the first title in franchise history in 2017.

There was one massive problem, I learned during that 2018 postseason. Sitting in a hotel room within walking distance of the Astros' stadium, I spoke with people who had firsthand knowledge of how the Astros had cheated in that championship season. These were not sources on the outside pointing fingers, but people who knew—who had lived it.

I learned how the Astros used a camera in center field to zoom in on the signs the catcher flashed the pitcher before the pitch. How the Astros had set up a television monitor near their dugout, where the players sit during games, to be able to see that video feed, and how they brazenly banged on a garbage can with a baseball bat and other devices to communicate what they gleaned from that screen. It was an advantage, many players felt, to know what was coming, be it a straight fastball or a bending curveball. And to use technology to gain that knowledge was beyond the pale.

This wasn't just one player breaking the rules, either. This was a World Series–winning team that had collectively cheated, and the public didn't know it.

I was floored. It was a massive story, the kind, frankly, many reporters dream of, and some might even dread. I was confident in everything I had at the outset—indeed, it all proved to be true. But to get a story done, I would need further corroboration.

One Astros source warned of the context of cheating in the sport, an encouragement that in hindsight could have both been earnest, but also self-serving, meant to deflect attention away from what the Astros had done. Nonetheless, I wanted to learn for myself and include it in my reporting—in what environment did this behavior arise?

During batting practice before one of the Red Sox–Astros playoff games at Houston's Minute Maid Park in 2018, Houston's general manager, Jeff Luhnow, stood near the top step of the Astros dugout. He was the architect of the team, and I tried to get his attention as he was walking away from me. "You won't find anything," he said defensively, making clear he wouldn't talk to me.

Luhnow quickly disappeared down the dugout steps into the tunnel, walking, ironically, right into the area where I had just learned the team had conducted its cheating.

On the night the Red Sox won that series in Houston, eliminating the Astros, I shot my television spots on the dimly lit, empty field. The Astros' dugout, on the first-base side, was a short distance away. Down a few steps to the tunnel I went, to a short but wide corridor that leads to the locker room. I wanted to check out the scene of the prior year's crime for myself.

There was the garbage can, near to the wall on my right, and an empty space with wires hanging nearby indicated where a TV had once been—exactly as the setup had been described to me. I took a few photos, hoping someday one would accompany a story.

The Red Sox had moved on to the World Series, where they faced the Los Angeles Dodgers. I met with a pair of MLB officials at Dodger Stadium, trying to understand what MLB was undertaking to combat electronic sign-stealing. I told them I had multiple accounts of the Astros stealing signs via electronic means in the prior year.

"I think that every club is always suspicious, but again—" one official said.

I cut the official off: "This is from within the Astros."

"Within the Astros, they're acknowledging that they've done this?" one shot back, surprised.

Yes.

"They have acknowledged that?" one said. "I mean, I can't speak to that. I mean, to our knowledge—you have your information, and we have ours, and that's all we can go off. As to whether that has occurred, to our knowledge we are completely unaware. I am confident in the measures that we've taken."

I was curious how seriously the league would treat the matter and was told it would ultimately be up to Commissioner Rob Manfred. I wasn't contacting the league attempting to steer its own investigative work, to be a friendly tipster. Rather, were MLB looking deeper into the Astros' cheating, and I could ascertain as much, then I might have an entrée to a story sooner rather than later.

It was one of a handful of brief communications I had in 2018 with baseball's central office over what I understood had happened.

"If you can tell your sources that they should—if they want to speak to the commissioners' office, we're all ears," a different official told me once the World Series ended. "The problem is, nobody talks to us."

Of course, no such redirection would take place. It's not a reporter's job to steer sources to the league. But it was clear to me the league was not of a mind to act.

As the offseason began, I was leery of publishing what I had learned about the Astros to that point. For one, none of my sources were on the record, and if the story was going to be based solely on unnamed sources, I wanted more than I had at the time. I also knew that finding someone to go on the record about cheating might be impossible, but I still wanted to see if that person was out there.

I also considered how the story would be received, and, frankly, whether it would be believed. I was no longer in Houston, but covering a rival team in Boston. The Astros, I knew well, were aggressive with the media, and I suspected they would do everything in their power to attack me and my reporting.

During my time covering the Astros, from late 2013 into 2016, they were a controversial franchise. I reported on questions about their management culture and decision-making with the support of my newspaper, the *Houston Chronicle*, which was the only outlet in the city that covered the team on the road and was not also owned by the team.

The Astros had tried to bully me into submission. In 2015, the owner of the team and the head spokesperson attempted to remove me from the beat in a meeting with a pair of *Chronicle* editors simply because they didn't like my coverage. Thankfully, my editors stood by me.

Now, the truth is the truth, and years later, I wasn't going to back away from reporting on the Astros' cheating for fear of reception—not alone. But there was one other major wrinkle. I didn't think the outlet I was working for at the time was equipped to support this reporting.

This was not a major newspaper with the backbone and support staff for a major investigation. I was working for a TV station whose primary reason for existence was televising Boston Celtics basketball games and reacting to sports-talk radio.

I took the conservative route, and really, the only route I could: to keep reporting. I wrote a general piece on electronic sign-stealing in November 2018.

Very quickly, my doubts about the support I had at NBC Sports Boston proved correct. When they fired me in February 2019, I was blindsided, but perhaps I shouldn't have been.

Days passed slowly with some part-time work on the radio in Boston, talking to fans after games: "Six-one-seven, seven-seven-nine, seven-ninety-three-seven, taking your calls up until midnight on your home for Red Sox baseball. Chris in Natick, what's up, Chris?"

Eventually, The Athletic, now owned by the *New York Times*, brought me on. In my new role, I would be working closely with the best baseball writer in the world, Ken Rosenthal. He's recognizable by the bow ties he wears for charity during Fox national telecasts, including the World Series.

Together, we would pick up my reporting on the Astros.

O

This is a book about what happens when business leaders decide that the bottom-line result is all that matters, in a setting many MBAs only dream to occupy. About what happens when a baseball team believes that no matter how great a mess it creates, a championship parade can erase all sins.

The Astros were an experiment. Playing in a stadium that once bore Enron's name, the team was built around innovation, on outsmarting the competition. When a wheeling-and-dealing billionaire with a checkered history in his outside logistics businesses, Jim Crane, bought the team in 2011 and installed an ex–McKinsey consultant, Jeff Luhnow, as general manager, the messaging around the Astros was that they were going to be a franchise built the right way—with patience and discipline and an adherence to a still-nascent area in the sport, analytics.

The last decade was a period of rapid change in Houston and the sport overall. But Houston's transformation was not a well-thought-out program of change management. The substance of the Astros' pursuits, the core calculations as to what could sustain a winning team, were almost always sound. Yet the implementation, the ability to win hearts and minds, lacked to the point that it amounted, at times, to blatant disregard.

To make changes, the Astros were convinced, feelings would be hurt; people would be unhappy. What great empire was built otherwise? So long as the team eventually won, then everything would be fine. Everything would be fixed.

"Perception will change when we succeed," Luhnow told me in 2014 when I was reporting on the Astros' industry reputation. "When we win a division, all that perception will turn from negative to positive.

That's how it works. You think if Oakland didn't have success—how many people hated Moneyball, the idea of Moneyball? But Oakland has proven over and over again how successful they are, by being creative, by being innovative. So they're heroes."

The Astros were right to believe they had to push. But they didn't know which boundaries amounted to a bridge too far, and their culture suffered for it. Steadily, and in different ways, the Astros were blowing through stop signs, or running right past accidents that should have led them to erect some. Not even winning the 2017 World Series was enough to protect the team when the world learned what they had done along the way.

We'll look closely at how Luhnow built his career, and how Luhnow and Crane built a franchise. We'll see them reach the height of on-field success and enough falls and hubris to stock a Shakespearean tragedy.

Through these stories, I want to explore two ideas.

First, that all players and fans want, and should want, is the champagne spray of postseason wins. There has been a simple formula in sports narratives for ages: win, and they'll write glowing things about you. Change the game, take the glory. And the full-steam-ahead worship of innovation in the sport that arose almost two decades ago, when *Moneyball* was published, set up a carrot so big for these aspiring executives—and writers who wanted to be the next Michael Lewis—that you can hardly blame the participants for their rush to the top.

This book does not find that analytics are bad, or its practitioners dim-witted. It highlights the many questions too few people were asking in the throes of massive change. What attention should be paid to not just the result, but the means? To the impact on key stakeholders, like the fans and the players themselves, or even the average workers who make average salaries in the industry, like scouts and coaches and back-office staff?

Indeed, change came with an ugly side, and often came without full context in the press. What was sold as good for baseball teams—tanking, finding cheap players—really was good for owners' pockets above all else.

The second issue runs parallel: How did one of the great scandals in baseball history develop? How did we arrive at a cheating scheme that was still creating jeers and back-page stories years after the fact?

Electronic sign-stealing, the undertaking that ultimately brought down Luhnow's Astros, rose in baseball through negligence—not just that of Houston management, but baseball's central office. But to understand how the Astros operated in the years prior to and during electronic sign-stealing leaves no surprise that the Astros would push too far, that they would be the ones to cross the line, and dramatically so.

In 2014, I wrote a piece for the *Houston Chronicle* that was the first to prominently shine light on concerns industry stakeholders had about how the Astros were operating. "Radical Methods Paint Astros as 'Outcast'" was the headline.

A couple of years later, I wrote a piece for Baseball Prospectus that was perhaps even more prescient.

"The Astros haven't been shown to have broken a rule," I wrote in 2016. "Yet how they have maneuvered and molded draft plans to the collective bargaining agreement is fodder for sports management courses. How should major league teams—big businesses acting as public trusts—morally operate? And even in situations absent any moral question, where do baseball's rules prove the most opportunistic or weakest? Where does shrewdness cross over into impropriety?"

That piece, published more than a year before the Astros' tainted championship season, ended with a prediction.

"But where the Astros have operated and at times succeeded is the grey realm inside the framework of those rules—one where few precedents exist. . . . What we can say, with assurance, is that the Astros alone did not make the rules. They may singularly make us rethink some."

When Jeff Luhnow was winning, it was easy for some to jump to the conclusion he was doing everything right. When he was fired, it was easy to dismiss him and everything he built as the result of foul play. The reality is much more complicated.

What follows is baseball without the varnish, without the myth-spinning and mystique hucksters. It is the cruel, number-crunching, dollar-focused, sometimes amusing, and oft-maddening reality of how really smart and successful people run a ball club. It's what happens when corporate America meets America's pastime.

# 1

# A MONEYBALL MAN

ROBERT HOLLOWAY WENT TO OAKLAND COLISEUM EXPECTING "A CULTURAL experience," which meant the vile stadium food wasn't strictly a disappointment. A sarcastic Brit, Holloway didn't know baseball, and didn't particularly care to. Really, he was only at the ballpark because it was where his colleague Jeff Luhnow wanted to be.

Holloway was the CEO of a Bay Area start-up called Archetype Solutions during the first dot-com boom, and Luhnow, his chief operating officer, was baseball obsessed. They shared an office together at the venture capital–backed operation's first office, "a shitty little space," Holloway said, before they moved to an old converted brick bakery in Emeryville, California. The Coliseum was a stone's throw away.

The mission at Archetype Solutions was to design better-fitting clothes using algorithms, and right as the year 2000 began, Holloway had come across Luhnow through a network of elite business connections. Luhnow became "the boffin behind the scenes," as Holloway put it, noting the very British expression.

"The professor, the expert," Holloway said. "And I was the flimflam at the front. That's one of the reasons we worked so well, is we were so different."

A former management consultant, Luhnow was introverted and quiet, but carried a conventionally glamorous resume: an MBA from

Northwestern University, plus dual undergraduate degrees from the University of Pennsylvania, in economics and engineering. At the turn of the century, then, Luhnow had the credentials to do most anything he wanted, except for what he wanted to do most. So he spent his free time in a fantasy world instead.

Luhnow wasn't just an avid follower of Major League Baseball. He was, from a great, fictional distance, managing his own team. He was playing fantasy baseball, a budding national phenomenon in the US, and one that had engulfed him since his days at Penn. "I mean, literally, he was obsessed with it," Holloway said. "It's all he fucking did was just fantasy baseball. Was that online? I can't remember."

Many variants have sprung up, but the core concepts remain unchanged: participants draft players, and the fantasy participant's fortunes depend on how those players perform in the real world.

At its inception in the 1980s, fantasy baseball was called "Rotisserie baseball," named after a French restaurant in New York where a group of friends started the craze. Back then, fantasy baseball was a labor of pen and paper and newspaper box scores. A league's members would tally up the results themselves. But the dot-com boom made the game more readily available as major companies like Yahoo and CBS caught on. The competition moved just a few dial-up modem tones away, and computers took over the tabulation of results.

One of Luhnow's closest friends at Archetype Solutions, Steve Campo, was his fellow enthusiast. They not only roomed together at Penn, but also worked together at a previous job, a different start-up, and they were always talking about their fantasy teams.

Luhnow even tried to explain how fantasy baseball worked to Holloway, who, years later, thought the term was "fancy" baseball.

"It was over my head because, one, I didn't know the sport," Holloway said. "Although basically my understanding of it was that he and thousands of other people all had teams that they built up and they got points for the performance of those teams. And they competed against each other, and so they were the team managers. And Jeff always used to say that he had more data, and more knowledge and more facts, than anyone else, and he was really good at it."

Plenty of children have grown up dreaming they can swing a baseball bat like Mickey Mantle, or throw a fastball like Bob Gibson. Some, too, have always fallen in love with the idea of running a team, of becoming the general manager who handles all the baseball decisions: the trades, the signings. But fantasy baseball made the dream of being a baseball executive more accessible. It allowed people to believe, and in the most narrow of ways, even demonstrate, that they could manage a roster. Friends and colleagues playing fantasy, as it's called for short, were all trying to show off their decision-making prowess, to prove just how much more they understood about the sport than the next schmo.

Naturally, new dreams were stoked. Armchair general managers everywhere thought to themselves something like, I bet I actually could do this, if I could ever get a shot. Most, of course, would never have the skills to do the real thing, because baseball GMs do much more than just build a roster. Real-life executives oversee large operations, and scores of people. But Luhnow had a different background than most. He had the training—a management consultant's commitment to the numbers and research—to make him, at the very least, an exceptionally strong pretend GM.

"It seemed to me a somewhat odd thing to do, but you know, whatever floats your boat," Holloway said. "He was very starstruck with baseball. He was so into all the stats and the numbers. And that was his gig. That's why he liked that company, he was perfect for our company: essentially we were an algorithmic, stat-driven operation that could work out the shape of your body."

O

Nerdy, with glasses and a duck-footed stance, Luhnow isn't imposing. He was raised in a posh neighborhood in Mexico City, the son of a travel-guide writer whose work was distributed in hotels across the country. He played some baseball as a youth in Mexico, and left for California in the 1980s to finish high school. His fifteenth birthday was in 1981, the year that produced "Fernandomania," when Fernando Valenzuela, a sterling young Mexican pitcher on the Los Angeles Dodgers, stormed the league and produced a national rooting interest for Luhnow's home country.

At Penn, Luhnow wound up writing to Dodgers owner Peter O'Malley, but never heard back. As an industry, baseball didn't value his credentials, not yet. The most coveted front-office jobs—designing the roster, evaluating players, discussing trades—were reserved for "baseball people," usually those who had themselves played the game at a high level. Luhnow could have gotten *some* job in the sport early in adulthood, but likely one that would have left him on the business side to analyze the sales of tickets and hot dogs.

Luhnow, though, had long believed in checking under every rock. "I grew up a son of an entrepreneur, grandson of an entrepreneur, and I remember thinking in high school, Gosh, all the good ideas are taken," Luhnow said. "There's no way to make money anymore by being an entrepreneur. Because everything that is profitable has probably already been thought of. And yet, we have an example of Uber, very successful organization—like, why didn't we think of that, right? It's such a simple idea having everybody that's in their cars sort of provide rides to other people and charging for it and making it easier. There are always frontiers. We may think that there aren't, but there are, and it's just a matter of finding it."

In 2003, a former player and an author changed everything. Billy Beane, a hot prospect who fizzled out before becoming the real GM of the real Oakland Athletics, was the star of a new book by Michael Lewis. Their collaboration blew the door to the sport wide open for brainy fantasy mavens everywhere, for people just like Luhnow. "There was a book that had come out that Jeff was infatuated with," Holloway said. "I remember that. What the hell was it called?"

*Moneyball.*

○

Luhnow spent much of the 1990s as a McKinsey & Company consultant in deployment from their Chicago office, serving as a generalist across various industries: oil and gas, financial services, retail, consumer package goods. Retail, though, had become his specialty, as well as hospitality.

For top business school students who want to go into management consulting, applying for a job at McKinsey is a little like applying for college. The other places you're looking at could teach you just as well, and the work might be similar, but slapping Harvard or Stanford on a resume nets the extra glance, and only the best need apply. The same is true for McKinsey, the ultimate brand name in consulting. The company could be called the McDonald's of the industry for its ubiquity and power, although the firm's rates are hardly reminiscent of fast-food pricing.

Two other firms are considered peers: Boston Consulting Group and Bain & Company, which along with McKinsey are colloquially known as "the Big Three," or "MBB." Smaller firms exist, but the Big Three boast the largest and most prominent clientele. In 2021, McKinsey's website cited thirty thousand employees, spanning more than sixty-five countries.

McKinsey also bathes in controversy, and increasingly so. The firm rose to prominence in the 1960s, its work deeply tied into the evolution of major corporations, and by extension, the overall economy. In 1970, the economist Milton Friedman posited that a business's duty was to increase profits above all, that its obligation was to the shareholder. That ethos gave "the newly ambitious management consultants a guiding purpose," wrote Daniel Markovits, a Yale law professor, for the *Atlantic*. "During the 1970s, and accelerating into the '80s and '90s, the upgraded management consultants pursued this duty by expressly and relentlessly taking aim at the middle managers who had dominated mid-century firms, and whose wages weighed down the bottom line. . . . The downsizing peaked during the extraordinary economic boom of the 1990s."

The headline for Markovits's story, which ran in 2020, was "How McKinsey Destroyed the Middle Class." Reporters for the *New York Times*, Walt Bogdanich and Michael Forsythe, wrote a 2018 piece with a similarly striking title: "How McKinsey Has Helped Raise the Stature of Authoritarian Governments." The investigation cited McKinsey's work rehabilitating the image of Ukrainian president Viktor Yanukovych, who has since been found guilty of treason, as well as other unsavory McKinsey engagements in countries like China and Saudi Arabia.

"The firm produced a report tracking how some of Saudi Arabia's most important policies were viewed by the public, singling out three individuals who drove often negative conversations on Twitter," the *Times* reported. "One was later arrested, according to a human rights group." Saudi Arabia is such a large client for the firm that McKinsey participated in a major investment conference there in 2018, even after others pulled out following the slaying of *Washington Post* columnist Jamal Khashoggi the same year.

The *Times* too reported on McKinsey's involvement in the marketing of a drug at the center of the opioid crisis, OxyContin, made by Purdue Pharma. In 2017, McKinsey suggested Purdue could give "distributors a rebate for every OxyContin overdose attributable to pills they sold," according to the *Times*. McKinsey agreed to a $573 million settlement over that engagement, and the firm's top partner, Kevin Sneader, personally apologized.

The name McKinsey still carries major clout inside the business world, even as onlookers, and some reformed insiders, malign it. But its reputation has also taken a hit: Sneader was voted out in 2021.

Certainly back in the 1990s, at the time when Luhnow was a young professional, McKinsey was an unquestioned destination for those who prized the doors it opens, and its handsome salaries.

Consulting firms have all sorts of specialized teams, but they typically train employees to have a religious devotion to numbers. Opinions have to be backed up by data, not merely belief. Consultants are taught to drill a layer deeper, to peel back the proverbial onion and focus on how the laws of economics are behaving in a particular situation. If one department in a company is losing money, the goal would be to determine root causes.

At McKinsey in May 1999, Luhnow held the title of associate principal and was inside the window to be made partner when he left for his first entrepreneurial adventure. "He was with a company called Pet foods dot com, or Pets dot com, I can't remember what it was called now," Holloway said. "They were delivering dog food. I always thought, That's a strange business model, but, whatever. That business was cratering, and timing was good."

Luhnow's company was Petstore.com, which was later acquired by Pets.com, and the eventual failure of the businesses is considered one of the most memorable flops of the dot-com bubble. (They were going to fail with or without Luhnow, though.)

Just like his eventual introduction to Holloway, Luhnow's arrival at Petstore.com had been owed to his gilded circle. When starting Archetype Solutions, Holloway, in fact, had spoken to two Luhnows: Jeff and his older brother, Chris. Chris Luhnow had been a management consultant, too, at Boston Consulting Group.

At the behest of a venture capital firm, one of Chris's former colleagues at BCG started the pet supply company in the 1990s and invited Chris to join him there. Jeff came over, too, and headed up marketing.

Petstore.com went from zero to seventy people in maybe three months. When a human resources employee was hired, a bit late, one of their first tasks was to walk around with a clipboard and ask everyone what exactly their job was.

The company was spending an awful lot of money to try to acquire customers, placing Luhnow in charge of a sizable budget. One Petstore .com colleague said Luhnow was successful in his role, recalling a deal with Yahoo worth a couple of million bucks. "Jeff was a very smart guy," they said. "And we were all kind of inventing it as we went along. He was quite inventive and hardworking, all that stuff. On the spectrum, he was more kind of self-interested than group-interested. But not to an uncharacteristically high degree in the context of the time."

In November 1999, just a few months before Luhnow left for Archetype, Petstore.com announced its first national advertising campaign, with a new website and six TV commercials, as well as radio and magazine ads, at a cost of more than $15 million. "We focus on the emotional attachment between people and animals in both our ads and on our site because we truly understand pet owners and their needs," read the lead quote in the press release, from the vice president of customer service, Jeff Luhnow. "We are pet lovers ourselves so we know the deep bond that exists between pets and people. We also know the importance of getting the right information and advice from people who are experts in animal care and behavior."

Once Luhnow jumped ship for Archetype, Holloway and he formed a classic CEO-COO duo. Holloway handled the sales and legal and marketing, while Luhnow ran the operations, strategic analysis, and product development. The staff grew to about thirty and the business took off, with clients that included JCPenney, Sears, and QVC. "We were so far ahead," Holloway said, in no small part because of the intellectual property, the analytics, that were manufactured at Luhnow's direction.

Archetype developed algorithms that could forecast one's body shape to produce a unique cloth pattern, and make a product that, allegedly, would fit perfectly. A 2001 story in the *Capital Times* of Madison, Wisconsin, cited Lands' End as the first company to use Archetype's tools on a wide scale. Customers were asked fifteen questions to produce the right cut. The cost for pants: $54 and a shipping time of two to three weeks.

Pushback was inherent to the business. Established retail behemoths were not easily convinced they should behave differently, so client meetings required great answers for skeptics in senior management. Holloway was the lead figure externally, and although he said Luhnow too handled external meetings well, Luhnow's work was more internally focused. "The area that he probably most needed to develop—I had no doubts that he would—was his ability to deal outside the organization versus inside," Holloway said. "But that's just an experience thing, that's all."

On the Myers-Briggs personality scale, Holloway wagered, Luhnow would come down as an ISTJ: introverted, sensing, thinking, and judging. A logistician.

O

That book Luhnow couldn't stop talking about in his time at Archetype, *Moneyball*, told the story of the 2002 Oakland Athletics, or the A's for short.

The A's were a smaller-market team that had become successful even though they didn't spend on top players like the deep-pocketed New York Yankees. Author Michael Lewis largely explained why and how. Oakland had found an edge under the guidance of Billy Beane, a former player who eschewed traditional baseball thinking and searched for inefficiencies. He paid attention to the work of baseball outsiders like Bill James, the godfather of the advanced numbers in the sport, known as Sabermetrics, or colloquially these days, analytics. Going back to the 1970s, James had championed oppositional views grounded in math, and his work had long deserved wider attention beyond the cult following he had developed.

Even once *Moneyball* had fully pushed James into the spotlight, blowback for his thinking was common. "The baseball community was not ready to hear what I was saying, and everything I wrote, somebody would pick it up and ask three or four players what they thought about it and they'd find a player who thought I was full of shit," James said in an interview. "Everything I wrote would be immediately confronted by this professional expertise." He dealt, he said, "with that kind of artificial blowback for forty-five years."

Beane, like James, realized that batting average, the classic statistic that measures how frequently a player gets a hit, was not as useful as on-base percentage. OBP measures a combination of how often a player gets a hit, like batting average did, with how often a player draws a walk, which has the same result as a base hit: the hitter takes first base, and does not make an out. Walks in the sport, and players who drew them, were drastically undervalued. The numbers the baseball establishment had long relied on really did not come close to fully capturing a player's contribution.

The A's also began to approach their amateur draft differently, selecting more college players, who statistics showed were safer bets to excel once they made their way through baseball's winding minor leagues up to the sport's highest level, the majors. Young players are particularly valuable in baseball, because they have to spend six seasons in the majors before reaching free agency. Until that point, a team can retain them without having to ward off other bidders, although salaries start to increase usually after a player's third year. A sport that had long valued grizzled veterans and star power was undervaluing its youth and their inherently low salaries.

*Moneyball*'s impact was profound, both for fans and decision makers in the sport. Nothing is more appealing to owners than winning and doing so at a discount, and *Moneyball* provided the blueprint: act differently, use better evaluative tools, and challenge convention. A crossover hit outside of baseball as well, Beane's approach altered the flow of human capital into the game. Players who previously would have been appealing to GMs were less so, and others were newly coveted.

The same was true in front offices: the book changed whom owners and GMs sought to hire to manage clubs.

The tale carved out a path for a new swath of off-field talent, and endangered those who were already in place, people who, in nearly all cases, had dedicated their professional lives to the sport, and in some cases, had come to rest too comfortably on their laurels.

Opportunity in baseball is still limited in profound ways. Both the sport's owners and the executives they hire have always been predominantly white and male, a trend the sport's owners still have not fully reckoned with or sufficiently moved to fix.

Those who would ride the *Moneyball* wave into the game would face a problem: What if you changed the system and lost? This kind of disruption doesn't always breed second chances.

Luhnow's ex-wife bought him *Moneyball* in June 2003, for his birthday. "I was interested, but that was about it," Luhnow told the author Howard Megdal in the book *The Cardinals Way*. Luhnow was perhaps downplaying *Moneyball*'s impact on his own plans.

"Jeff was infatuated with it," Holloway said, "and he wanted to take it to the next step."

"The minute 'Moneyball' came out, he read it and immediately was talking to me about, 'This is perfect—this is what I need to do,'" Steve Campo, Luhnow's fantasy-baseball-playing buddy at Petstore.com and Archetype, told the *New York Times*.

Suddenly, Luhnow's McKinsey connections were worth something in baseball.

A former colleague at the firm had married the daughter of St. Louis Cardinals owner Bill DeWitt Jr., and in the summer of 2003, the owner's son-in-law told Luhnow that DeWitt wanted to speak with him. DeWitt was looking for someone with Luhnow's skill set, a Moneyball type. He wasn't set on someone with a management consultant background necessarily, DeWitt said, but he considered that a plus.

At McKinsey, Luhnow had worked for a long time with a large casino company, and his understanding of odds and probabilities was something he leveraged in his interview. An offer to join the Cardinals followed, the fantasy a new reality.

"You can talk people out of things, but for Jeff, the opportunity to get involved with a major baseball team, or whatever your league is called," Holloway quipped, "it just was so perfect for him. He said, 'What do you think?' And I said, 'You should fucking do it.'"

# 2

# THE CARDINALS YEARS

EVERY YEAR, THE BASEBALL INDUSTRY CONVERGES IN DECEMBER FOR ITS winter meetings. General managers host player agents and rival executives in suites while reporters chase rumors at the hotel bar, and in a week's time, a major convention passes. Player moves, the trades and signings, can be fast and furious. That was particularly true two decades ago, when in-person meetings had not yet been supplanted by texting.

John Mozeliak, today the Cardinals' president of baseball operations—a rank that some organizations use for their top official rather than general manager—was already in St. Louis in 2003, rising through the ranks. At the meetings in New Orleans, the Cardinals were developing a trade for a pitcher who would become a staple of theirs, Adam Wainwright of the Atlanta Braves. Newly hired Jeff Luhnow was on hand, working in the suite with the team's other execs.

Luhnow had arrived on the inside, and yet, he hadn't. "He wasn't in sort of that normal inclusion of the baseball group," Mozeliak said. "And I remember kind of like feeling bad for him, so I would hang out with him at night when we were just sitting in the suite. And you know, we'd both be basically staring at our laptops and our Excel files and trying to work on things to sort of help make the right decisions. But when I think back to those times, it was just someone, like, trying to find his footing in this game."

Above all, Cardinals owner Bill DeWitt Jr. brought in Luhnow as an agent of change. But the sport looked nothing like a start-up or the high-octane smarts of McKinsey, the circles he well knew. Innovation was not endemic to baseball, certainly not at a fast pace. And the breadth of backgrounds, ages, and lifestyles of its workers was also much wider than what Luhnow was used to, even when accounting for the variety of industries he interacted with as a consultant. The players sometimes turn pro as teenagers, and the coaches might be near retirement age.

"I think that was part of Jeff's problems when he got in here: he understood more of the corporate mantra of how you run a business, and some of that is helpful to create innovation and modernization of a company," Mozeliak said. "But some of it can also be a bit frustrating to employees that aren't used to that."

Across the industry, a groundswell of opposition to people like Luhnow had been building, spurred on by *Moneyball*. The book highlighted a rift in the sport, the divide between the old school and the burgeoning new, between scouting and statistics.

For all of time, teams had found the best baseball players by reviewing common statistics and watching players, live and in person. Each club employs a small army of scouts, evaluators who travel across the country and abroad to pick out players. They judge bat speed and fielding ability and make projections based on intuition and experience, on comparisons to the memory of thousands of other ballplayers they've seen. Anyone could recognize it's good when a minor league player is hitting .350. But traditionally, it had taken a scout to know which players were feasting on bad pitching, and which could make the adjustments to thrive at the next level. They're searching for gold, and their roles have long been woven into the romanticism of the sport: the scout, chomping on a cigar, who ventures miles off the beaten path to find the superstar no one else had unearthed.

Scouting, too, was a track that had produced many of the sport's executives. Some decision makers had dabbled in advanced numbers before, but after *Moneyball*, the mandate was newly explicit: the book was an existential warning to much of the old guard, and that made Luhnow persona non grata.

Walt Jocketty was the big cheese in St. Louis in 2003, the Cardinals'

GM. Coincidentally, he was on the road with the Cardinals in Houston on the day he got a call from DeWitt telling him of Luhnow's arrival. "I didn't know him," Jocketty said. "I knew he had no baseball background. He was running that company, online company of some sort. So anyhow, the first time we met, he just told me that he wasn't after my job, he was just there to help us make better decisions—and da, da, da."

Under Jocketty, the Cardinals were not in a state of disrepair, at least not one that was easily understood. They perennially packed the stands as one of baseball's oldest, most prized franchises. Then and now, the Cards have more World Series titles than all but one team, the New York Yankees. They took a middling third-place finish in 2003, but had been to the playoffs the three previous seasons, twice making it to the penultimate round. Albert Pujols, one of the greatest hitters ever, was still young, in his third season.

But as an investor in his outside life, DeWitt had trained his focus over the horizon. Once the current group of players had moved on, he didn't want to be left holding the bag. DeWitt gave Luhnow the title of vice president of baseball development, charging him with modernization and improving the Cardinals' decision-making ability, mainly in two ways: to better evaluate major league players so the Cardinals could compensate them appropriately, and to be a force in the amateur draft.

"The challenge at the time was to change the organizational culture, and it wasn't easy, particularly with the on-field success we were having," DeWitt said in Megdal's *The Cardinals Way*, and confirmed again in a 2021 interview. "It was easy for those who disagreed with the approach to be critical, and this worked its way into the media. There was never any question in my mind, however, that this was the correct path for the Cardinals, and I was prepared to live with the results despite the disruption and scrutiny."

Disruption and scrutiny followed, indeed.

"There was pushback, there was resentment, there was sabotage, there was one person that refused to talk to him," a Cardinals colleague remembered. But what, that executive asked, would one think would happen? The owner had just given large responsibilities to someone whom his son-in-law had worked with, someone who had no playing or front-office experience.

DeWitt had done something very unusual by the industry's norms: he had given Luhnow the title of vice president straightaway, despite his inexperience. Along with Luhnow's title, too, came a particular privilege: he had the owner's ear, just as a McKinsey consultant would have a direct line to a client's top executive.

Normally in baseball organizations, the GM or president—the occupant of Jocketty's role—is the point person for ownership, the vessel through whom all decisions flow. "I took offense to it at first," Jocketty said. "I just felt like he was reporting to DeWitt and was telling him a lot of things that I wasn't privy to, and it was a bad, bad relationship."

Luhnow got to work, and to peers, his intelligence and ambition were immediately detectible. He didn't walk in and flag down team vice presidents to demand changes, partly because his relationship with Jocketty was so poor from the get-go. But Luhnow "had access to Bill, and that was probably enough for him to just keep charging and implementing," a colleague remembered.

The draft was to be Luhnow's centerpiece, and because of the politics inside the organization, it was all he could really touch. The first one he contributed to was a notorious dud. In 2004, the Cardinals, for the first time, would try to emulate the A's, incorporating numbers and analytics more heavily into their selection process. Mozeliak technically ran the draft, reprising an old role until the franchise had full confidence to turn it over to Luhnow. But the numbers the Cardinals were relying on at that time were rather shallow. College players were considered a safer bet, as *Moneyball* and the A's had shown, but the Cardinals' draft skewed too far in that direction.

The fruits of drafts are never fully understood right away, because players usually take a few years to scale the minor leagues. But at the most important level, the major leagues, the Cardinals were highly successful in 2004, winning 105 games in the regular season, an abnormally high number. They made the World Series, only to be swept in four games by the darlings of the sport, the Boston Red Sox, who won their first championship in eighty-six years with a young Moneyball-savvy GM, Theo Epstein.

That first draft hadn't helped Luhnow's cachet, but he plowed forward. He revived the Cardinals' international scouting efforts, taking it on himself as a Spanish-speaker from Mexico to reestablish the team's presence in Latin America. No one else was going to do it, so Luhnow seized the opportunity and added another title: international director. The 2005 draft was more successful, too.

Come 2006, the Cardinals were on top of the sport, winning the World Series over the Detroit Tigers. The championship was a surprise, because the Cards weren't a juggernaut prior to the playoffs. But the relationship Luhnow held with Jocketty, with field manager Tony La Russa, and another executive, farm director Bruce Manno, was festering, and allegiances had been pledged.

Among the tales told: Luhnow would say good morning to someone who was not a fan of his, and that person would walk right past him like they were in grade school. One Cardinals executive had a title that would typically have landed him his own office, but he was in a cubicle instead. The executive had given up that office because he didn't want to share a wall with Luhnow.

"Yeah, there were silos," remembered a colleague. "There were cliques, there were people who had been there a long time generally, or looked at the world a certain way, and they tended to move in hoops together."

To DeWitt, one of Luhnow's strengths was his ability to identify what changes to actually pursue. But no matter how much confidence Luhnow had that his new approaches were correct, trial and error was involved, experimentation. Failures and false starts were expected, and failure encouraged sniping. Luhnow, for example, made tweaks to the way scouts went about watching young players, only to later abandon some.

"I tried a couple of new configurations how to align the scouts; some of them made sense and worked and got results, and we implemented them further, others didn't," Luhnow said. "One year, I had a guy just dedicated to high school players and one guy just dedicated to college players. They were called a high school and college specialist. We realized after a year of trying it and getting people's feedback and seeing the results that it wasn't an optimal system; there was a better way to go so we abandoned it. I'm not afraid to abandon something if it doesn't look like it's the right idea. I'm not afraid to change something if it's not producing results."

Inside and outside the Cardinals, they began to call him "Harry Potter" or "the accountant." Some derision was inevitable. But it's possible that a different approach, be it from DeWitt, Jocketty, or Luhnow himself, could have tempered the acrimony.

"He'd agree with certain things I'd say, but I knew in the background that he was thinking something else and doing other things," Jocketty said of Luhnow. "He was doing things behind my back, which I found out later. It was not a healthy environment. And I think he had a lot of people upset at him."

Tact was not Luhnow's strong suit. But even if it had been, tact can only go so far when the mission is to tell members of the establishment how wrong they are.

In his first spring training with the team, Luhnow held a meeting with La Russa, pitching coach Dave Duncan, and Jocketty. Luhnow tried to tell La Russa how to use his bullpen and build his roster, "and it didn't go over well at all," Jocketty said.

DeWitt met with Luhnow often and the owner told Luhnow he didn't need to try to deal with the major league staff, because they didn't value the work he was doing. Luhnow was firm, however, that he was going to give the staff the information that was good for them, even if they didn't realize it.

The power struggle between Jocketty and Luhnow was clearly favoring one person: the owner's handpicked man. In 2005, Luhnow was given full control of the draft. A year later, DeWitt bestowed more responsibility: Luhnow was now the VP overseeing both amateur scouting and player development. He was now guiding both the acquisition of the players and their grooming as minor leaguers, and made changes to the farm system that "were contrary to what we had done in the past as far as the traditional player development," Jocketty said.

In a sense, that was the point.

"You got to remember the St. Louis Cardinals were one of the best organizations at developing players over the years," Jocketty said. "And we had a program in place that was very successful over the years and I think they still follow that pretty much today. So he came up with some different ideas. I really don't remember all of it. Off-the-wall kind of stuff, and guys just kind of scratched their head. It was a tough environment for quite a while."

It was an unsustainable environment, too, and by 2007, Luhnow had won. DeWitt fired Jocketty and replaced him as GM with Mozeliak.

After the fact, Jocketty partially pointed the finger at himself. He realized he missed the boat in a new age, and that if he wanted to keep working in the sport, he'd have to adapt to the new wave of baseball thinking, the brand Luhnow stood for, more than he had. He landed with the Cincinnati Reds in an advisory role. "It took me a while to come around to it, but it was probably too late," Jocketty said. If he could do it again, Jocketty said, he would have been more cooperative, "at least willing to learn more about the analytics and how they were using them and how they were applying them, try to figure out a way that we could work together on it."

Nonetheless, Jocketty resented Luhnow's approach, and so too did others. For a month, in October 2007, Mozeliak was technically interim GM before DeWitt handed him the reins full-time. One day in that window, Mozeliak asked Luhnow to stay out of the office. Another high-ranking Cardinals executive allegedly had threatened to kick Luhnow's ass if he showed his face at the office.

Luhnow's reputation had already reached the media, but after Jocketty's firing, Luhnow was in damage-control mode. "I didn't want to be involved in this to the extent that I have," Luhnow told the *St. Louis Post-Dispatch*'s Derrick Goold. "I feel like for whatever reason I have become a lightning rod for it in the last week. . . . I have picked up a few labels over the years. I hope that I shed a few of them in the next few years."

Neither Luhnow nor Jocketty ever stood a chance to emerge cleanly. A Cardinals contemporary noted that DeWitt has since said all the right things, that he knew disruption was on the way, yet the process the owner put into place had been half-baked. Was this an organization that had planned for and prepared its people for change?

Jocketty wasn't sure just how much DeWitt knew of the troubles. He remembered DeWitt describing "a tenor" in the organization of people not getting along. "He was blaming me for it," Jocketty claimed. "I think Jeff was the one who caused all this. Because a lot of people were very loyal to me over the years and still are today."

Although regretful, Jocketty made no bones about how Luhnow's maneuvering registered. "I'm gonna get my ass up on it," because "anybody would, if you're supposed to be the man in charge and you got a subordinate that's going behind your back."

DeWitt said the intent was, actually, for Luhnow to be positioned under Jocketty.

"Everyone knew that I believed it to be a position of high priority," DeWitt said. "It was clear that Walt didn't value the position the same as I did; as a result, Jeff communicated more with me. . . . I was totally committed to the project, and wanted feedback on a continuing basis."

Change management, the design and method of enacting change, is so complicated and difficult that a field of study is dedicated to it. In 1995, Harvard professor John Kotter wrote a paper for *Harvard Business Review*, "Leading Change: Why Transformation Efforts Fail," which listed eight common errors.

"Making change in even relatively small organizations that have been around for a while is no small challenge," Kotter said in an interview. The model of large organizations in many industries, be it higher education or newspapers or pharmaceutical companies, was a function of the late nineteenth century, of the industrial revolution. Businesses were built for efficiency and reliability. "They were not designed to be agile, flexible," Kotter said. "And once they'd been around for a while, organizations develop cultures, and cultures are even a bigger anchor often on change. And when it happens these days, it is because people literally start a movement. It's not a small group of the smartest guys in the room over there calculating, and then giving out instructions."

The prevailing philosophies, then, did not recommend bringing in one outsider to work his magic, sitting back, and watching the fireworks. "It's coming up with something that can win over hearts and minds to a diverse crowd of people who somehow have a stake in whatever the venture is," Kotter said. "And you get enough people who want to help out and not want to resist and who want to lose the local knowledge that they have as a result of where they sit, so to speak. With a little bit of time of trying things in a new way and getting better results, then more people try things in a new way. You get better results; you get new mindsets and new habits and a whole new way of doing things."

Asked in 2021 if he had considered change management best practices, or had been familiar with them, DeWitt said he had not.

A lasting lesson for Luhnow, though, was that he needed more like-minded thinkers alongside him.

○

Sig Mejdal will occasionally remind you how poor an idea it is to drive while tired, that fatigue can disorient someone just as drunk driving can. His last job before joining the Cardinals, at NASA, was examining how much wakefulness debilitated humans, and how much sleep enabled them to recover. Understanding rest was an exercise in math, and for Mejdal, an exciting problem to attack. He studied engineering as an undergrad, and had a master's in cognitive psychology and operations research—the study of mathematical models under the constraints of the real world. He had worked at Lockheed Martin, too.

In short, Mejdal is brilliant, and from ten thousand feet, was an analogue to Luhnow as an outsider. Prior to *Moneyball*, Mejdal didn't have the imagination to believe he could work in the sport. Once it was released, he tried to claw his way into baseball, without the benefit of a gilded circle to propel him.

Mejdal was doing baseball research on the side and had an understanding of how human beings react to change, which is to say, poorly. He, like Luhnow, had some professional experience with casinos, but in a very different role. Mejdal had worked as a blackjack dealer, and liked to dip back into that world when socializing his ideas. "Intellectually, you know that hitting a sixteen when the dealer has a seven up is a proper action," Mejdal said, "but that doesn't mean that it feels right. If I have a large wager on the line, it feels even less right, and my stomach tells me that very clearly.

"In my experience, change in any industry is difficult. Supporting a change that doesn't feel right is extraordinarily difficult. The things that persons with my background have to add are almost without exception changes that don't feel right. If they felt right, they would have already been done."

Mejdal didn't know Luhnow existed, but one of Mejdal's emails to the Cardinals eventually made its way to Luhnow's inbox. They met at the 2004 winter meetings, and Luhnow wanted Jocketty and Mozeliak to meet Mejdal as well. Mejdal switched his flight to a connection through St. Louis, purposely missed the second leg, and landed a job, at first temporary.

Mejdal was a scientist, but more outgoing than Luhnow, more innately personable. A 2010 story in the *Post-Dispatch* noted that Mejdal had, somehow, been to eighty-three weddings.

With Mejdal as his right-hand man on board in 2005, Luhnow didn't have a particularly large audience inside the Cardinals, but the duo's greatest opportunity was the area they had the most control over, the draft. "Jeff was relentless in his effort to identify everything he could find in the public domain, no matter how far-fetched it might sound," DeWitt said.

Like every team, the Cardinals were in the prediction business, yet they didn't have their own statistics database, nor someone who had college-level statistics skills to mine it. Mejdal was not a computer scientist by trade, but at that point, the work was rather rudimentary. He started to build a draft model that would project future player performance, which at that time was simply looking at college performance and combining it with scouting information.

Mejdal was the evangelist, water-torturing Luhnow every year to move faster. But they felt they had to baby-step—even if others didn't see the restraint they thought they were displaying.

Mozeliak's promotion to GM had settled the major drama in the Cardinals front office. Luhnow had greater access to the rest of the organization, and Mozeliak was more clearly in charge. "Jeff maintained his line to me, but less frequently," DeWitt said. "There was clearly a lot less tension up and down the organization." Mozeliak was a moderate, much more supportive of Luhnow and Mejdal than Jocketty, yet not nearly as aggressive as the new duo felt he should have been, as they wanted to be themselves. "My relationship with Jeff was, I thought, pretty healthy during those times," Mozeliak said.

Luhnow's ambition had been obvious from the time he arrived in St. Louis. He hadn't punted his old career, nor built such a resume, just to arrive in baseball and peter out. Luhnow had a connection to the McCourts, then owners of the Dodgers (and a different owner than the one he wrote to years before), and Luhnow quietly expressed hopes to a friend that he might be able to land in Los Angeles. Either way, he wanted to ascend, and he often rubbed people the wrong way.

As a manager, Luhnow drew positive reviews for giving his people room to spread their wings. "For all of the drama he was in the middle of, he was great about giving opportunities for people to experience and learn new parts of the game," one report said. Luhnow was also perfectly capable of throwing on the charm when he wanted to. Yet he was in some ways too hands-off and could be a challenge to track down. One Cardinals subordinate used to send him emails that eventually said simply: "I am going to do the following unless you stop me."

Those whom Luhnow did not believe in saw a very different side of him. Luhnow arranged for some reassigned employees to receive a copy of the 1998 book *Who Moved My Cheese?: An Amazing Way to Deal with Change in Your Work and in Your Life*, a business fable about mice and humans in a maze, searching for cheese that keeps on moving. For those who cannot find the cheese, death awaits. It's unclear how many people at the Cardinals actually read it, but it's doubtful many were thrilled by the gift.

Multiple Cardinals colleagues noted how Luhnow approached the media in those days, how he often appeared in various publications and was seemingly always down on the field when a national sportswriter was in town. "A total self-promoter," a fellow Cards executive said. "If he could find someone that's going to write something flattering about him, he's in. And if it wasn't, he'll dodge you like a truck."

As he had done at McKinsey and at the start-ups, Luhnow was keen to tap outside expertise. In St. Louis, he brought in a cartoonist who had done work for the *New Yorker*, Mike Witte, as a pitching consultant. Witte, on the side, had studied pitching mechanics through video. Lo and behold, in 2005, Luhnow showed up in the *New Yorker*, which rarely covers sports. "Jeff Luhnow, the Cardinals' vice president of player procurement, admits that Witte at first seemed to have 'very little credibility,' but he nevertheless put him on the payroll. . . ."

Witte turned Luhnow on to a pitching coach whom Luhnow hired to work in the minor leagues, Brent Strom. A former major leaguer, Strom, too, had great ideas, but unsurprisingly, others could find them annoying. But Cardinals colleagues had some admiration for Luhnow's marketing sense, for his ability to sell ideas internally or to the media. It's easy to imagine that some who looked at Luhnow skeptically in St. Louis were simply jealous.

Although intelligent, Luhnow and Mejdal were still really green about the sport they were changing. Mejdal visited a psychology lab at Washington University in St. Louis around 2006. He was looking for students to help out with projects, and he connected with a minor league player, Garrett Broshuis, who was working at the university in the offseason. Mejdal and Broshuis went to Cardinals games together, sitting in the same area as the scouts who happened to be in town for that day's game.

"I was literally like teaching him the ins and outs of the game," said Broshuis, who has since become a lawyer and a leading advocate for minor league baseball players' rights. "Because he knew all the numbers stuff. But he couldn't approach one of their scouts, or one of their people to ask more basic questions, for the sake of embarrassment I guess, and he truly wanted to learn more. We'd sit down, and he'd just pick my brain on everything that was going on." Pitchers throw a variety of different pitches besides their fastball, and Mejdal wanted to know how to visually identify a changeup in real time: a pitch that's meant to look like a fastball but moves more slowly, fooling a hitter. The kind of question most scouts sitting around him would have laughed at.

For the draft, Luhnow himself went out on the scouting circuit and quite enjoyed it. When he got control of the farm system in 2006, he spent a lot of money to fly staffers to various fun parts of Latin America and do a lot of drinking. As farm director, Luhnow now would determine when a player moved between the team's minor league affiliates, each considered to have its own difficulty level.

Typically, players move between levels when their performance dictates it, because the goal of the minors is the development of big leaguers. Yet they crown champions in the minor leagues, too, and some coworkers believed Luhnow was overly concerned with designing minor league rosters around team success. That he was acting in self-interest: winning in the minors was good for players to experience, but it also would add a particular shine to Luhnow's work. Managing up was a forte: Luhnow knew what would be pleasing to clients, how to make himself glisten.

"He was very much from the mindset [that] if you can measure it, you can prove you're having success for that," Mozeliak said. "In any sport, what's the easiest way to measure, to keep score? Win or lose. And so even though when you think about what's the optimal player development model, it's creating major league players that are contributing to your big league club, then you're winning—but for him, there was a desire to have success in the win-loss column at the minor league level. I mean, I'll confirm that. I am one of those kind of people that absolutely, I do subscribe to that to some level. Because I don't think you can lose, lose, lose and then all of a sudden think, I can just turn on the winning mindset. I do think creating a winning environment in your player development system does have value."

In all facets, the more that could be quantified, the better for Luhnow. He was concerned with return on investment in every operational activity: putting a number on everything and everybody and cutting out whatever didn't add value relative to its cost. One of the statistics the Cardinals developed was present value, or PV.

The idea "was to put a single value on every single person and make sure that we were investing resources in the most valuable assets," a colleague said. "The analytics to some extent gave him cover, and even at times when he didn't understand what a number meant, he'd still at the end of the day go and say, well, 'This is how much this player was valued, this is how much this player was valued, here's a hard concrete number for you to look at, and this is why I made that decision.' It gives you a certain amount of cover. Just like scouts overvalue radar gun readings, and it's for the same reason because it's concrete, indisputable: 'I held up my radar gun. I saw ninety-six. You can't argue with me about that.'"

One of the better draft picks the Cardinals made under Luhnow was Matt Carpenter, a first baseman in the thirteenth round in 2009. As it was then, today it's cliché for teams to say that they always take "the best pick available," regardless of other factors. But at the time the Cardinals took him, Luhnow's focus was on the build of a particular farm team.

"He was like, 'This team has no offense,'" one colleague remembered. So he directed Mejdal to find a bat, which was "a weird way to draft, and those kinds of decisions were made all the time. And they often worked out very poorly. And in this one case, it worked out exceptionally well."

Carpenter was turning twenty-four in the winter after the draft, older than most college peers, which meant his prospect value just wasn't great. But for helping out a minor league team right away, the Cardinals were bullish. When Carpenter became a mainstay in the majors, their draft model had worked—even if the thinking on draft day had been different.

(Defying the "best available" mandate was not unheard-of, either. Teams usually make sure they draft enough players at a given position to fill out a roster, for example.)

Luhnow's work on the farm system was more contentious, and the pushback was growing. He introduced a new way of deploying pitchers that ruffled some feathers, using starting pitchers differently than they were used to: two to a game, in a piggyback or tandem, such that one of them in any given game was, in effect, a relief pitcher.

In 2010, Mozeliak took the farm system away from Luhnow, leaving him with the draft as his sole focus. Luhnow was spread thin, and most teams divvy up the roles he held. "It's a very difficult job to be a scouting director and a farm director simultaneously," Mozeliak said. "Being on parallel paths is just difficult. So as we were obviously having a lot of success in the draft, I felt like we needed to make sure we were putting a lot of emphasis on how we thought about development. And I just didn't think he had enough bandwidth to do both."

Mozeliak's motivation wasn't only that practicality, however. He wanted someone running the farm who was more intimate with the actual field of play and preparation. "I felt like we needed to put an emphasis back on making sure that we were properly training them."

Luhnow was still an integral figure, but losing the farm system was, at the least, a partial rebuke. "Certainly, I don't think Jeff was, like, ecstatic to have his sort of span of control reduced," one colleague remembered. "But I kind of always felt like he loved the draft, he liked scouting, he was out seeing players. He loved that and was still doing it, and we were expanding little by little our analytical footprint beyond just the amateur scouting into other areas of the organization."

Luhnow's welcome hadn't fully worn out in St. Louis, but he and Mejdal still wouldn't be able to move full throttle, not without more control. "Jeff had ascended as far as he was going to get," a colleague said.

○

In 2011, the Cardinals won the World Series again, their second championship in six seasons. Luhnow and Mejdal were seeing massive returns in the draft. "We had something that retrospectively, if you had applied this method to past drafts, you would have doubled your output," a Cardinals exec said.

To Mozeliak, Luhnow's greatest achievement in St. Louis was modernizing the team's player evaluation systems. Through all the acrimony, Luhnow had transformed the way the Cardinals front office handled its main function.

Luhnow was never exactly a made man, though. The *Post-Dispatch* noted the Cardinals had seen more drafted players reach the majors from 2005 to 2011 than any other team. More were on the way. And yet, that was "not a stat that tells the whole story of the Cardinals draft," wrote the beat writer, Goold. "Quantity should not be a mask for quality. The Cardinals, through the years, have developed a reputation in the industry for drafting safely and drafting predictable players."

Even a progressive member of the Cardinals organization, one whom Luhnow had hired, thought the approach had been skewed a little too far toward analytics. Luhnow did more than change the Cardinals' draft, of course, and he had help along the way.

Naturally, pioneers and visionaries always receive the bulk of the credit, but building an entire database of baseball information—"Red Bird Dog," the Cardinals called theirs—and developing proprietary models was not a one- or two-man act.

Jeremy Cohen, Chris Correa, Mike Girsch, and Dan Kantrovitz were all instrumental in Luhnow's time. All were bright, and Correa, Mozeliak said, "understood the game as well as anybody I've ever been around for not playing it."

"He had the ability to walk in and talk to people in uniform as he would have talking to a bunch of people in suits," Mozeliak said. "He just had incredible skill to do that. And was just extremely patient with anyone he was dealing with, and that's saying a lot because this was a very sophisticated thinker."

Luhnow and Mejdal deserved the spotlight, but also to an extent sought it. "Jeff and Sig don't mind people thinking that they do everything," a Cardinals colleague said. "Sig's built a brand about as well as anybody in baseball I've ever met, for a guy who's never run a team. He's done a very good job of that. First of all, he's just a personable, outgoing guy. But also, I think he's actually aware that he's trying to build a brand."

Their brands were thriving, too. When the Cardinals won the World Series, the new owner of the Houston Astros, Jim Crane, a Missouri native, was looking for a GM.

A billionaire through logistics, Crane had received permission to interview the GM of the small-market Tampa Bay Rays, Andrew Friedman. A Houston native, Friedman already had built strong teams with a very low payroll. But Crane couldn't woo him away, and Friedman later took a job with one of the game's jewel franchises, the Dodgers, instead.

So Crane, a businessman who had never owned a baseball team before but had dabbled in minor league hockey ownership, turned to the unproven commodity: the boffin behind the scenes.

Nearly a decade after an awkward first winter meetings with the Cardinals, at the 2011 convention, it wouldn't matter whether Luhnow's peers wanted to include him. He was named GM of the Astros while the meetings were under way, and it would be up to everyone else to adapt to him, not vice versa.

"We compared him with a lot of candidates and he came out on top in every area," Crane told the *Houston Chronicle*. "His previous business skills and his people skills and the way he goes about everything."

DeWitt said he wasn't surprised Luhnow got the offer from Crane. But some with the Cardinals were skeptical as to how it would play out, citing the lack of trust Luhnow engendered in St. Louis. "He was just a guy that never quite fit in," one colleague said. "I think those types of guys make tricky leaders."

Everyone started to scatter for Christmas. Inside the Cardinals front office, Mejdal was presumed to be following Luhnow out the door, but hadn't technically left just yet. Some colleagues were concerned, at the time, about what else could leave with them. After all, St. Louis's analytics department, and the intellectual property it developed, had started with Luhnow and Mejdal.

"We know that Sig's probably going to leave, but he hasn't left. We also know that Sig has tons of information on his laptop that we consider proprietary to us and access to other information," one Cardinals executive said. "So there was the awkward sort of what do we do here, how do we handle this?"

Baseball was behind in all sorts of best practices, and that included safeguarding IP and technology. Some members of the Cardinals front office were said to have shared passwords among each other, with functionally shared accounts.

One of the younger whiz kids, Chris Correa, was particularly concerned.

"Not everything was housed on a server," Mozeliak said. "And so there was a lot of information floating in different places. So, of course, there was some concern. But the bottom line is, I don't know exactly what happened."

# 3

# BLOOD IN THE HALLWAYS

TYPICALLY, A GENERAL MANAGER WALKING INTO A NEW JOB WOULD HAVE A handful of restrictions beyond the most obvious items, like the budget. In an early meeting between the first-time GM and the first-time owner, Jeff Luhnow asked Jim Crane directly, "What are my constraints?"

"You can't do this, you can't do that, you can't keep those people," was the message Luhnow expected to hear.

The owner had a curious response. He gave Luhnow a piece of paper with nothing on it. The implication: it's your oyster.

"That paper is still blank. I still have it," Luhnow said years later. "That was his way of saying we really do want to do this the best way possible: start with a clean sheet of paper."

Luhnow felt he did "better in an environment where I'm being guided by certain principles, and I can share that." Where he "can try and make sure the decisions we make are consistent with our goals and our principles."

To that end, Luhnow had prepared a twenty-five-page proposal for Crane, a general-strategy plan that covered every functional area in baseball operations. The franchise was turning sixty in 2012, and Houston had never won a World Series. Crane and Luhnow wanted not only a winner, but a sustained one, built the right way from the bottom up.

Even though he was no stranger to the business world, Luhnow wanted a second set of eyes on his plan before showing it to Crane. Luhnow's soon-to-be father-in-law, venture capitalist Kip Hagopian, had read a lot of investment plans and told Luhnow to tighten it up. Hagopian was quite successful, with early investments in Apple, and had served on Ronald Reagan's "Commission on Industrial Competitiveness." (More recently, Hagopian authored a paper, "The Inequity of the Progressive Income Tax," which began with an example of a fictionalized character, Harry, who was being disproportionately taxed "simply because his family works harder than the families of the society's other members.")

Luhnow knocked the draft down two pages, to twenty-three. He wouldn't show the plan to anyone else besides Crane for the next five years, if not longer. "Someday when I'm out of the industry I'll probably share it," he came to believe.

The plan didn't predict an exact timeline, but there were "several mentions of five years to playoff competitiveness." That was the mindset, the time frame in which Luhnow planned to turn the team around.

Unlike in St. Louis, Luhnow now had an audience, and control of the entire baseball operation. The Cardinals experience had validated Luhnow's thinking and shown that change was both possible and worthwhile. But Luhnow, too, knew how different the Astros plan would be compared to what the sport had seen, how much more boldly he wanted to move. He knew, as well, how disliked he was in some corners, and that his Astros plan wouldn't exactly make him newly beloved. Not right away, at least.

Early on, Luhnow gave different friends in the sport variants of the same message: when it ends in Houston, it won't end well. "He was aware his reputation in the industry wasn't great, and that Crane had given him an opportunity," a friend said. "And his sort of attitude was, I understand that if this doesn't work, I'm not going to get another shot at it. You can go through the list of GMs who failed one place and got another opportunity somewhere else, or who failed in one place and became another special assistant to the GM for another twenty years. Jeff understood, or his self-assessment was, that's not how this is going to go for me. It's either going to go really well, or I'm going to go become a professor or whatever the next stage of my life is.

"And this is what he told me: Given that, I'm doing it my way. Like, why would I not? What do I care what people think? Like, I know that there's no job at MLB Network, there's no special assistant to the GM coming after this. I'm going to do it my way."

○

The Astros hadn't made the playoffs since the 2005 World Series, when they were swept by the Chicago White Sox. Attendance cracked three million fans the following year but had declined every year since. The farm system was not deep, the roster was expensive, and their analytical capability was subpar. Most important to ownership: the team was losing money on an operational basis. Tens of millions, one person with knowledge of the books said.

An Ernst & Young audit of the Astros for 2010, submitted in court proceedings, showed about $165 million in revenues, excluding a major transaction with their regional sports network. Expenses were about $177 million, for a loss of about $12 million. But people in the industry point out that operational costs, and even the audits, do not capture the full financial picture tied to ownership. (For one, they don't consider growth in franchise value.)

The team was in the black in prior years. Per a prospectus prepared by Allen & Company in October 2010, which was also submitted in court, the team's EBITDA (earnings before interest, taxes, depreciation, and amortization) had been $5.6 million in 2009, $23.7 million in 2008, and $37.3 million in 2007.

In sports, rebuilds are usually publicly framed around the players: out with the old and in with the new. But in Houston, the entire organization was subject to change. Crane wanted to clean house. An executive at the league office who talked to Crane at the time described the process as going "in with a sickle," whacking people left and right.

George Postolos, the former CEO of the NBA team in town, the Rockets, had helped Crane buy the Astros and was named team president. A lawyer and a Harvard man, Postolos was nerdy and a different breed than Crane himself—not too unlike Luhnow, in that sense—and the kind the bottom-line-driven Crane could find use for.

Postolos's predecessor, Tal Smith, had been a fixture with the team. Minute Maid Park had an oddity on its playing field, an incline in center field where a flagpole jutted out. The steep climb and the pole both could wreak havoc on the rare occasion that a hitter drove the ball to the right spot, more than four hundred feet away. They named the incline "Tal's Hill." A few years into Crane's tenure, he would remove it.

Postolos led the more imminent demolition project and quickly became regarded as the Astros' angel of death. "It was blood in the hallways," said Enos Cabell, who played more than one thousand games for the Astros between the 1970s and '80s, and whom Crane retained as a special assistant. "Because they got rid of practically everybody, and that was Postolos. He came in, and he changed a lot of stuff, especially in the offices. So people that had been there for twenty, thirty years, they were let go."

Crane and Postolos had a simple outlook: They were running a business that was losing money. Therefore, the time to make changes was now. Everyone knew the Astros were going to be a bad team for quite a while, and the faster he and Crane could get the team in the black, the better the goal of winning would be served. Crane and Postolos also believed that employees who had worked for the Astros for a while would not immediately pivot to a different owner or management style. Conveniently, new and younger employees are also usually cheaper.

"Jim was unusual in making as many changes as he did," said the grocery magnate Crane bought the team from, Drayton McLane.

The transformation on the business side was immediate. In baseball ops, Luhnow let some people go, too, but he kept some senior baseball operations staff around for 2012, field manager Brad Mills among them. Some employees were clearly earmarked to be replaced in a year's time, and others Luhnow wanted to sniff out, to see if they might be malleable and progressive enough for him to retain.

Hiring managers were to turn over anyone they wouldn't hire themselves, to rip off the Band-Aid. At one point, one of Luhnow's subordinates argued that even though there were a handful of scouts he would let go, he didn't want to have to rehire the positions all in one winter. Postolos's message was clear: we're doing it all now. "If I could sum up Crane, and I'm saying this in an admiring way, because it's like, the way of the world . . . we weren't going to waste money to avoid having a difficult conversation with somebody," one member of Luhnow's regime said. "If you weren't an asset, if you weren't part of the future, he churns the company. It became very meritorious, very quickly."

Traci Dearing had been with the Astros since 1995, starting in the scouting department before becoming the executive assistant to the general manager. Luhnow was the fifth GM she had worked with in Houston. Her father, after he retired, worked as an usher at the stadium.

From the first day Luhnow arrived, the message to everyone was: "You better have your business in order, because you never know what's going to change," she said. There was also a book that he told staff to read, the same one Luhnow had pushed in St. Louis: *Who Moved My Cheese?*

Dearing thought Luhnow had a brilliant plan, but every Friday, or at least every Friday payday, she said, Astros employees were waiting for the hammer to fall. Once Dearing's own name was called, others held her up as an example of the cruelty of the firings: Why did *she* have to go? Dearing had lasted less than a year in the new regime, but wasn't resentful.

"Day one was I agitated? Sure. I put in almost eighteen years there. That's a long time. You sacrifice a lot with your family," Dearing said. "But at the same time, it's not something that any of us that were with the old regime shouldn't have expected, in my opinion. It's like any other company. Any time a new company comes in and buys it out, there's a chance that everybody could be changed."

Morale took a hit from the dismissals, and at least some employees signed a nondisparagement agreement once they were shown the door. Mills, the field manager, personally felt the pain of some of the firings, and simultaneously, some empathy for Postolos, who he said "was given a very tough task."

"That's hard, man. That's hard on anybody, I don't care what you say," Mills said.

John Kotter, the Harvard change management expert, said that restructuring can be a red flag in a change management program. Firings can be necessary for adoption, but it can also make the process considerably harder. In the last twenty years, he said, firings around an employee who remains have been shown to activate the strong survival system wired into human beings. "That system is constantly looking for threats, and when it starts to see job losses and impacts on families and careers and everything else, it can easily go into kind of a hyper state. And when it goes into a hyper state, your kind of survival mechanism, it doesn't do a very good job of making rational short-term decisions to help you survive. And it completely kills your capacity to think broadly, think in terms of opportunities, think positively.

"That period in which you're basically shut down from a people point of view—because everybody is into self-protection and hiding underneath their desks—no innovation happens."

○

Crane's predecessor, Drayton McLane, had won himself a lot of fans, even though the Astros hadn't won a championship. "He's a character. He's a sweetheart," Dearing said. "He'd go back and teach Sunday school. He was always there. He shook everybody's hand in the stadium. He talked to everyone."

At the time Crane took over, it would be difficult for the Astros or any other team to be called a "family" business. That description conjures a mom-and-pop image that would ignore how big the business really is. But when it comes to how employees were made to feel during McLane's time, many do refer to that f-word.

Today, MLB draws more than $10 billion annually, pandemic seasons aside. National and local media rights bring in huge dollars, and player salaries can be eye-popping, too: $200 million, or even $300 or $400 million, over a multiyear contract for the best of the best. But from the perspective of the sport's other labor force, the nonplayers, teams for most of the sports' history had been run in a way that actually often lived up to cliché of a family atmosphere. Owners generally were not cutthroat or hyperefficient with their employees. They had bought teams as trophies, expensive toys.

"Drayton rewarded you for loyalty and being a good employee," said Bobby Heck, the Astros' amateur scouting director at the time of the takeover. "There were a lot of people with twenty-plus years. Some of it was loyalty just because they signed the contract every year, but there was a lot of people that were good, and Drayton was generous. But probably someone walked in there, and they looked at it and said, 'Wow, this job's twenty thousand dollars more than it should be paid.' It was a family-first, personal-over-impersonal type of organization when Drayton was running it, as well as Ed [GM Ed Wade]. And then it became—it went from we to I, and from personal to impersonal."

The overall industry was in the midst of a shift to a more corporate outlook. GMs had begun to apply Moneyball principles to the most expensive part of their labor force, the roster, and owners ate it up. But elsewhere, the cost-cutting and drive for efficiency had not permeated every other corner of the businesses, not yet, and not to the extent Crane was pushing for.

Outside of baseball, Fortune 500 companies were already moving much more aggressively. That shouldn't be surprising, because most businesses exist in a very different environment. For one thing, baseball franchise values only go up. And that is in part because the sport is a closed circuit of thirty ownership groups who have the benefit of an antitrust exemption, granted by the Supreme Court in 1922. That exemption has helped preserve the power for the owners to act in ways that might run afoul of the laws that most every other business must abide.

If you own a store that sells mattresses, the value of that store would go down every time a new mattress store opened. MLB owners don't have to worry about that. Ted Turner, once the owner of the Atlanta Braves, was famously quoted in the seminal book on labor relations in baseball, *Lords of the Realm* by John Helyar, as telling his fellow owners, "Gentlemen, we have the only legal monopoly in the country—and we're fucking it up." Indeed, baseball owners could often be their own worst enemy, particularly in labor disputes.

But unlike proprietors in other industries, baseball's lords have never really run the risk of going out of business because they hadn't read and adopted the latest work of, say, Ray Dalio, one of Jeff Luhnow's preferred authors. Baseball club revenues were growing plenty without baseball teams mimicking every latest and greatest trend.

"In the beginning, as baseball owners came along it was all family-owned or small business, because the businesses themselves were not very big," said Fay Vincent, the former commissioner. "And indeed, to some extent, it's still true." Decades ago, when Vincent was an executive at Coca-Cola, he considered whether the company should pursue football ownership. The commissioner of the NFL at the time, Pete Rozelle, told him Coke presented a difficult problem. "He said, 'We have historically not wanted corporations to own franchises for the very simple reason that we were worried about the mob.'" Those concerns are gone, but major corporations still might turn away from team ownership because the largest profits come when a team is sold, rather than quarterly. "The American model of the company that sells stock publicly and trades publicly and has to generate earnings is to some extent in conflict with a sports franchise, which has ups and downs," Vincent said.

Of course, had Coca-Cola bought an NFL team, it probably wouldn't have had any regrets. McLane bought the Astros for $117 million, and two decades later, sold the club to Crane for about $615 million. McLane said he never would have imagined the price climbing so high.

Some teams have had actual corporate owners. Today Liberty Media is the parent company of the Braves. When they were owned by Turner, the Braves played a prominent role in pushing baseball's economics to its current model, one that present-day commissioner Rob Manfred has said can be thought of as two businesses: the in-person experience at the ballpark and media distribution. Turner, the television mogul, put his Braves on his superstation, TBS, reaching anyone whose cable providers carried his station, and making Braves fans all around the country. "All other teams were just broadcast in about a 150-mile radius of the city, and the Braves' broadcast began to change that in the middle to late eighties," McLane said. "So everybody wanted to emulate what the Braves did, and that's when cable TV came to almost every team."

The growth of games on television led to exploding revenues. In 1992, the Astros had a payroll of around $14 million. Individual salaries for top players alone exceeded that by the time McLane exited. "I paid Jeff Bagwell more than that," he said. "They weren't big businesses in those days, and the Astros were kind of in the middle. . . . As the cable TV money flowed in, and other sponsorships flowed in, that was the escalation of salaries."

When he was bidding on the team, Crane was very open about his plans for the Astros, partly because he was in the process of fundraising. Even more so today, the cost to buy a club has grown so large that it has effectively reduced the number of individuals who can afford a team on their own. Crane assembled a large group of investors and formed a board of directors that, according to the *Houston Chronicle* in 2012, consisted of thirteen votes. Each vote represented investments of at least $25 million, but many minority owners put in less, owning a partial piece of a vote. Crane had three full votes, plus a portion of another.

Crane said his job was "to keep no dissension in the ranks."

"We run it full disclosure," Crane said. "They see all the numbers, they know what's going on, they know why we're doing it, they know why we're spending it."

The treatment of employees inside baseball can garner more attention than the same topic in other industries, and that's for a few reasons. Baseball teams normally draw heavy media coverage, for one. Working in the sport is also aspirational, which might lead to more idealism than you'll find in discussions of, say, the working conditions at Walmart. Everyone involved in baseball typically has a sense of the massive amount of money coming into the industry as well.

Cushy jobs exist for senior staffers, but more often, pay is poor, particularly compared to comparable jobs in outside industry—for those in positions where comparable jobs actually exist. The typical trade-off had always been the privilege of saying you worked in the game—what could be cooler than that?—and a sense of comfort that your job would not disappear, so long as you did your job.

"It's not a free labor market, right," said an executive with a rival team. "It's heavily constrained, and all the leverage is in the hands of the employers. Which creates this, 'OK, I'm doing this because I love it, I'm making the sacrifices.'"

"It's one of the smaller businesses I've ever been responsible for," said McLane. "There's only 25 players on the team, there's about 190 in the minor leagues, and then you have about 200 of coaches, trainers, office people. So it's not a really big, big organization. But it's so prominent. I was in the grocery business all over the United States when I bought the team and had about 9,000 employees. And nobody had ever heard of me."

Back when he took over the Astros, McLane didn't fire a lot of people. Like many new owners, he didn't consider himself a baseball expert, and chose to be deferential. Now, McLane could be plenty demanding in his own right, but he was ultimately well liked. "With Drayton, it just seemed like he really cared about everybody," Mills said.

Firings are never comfortable, but Crane and Luhnow weren't exactly gentle. The incumbent farm director, Fred Nelson, was on hand for a press conference that was about to start in 2012. "Jeff walked up to him and stood right next to him. And he had just fired a lot of people, and said, 'So, last man standing, huh?'" said Jay Edmiston, who started at the Astros in 1986. "He said that to him." Nelson was gone by the next year.

Edmiston was a teenager when he first joined the Astros as a bat boy. He worked his way up and eventually became the point man for its Florida operations. McLane used to call him the "Mayor of Kissimmee," after the town where the team held its training camp. Starting in 2012, Edmiston watched a lot of friends walk out the door.

"I saw how it affected Fred," Edmiston said. "And I just said, 'Well, this is what we're dealing with, Fred.' And so that's the person that Jeff was: he doesn't care about your feelings or what you've done, nothing. It's what you can do for him in order to gain success or knowledge his way."

Gene Coleman was the Astros' head strength coach. Coleman helped Luhnow work out one day, and then twenty minutes later, after they were done, Luhnow called Coleman and let him go. "Gene calls me and said, 'You're not going to believe this shit,'" remembered former Astros athletic trainer Nate Lucero. "I said, 'What's that?'"

"I just got fired," Coleman said.

"Shut the fuck up," Lucero said.

"I swear to God, I just got fired."

"Gene, you just were working out with him—when did it happen?"

"He called me on my way home."

Jackie Traywick, the senior vice president for finance and administration, phoned a friend in the sport, a high-ranking executive outside of Houston, when she was fired. "They basically called her in and said, 'Because you're not performing, we're going to fire you for cause, so we don't have to pay out your contract,'" the friend recalled. "And to say that she was being fired for cause was, like, mythical. So, that's Jim."

○

The first grand stage Jeff Luhnow and Sig Mejdal took with the Astros was the 2012 draft, and one of Luhnow's favorite colleagues from St. Louis was front and center.

A former baseball player at Yale, Mike Elias climbed through the Cardinals' amateur scouting department, and Luhnow eventually put him in charge of the day-to-day operations there. He was the air traffic controller in St. Louis, requisite experience for Elias to become the Astros' amateur scouting director.

Luhnow did hire Elias right away, but he didn't give Elias the top title off the bat—the 2012 draft was too near, the scouting process too deeply under way to make a switch prudent. Elias instead became a special assistant in Houston, although many people assumed he would replace the talented incumbent scouting director, Bobby Heck, sooner rather than later.

All drafts are important, but 2012's would be a significant test for a franchise that had pinned itself to the future. Luhnow and company were picking first overall, which brings pressure unto itself. But the whole draft system had changed in baseball's new collective bargaining agreement.

In the past, teams could give signing bonuses to draft picks as they pleased, although the commissioner's office was never pleased if teams exceeded its suggested values at each pick. For the 2012 draft, and for the first time, every team functionally had a soft cap—a predetermined pool of money to distribute among all their picks, and the penalties to spend significantly more were onerous. The new system was a win for team owners, in part because it brought greater cost certainty compared to the past.

Every draft pick would have a dollar amount attached to it. Houston's first overall pick in 2012, for example, was worth $7.2 million, and each pick would decline a bit from there. (Minnesota's second overall pick was $6.2 million.) Add up every pick a team has and you arrive at the team's total bonus pool. Houston was a little north of $11 million.

There was a catch. Not every dollar assigned to a particular pick had to be used on the player taken at that spot. For example, if the Astros could find someone to sign for $4 million with the first pick in the draft, they could use the remaining $3.2 million to sign another talented pick, someone who might otherwise have declined to sign because their slotted number was too low.

A great advantage, then, could go to teams drafting capable players who would take bonuses below the value assigned to their pick. No one had actually employed such a strategy before, because the system was brand new. But the Astros were bold. The trick for Elias, Mejdal, and Luhnow would be to find a player whom they really liked with the first overall pick who would also be willing to take a reduced bonus.

But the player taken first overall still had to be really good.

"The strategy of 'Let me give up value to save money, to then spend that money to make up the value I gave up, but somehow get more value' is not a smart strategy," an Astros executive said. "I would have been screaming like a crazy man if we were passing on what I thought was the best player."

A tall Puerto Rican shortstop who was particularly young for his age and oozing with talent and poise, Carlos Correa, fit the bill precisely. (He is no relation to Cardinals executive Chris Correa.)

Because Correa was playing outside of the continental US, he wasn't scouted as often as players in the forty-eight contiguous states. That didn't make him a secret, but he wasn't close to a consensus No. 1 pick, and that ambiguity only helped the Astros. In a way, they fostered it.

Elias, in particular, fancied Correa. But while other teams leaked or hinted at their favorites through media outlets, Elias didn't even tell the scouting staff whom the Astros were picking until the day of the draft, in June.

"It was brutal," said Dave Post, the No. 2 in the amateur scouting department. "You spend a year working, living it and then you find out that you've taken a kid thirty seconds before the rest of the world does.

"It was strategic. It was, 'We're not going to let anybody know what we're going to do.' Mike loved Correa the whole year. He was right. It wasn't that anybody disliked Correa. It was just, me personally, I liked Byron Buxton [who went second overall]. He was the one I wanted, personally. Everybody wanted somebody else.

"And hey man, the fact that Correa played in the infield and he was super young and he was super cheap—they kept it very quiet. Correa worked out for Jeff and Enos down in Kissimmee one day, closed workout, quiet. Information wasn't divulged, you were kind of in the dark."

Correa signed for $4.8 million, well below the actual slot of $7.2 million. (The first overall pick the year before him, in the last year of the old system without a bonus pool, was a pitcher, Gerrit Cole, who signed for an $8 million bonus. Five players in the 2011 draft, in fact, had received more money than Correa did.)

With their savings, the Astros were able to sign their next pick, Lance McCullers Jr., a high schooler who had a great fastball-curveball combination and the leverage of going to college if he didn't receive his desired bonus.

"It was a very immediate thought: you can manipulate your money," an Astros exec said. "And we really felt like Carlos Correa was arguably, or secretly, or very possibly going to be the best player out of the draft: let's take a chance on him, spread the risk around. I remember Crane liking the idea of spreading the risk around. But it was very premeditated."

Correa likely had his own reasons for taking a below-slot bonus. Hypercompetitive, he probably wanted to be the first overall selection, and might have slid a few picks down had he passed on the Astros offer.

Ultimately, the entire process, guided by Elias before he formally ran the department, reflected the Astros' attention to detail, their effort to make sure they used the sport's rules and collective bargaining agreement to the greatest possible advantage. But Bobby Heck, who was still leading the scouts on the ground, was also crucial.

"I really think that Bobby did his best job of leading the staff that year," Post said. "He had one hundred percent approval rating inside the group. That's really hard to do in any business, let alone twenty hardheaded men."

Heck's path to the Astros had been winding. A former minor league catcher who could catch and throw well but couldn't hit a lick, he went back to school when the writing was on the wall that his playing days were done. He wound up in scouting, eventually, and as an ex-player was undeniably of a different cloth than Luhnow and Mejdal.

He had to manage the clash of the incumbent scouting staff and the new bosses, and Heck knew that some of the internal animosity Luhnow faced was unfair.

"It was the us versus them," Heck said. "The industry as a whole wasn't very nice to him, or respectful to him, just because he came from a different walk.

"I had mostly old-school scouts on my staff, and you know they were like, 'Well, they didn't play.' Part of it was educating our guys, too: there's more than one way to skin the cat. The one thing I did: I did an exercise in early January and showed 'em basically, we're not as good as we think we are."

Over time and across the sport, if a player does well after being drafted, a scout who had watched that player will often after the fact say something like, "I had him in the third round."

Heck would say, "But who did you have in front of him?"

"'Yeah, this guy went here, but you had these other two turds in front of 'em on your list,'" he explained.

As was the case for many Astros employees over time, Heck got to know Mejdal better than Luhnow.

"We had some of the best conversations," Heck said. "Challenged me, helped me grow. But he was like, always intrigued, why for the [prior] drafts, we always took a high school right-hander with our second pick, because he thought that was such a bad bet."

Ironically, in 2012, the draft where Heck and Elias worked together, the Astros took a high school right-hander with their second pick: McCullers.

In August, a couple of months after the draft, Luhnow texted Heck and asked to meet. Heck thought one of two things was happening: he was getting an extension or he was getting fired. Luhnow had played everything close to the vest.

It was the latter. Elias was taking over.

This was a Saturday. "And then that Monday, six or seven area scouts got let go," Heck said. "I was more pissed on Monday. . . . Because I knew I had a chance of getting fired. I knew I would get another job." He wasn't sure all of the others would find work as quickly.

"You liked to see what you were building until the end of it," Heck said, "but that wasn't exactly the people I wanted to be in the huddle with, either."

O

In 2012, Jim Crane had a plan to tap into his connections to CEOs across Houston, at businesses like Halliburton, National Oilwell Varco, and Schlumberger, for a grand sponsorship project dubbed the "Community Leaders" program. If those companies put in a few million dollars, they would get a huge sign in left field at Minute Maid Park, along the light tower. The plan was to have a charitable component, too, with some of the money going toward building youth fields.

The first mistake was that the signs were hideous and poorly placed. But Crane wanted to trumpet the effort in a preeminent industry magazine, *Sports Business Journal*. He was warned not to, because the underlying financials wouldn't look good for the team. But he went ahead with it anyway, and the story mentioned that the twelve signs would bring in $40 million—and that only $18 million would go to the community effort. The local newspaper picked up on it.

"That means less than half the money that sponsors put up would flow to the parks," wrote *Houston Chronicle* columnist Lisa Gray. "The rest, essentially, is advertising, which generates a nice profit for the Astros."

Gray's column ran with the headline "Loot, Loot, Loot by the Home Team."

Lance Berkman, a former Astros star who was with another team when Crane took over, was quoted as saying he hated the look of the new outfield.

Gray pointed out that even in a dismal season, one of the joys Minute Maid Park provided was a glimpse of the city skyline in left field: "This rotten summer, though, even that view is gone—blocked by an ugly bank of billboards." Minute Maid Park, she noted, was also a taxpayer-funded stadium, and changes required approval from the county sports authority.

A year and a half later, Crane did move the signs to a different spot in the stadium, citing fan feedback. But Crane was said to be furious at the column. "He was like, 'No one has ever called me a thief,'" an executive remembered. The comment registered ironically to Astros staff who recalled that Crane's outside business, Eagle Global Logistics, had seen employees go to prison over war profiteering charges. Crane, too, was angry that no one at the Astros had gotten the piece killed, a preposterous notion unto itself. But he seemingly didn't understand how the media worked, and appeared to have virtually no patience for anything but glowing coverage, after high-profile coverage of one of his divorces.

Using court records, the *Houston Press* in 2000 reported that Crane's ex-wife, Theresa, informed him that their son Jared "no longer wants to play on the little league team coached by him," when Crane believed otherwise.

"In a 1992 note under the letterhead carrying all the full weight and authority of the then Eagle USA corporate emblem, Jim lets

Theresa know he's pissed, mightily," the *Press* story went. "If the boy doesn't stay on the team, 'I will be left with no other alternative than to pursue this issue legally.'

"Apparently, the threat of kids' league litigation keeps the boy playing. The court record shows a similar 1994 corporate letterhead correspondence from Jim Crane detailing his latest furor. Jared had called at 5:25 p.m. asking him for a ride to the 6 p.m. game because Theresa was too busy to take him there. 'Further, I offered to pay for a cab to take Jared to his games which you denied him, stating I would not pay for the cab.'"

Daughter Krystal Crane was involved, as well.

"I cannot trust you," the *Press* reported she wrote her father. "From everything to cheating on mom, paying people off, not being there when I needed you and, worst of all, manipulating anyone and everyone."

Crane and his company Eagle Global Logistics were also prominently in the press when Eagle was charged with discrimination against Blacks, Hispanics, and women by the Equal Employment Opportunity Commission. The ugly case predated the ubiquity of the internet and did not dissuade MLB's owners from letting Crane into their fraternity.

○

Inside the offices, the atmosphere at Minute Maid Park took more subtle turns. "Corporate culture can manifest itself in different ways, and you can create corporate culture in many different ways," an Astros executive said. "One very easy, somewhat seemingly meaningless example, but it has an impact: dress code." Luhnow wore a suit and tie every day. Postolos the same. Particularly in baseball ops, other teams were usually more dressed down.

The attitudes changed as well. Everyone with the Astros was to think critically about what they spent, with no cost to be left unconsidered. Like Crane, Luhnow was programmed for efficiency, but Luhnow also leaned into it in this role, knowing well what would make him most valued to his owner.

Travel was an early area of focus. Employees had always been afforded their own rental car in spring training, and now some would have to share. The suitcases that big league teams usually provide to major league staff also were not offered for a time.

Outside of the season, the most important event in baseball is the winter meetings. For every team, dispatching large contingents was de rigueur, even though doing so was costly. Now Luhnow wanted everyone to justify their presence at the meetings by explaining what they hoped to accomplish. Most were still allowed to go, but the inquisition was not well taken.

Mills and Luhnow sat down and talked often, as GMs and field managers are wont to do. In spring training, the method of distributing meal money to players was up for debate.

Moving baseball teams from stadium to stadium is no small feat and is handled by a dedicated employee, the traveling secretary. They're responsible for making sure players have hotel rooms, and tickets to give to family and friends, and for myriad other logistical odds and ends, including the players' contractually obligated per diem. In 2012, Luhnow replaced their man in the position, Barry Waters, who had been with the club since 1979.

Each minor league team did not have a dedicated traveling secretary, and instead typically relied on their athletic trainer—the first responder when a player gets injured—to hand out meal money. Luhnow noticed this, and thought it was a replicable approach in the big leagues, too. "They wanted to have meal money on little cards, like debit cards," Mills said. He told Luhnow it wouldn't work.

"Well, why not?" Luhnow asked.

"Those things might work in the future," Mills said. "But right now, going cold turkey on a lot of those things, it's not going to happen, because you need a body on road trips to hand out meal money."

"Why?"

Mills pointed to how frequently players move to and from the minor leagues. "You're going to go ask a guy for a debit card, or they're going to have to cancel out the debit card?" Trainers have other, more pressing responsibilities, too.

"Your trainers, or whoever have to be at the ballpark early in the day, you're going to have them take away from their other job to do this?" Mills asked. The Astros didn't go through with the change, but to Mills, a search for a separator was invading every discussion.

Naturally, Luhnow wanted changes on the field as well, not just in travel budgets. "It almost felt like they came in [thinking] that everything we were doing in baseball—not just with Houston, with baseball—was wrong," Mills said. "And they were going to revamp it." Mills offered the other side of the coin, too: "The way you'd look at it is like, the system's broken, and we want to fix everything."

To Luhnow, player usage was a small piece of a larger picture, one way in which the Astros could slowly capture different edges. But Mills, like many peers, felt that baseball's norms, and the way the Astros had done things, were not actually broken. Losing environments always create stress, and the Astros in 2012 would lose 107 games, one more than they had lost in 2011.

Even in the best of times, managers and their GMs have love-hate relationships. Their responsibilities are distinct but intertwined, with the GM in charge of the roster and the manager, theoretically, its usage. GMs normally watch games from a suite at the home stadium and might not regularly travel on the road. The manager, meanwhile, is in the thick of the action, sitting in the dugout with the players during games and working out of the clubhouse (what they call locker rooms in baseball) before and afterward. Occupants of both positions have to reach some level of cooperation, because to an extent, the design of the roster is built around usage, and vice versa.

In 2012, GMs were starting to increase attention on managerial decisions. Advanced statistics could be newly applied to in-game management, too, not just trades and signings.

"His idea was to run it by a computer and numbers and everything else," Mills said of Luhnow. "So the conversation went quite long, simply because I gave my side, he gave his side. My side was for the fans. It was for the players. It was for these guys playing their hearts out on the field and wanting to play together as a team and playing for the fans."

But the power is in the GM's hands, ultimately—the manager is a subordinate. Quickly in Houston, frustration built.

"My vision is not to have an ex–baseball player as the manager," Mills said Luhnow once told him.

"Well, I guess I don't fit into your vision then, huh?" Mills replied.

Pitcher usage was a common fight between them in 2012, Luhnow's first season of play with the team. Late in games, managers have to deploy their relievers in a way that positions the team to win while also protecting those pitchers' health. Sometimes relievers throw on multiple days in a row, increasing fatigue and the chance of injury. Even if a reliever does not enter a game, just warming up in the bullpen can be taxing.

Luhnow wanted Mills to use his better relievers more frequently.

"What if his arm isn't feeling well?" Mills said. "We can't do that, because we're going to kill this guy."

"What do you mean we're going to kill this guy?" Luhnow said.

"He can't throw four or five days in a row," Mills said.

"Well, he can, if he only throws an inning here, two-thirds of an inning here, or whatever," Luhnow said.

"No, he can't. Because he has to warm up," Mills shot back. "We just can't walk up there and get this guy to come in the game. He has to warm up; his arm has to get hot."

On and on they went, and the conversations grew more contentious. When the Astros returned to Houston after most road trips, Luhnow would call Mills to his office before the first game of the home stand, debriefing Mills on where the field manager had most recently failed.

Luhnow began pushing a strategy limiting how long starting pitchers should remain in the game. The goal for starting pitchers had always been to pitch as long as possible on a given day. Otherwise, there's more work, and fatigue, for the bullpen.

Statistics then and now clearly showed, however, that pitchers get hit harder every subsequent time they cycle through the opponent's lineup. Most of the damage is done the third time through, regardless of inning, score, or pitch count. The batters have figured out what to do by the third crack. Luhnow wanted his manager to heed those numbers. "He came in with an edict that he didn't want starting pitchers facing the lineup the third time around," Mills said.

In turn, the manager had a demand.

"That's OK, if that's what we need, but we're going to need thirteen pitchers," Mills said.

"No, you do it with the eleven you have," Luhnow said.

"Jeff, we're going to kill these guys," Mills said, "and it's not fair."

"No, it can be done, and you can do it."

On August 17 in Houston, one of the Astros' young starting pitchers, Dallas Keuchel, was in the fifth inning of a game when the lineup turned over a third time. There were two out in the inning, one more needed to escape, and Mills let Keuchel stay in the game—an act of insubordination. The batter hit a double to put the Arizona Diamondbacks further ahead. Keuchel would pitch for a while longer, and the Astros lost.

The next night at Minute Maid Park, another young pitcher, Jordan Lyles, had allowed one run through four innings and the Astros held a 3–1 advantage. The very top of the Diamondbacks' lineup was due to bat in the next inning, marking the third time through the order. Mills left him in.

All hell broke loose. Lyles couldn't record an out in the inning, but did throw one wild pitch that missed the catcher. By the time the inning ended, the Diamondbacks led 10–3. In the dugout, Mills looked to his pitching coach and told him, "This is the worst thing that could have happened tonight because of what happened the night before."

Often right after games, Luhnow would be in the manager's office, hanging around while Mills worked on the next day's lineup with his bench coach. "It always felt like he wanted to be there, because he wanted to give his input on who was going to play the next day," Mills said. Sometimes Luhnow would ask Mills how he would feel if he directed someone to deliver his own suggested lineup to Mills's desk.

"I said, 'Well, I'd look at it, and for sure, I'd give it some thought,'" Mills said. "'But I'm not going to blindly put it in. There's things there's no way that you can be aware of, and I'd like to talk to you about it.'"

After Lyles got creamed in the fifth inning, Luhnow didn't show up for that discussion. Luhnow called Mills to tell him that he would come down for a chat after Mills did his standard postgame media session. When they met, they talked, and talked some more. Then Luhnow fired his manager.

The GM had one request in addendum: Although he had been fired, could Mills still manage the next day's game?

"I could tell that he expected me to do that, to say yes and to come back," Mills said. "But I think you can understand what my frustration level was at this point."

Luhnow's search for a new manager for the 2013 season led him to a former player who had gone to Stanford and had a particularly desirable trait: front-office experience. A.J. Hinch, in fact, had leapt directly out of the front office into the dugout at a young age, managing the Diamondbacks in 2009.

GMs always wanted managers with coaching experience, and Hinch didn't have any when he became Arizona's manager. But he had been a big-league catcher, a position that had always produced strong thinkers and, subsequently, many managers.

The sport, or at least Arizona's particular group of players, wasn't quite ready for a new-age, younger leader. Hinch didn't make it through his second season there before being fired, in 2010.

Luhnow now wanted Hinch to replace Mills, but Hinch saw a problem. Houston was a bad, bad team, and would be for a while. All those losses would pile up on Hinch's record. Hinch knew that if he didn't survive the rebuild—if he took the Houston job and didn't win quickly—his managerial record would be so poor that he might not get another chance. Luhnow had to keep looking.

Bo Porter, a coach for the Washington Nationals and former player, would take over the Astros for the 2013 season. In his first year, he would oversee the worst team in franchise history.

# 4

# AN IDIOT STRATEGY

THE PLAN TO REMAKE THE ASTROS CARRIED ONE PROMINENT CAVEAT: there would be losing, and lots of it. At his introductory press conference, Jeff Luhnow described his plan as "responsible," because he would not "steal from the future to make things a little bit better in the present."

"I know it's going to be a challenge, and I know it's going to be years," he said. "My guarantee is that we're going to work as hard as we can to make that time as short as possible."

Petstore.com ads notwithstanding, the tallest task of Luhnow's marketing career was selling fans on the one thing they innately dread: absolutely terrible baseball.

At this time, the order of baseball's amateur draft every June was determined by record. The worse a team fared in the previous season, the earlier they pick the next year, and the better the talent pool. Pick at the very top of the draft and, theoretically, the best player should be yours. The Astros, and any team of a certain mind, were literally incentivized to lose if they wanted to improve their odds in the draft—even more so starting in 2012 because of changes to the sport's collective bargaining agreement. Tanking, the process has been dubbed, and the Astros were not the only team that embarked on such a mission around this time. The Chicago Cubs were trying the same thing—at least to an extent.

"I think there's a bit of a difference between what we did and what the Astros did and especially how we operated versus how they operated," a Cubs executive said. "We invested in people, too. . . . We took the size of our front office way up. We paid people well; we treated people really well. Where Jeff was slashing and cutting and loyal only to the bottom line and trusting of no one. I think it was a completely different sensibility and culture. And we saw some of the same basic baseball efficiency principles that we were keeping in my mind, but it was manifesting in a different way."

For three straight years, from 2011 to 2013, the Astros would finish with the worst record in baseball, losing more than one hundred games each time. And for three straight years, the Astros would pick first in the draft.

Homegrown players had always been understood to be particularly valuable in the sport, in no small part because they're cheap. But they're fun to root for, too, and sometimes take on the identity of the franchise that shepherds them, and vice versa. Fans feel a particular pride when they succeed.

Pure roster-building pragmatism also made for a great selling point for Luhnow: the Astros would build a team in a way that was implied to be smarter and essentially better than the rest. The Astros sold T-shirts with the word "Process" on them.

Luhnow and his right-hand man, Sig Mejdal, were not inclined to do what merely had felt right historically, or what would look good to sporting moralists. One of their core goals was to be unflinchingly disciplined, and they oriented themselves around the odds.

But a few nuances were not spoken so loudly.

Losing is by no means an easy process to endure. Yet, if building a winning roster is a matter of skill, then arguably, Luhnow and company were taking the easiest, or at least cheapest, route possible. The most skillful effort a GM could undertake could be argued to be the one that keeps a fan base from years of misery prior to winning, rather than the one that embraces bad baseball wholeheartedly.

The New York Yankees, in the most impatient sports market in the world, for years had been accused of buying championships by outspending everyone. Whether an owner spending on the team, the product that fans consume, should be the basis for an accusation is an interesting question.

The Yankees had long been the game's premier franchise, playing in New York's spotlight with the revenues to match. Yet the team's longtime general manager, Brian Cashman, bristled at the notion that his job was much easier for it. "This is a very fast-moving Ferrari," Cashman said. "And in many cases, those same people who talk that talk would be an insect smashing against the windshield and getting splattered all over the place because they can't believe the amount of velocity that this car is moving at.

"You have to manage and deal with expectations, and that's a big thing. It's a lot of pressure when you're expected to win on a daily basis. So yeah, it's an easy thing to throw around all the time about, 'I wish I could do it that way [by spending],'" he said.

In Houston, even one or two free agents wouldn't have turned around the team immediately. But it is possible to sign players with an eye on trading them away for prospects in the middle of the season. Even that supplementary method for rebuilding would have required Crane to do the thing that he did not want: spend.

Crane and Luhnow were working with a much more docile fan base than the Yankees, and Houstonians were in many ways desperate. They had never seen a baseball championship parade, so they were more willing to sit through something radical if it meant getting over the hump.

But a drawn-out rebuild also quietly provides a perk for the executive who oversees it, for someone in Luhnow's role. The process takes time, and time amounts to job security. It can be half a decade before the process produces visible results, if not more.

A more glaring point the Astros did not silk-screen on shirts: the fact that draft picks are not guarantees, or anything close.

Bill James, the godfather of Sabermetrics, spoke on a panel during the early years of the rebuild, and someone asked whether he believed in five years the team would be winning ninety games. "The other people on the panel wouldn't answer it," James said. "I said, 'In five years, they're going to be winning way more than ninety games a year.'"

Jim Crane caught wind of the answer and sent James a nice letter, thanking him for sticking up for the team. But the reason James felt strongly about the Astros was not owed to the draft strategy that had become overstated as the lynchpin of the Astros plan.

"Tanking is an idiot strategy, to be blunt," James said. "Nobody ever improves their team by losing to get a high draft pick, because the high draft pick doesn't do that much for you. I think that's a complete misunderstanding of what happened and how that whole thing developed.

"I thought they'd be winning more than ninety games a year in five years because there were smart people in charge of the organization and there was a lot of money in Houston. If you've been to Houston, it's a lot of money down there, right? You put money and smart people together, you're going to win. That's all I meant by it. I wasn't referring to tanking."

Money, indeed, was the thing. The greatest benefit the Astros stood to take from tanking was financial. One of baseball's buzzwords, "sustainability," refers to having a pipeline of playing talent coming up through the farm system. But it's also a euphemism for cost control, because young, cheap players help keep the roster "affordable"—a moving threshold every owner defines as they choose.

Now spending prudently is also, undoubtedly, part of the puzzle of winning.

"I would argue if you're not trying to win in the most cost-effective manner, you are not trying to win," James said. "Everybody's budget is on some level finite. Nobody's spending two billion on salaries."

But in the short term, Luhnow and Crane had created a world for themselves where they could spend close to nothing on their major league players and have some roster-related justification for doing so. Payroll would, and did, drop to its bare bones, because the message to fans was that there was no other way.

The Astros were probably right to believe their revenues wouldn't likely improve with only small upgrades. Houston fans weren't going to show up to see a team just a hair better.

"There wasn't really a point in spending money on free agency," one Astros exec said. "The people in finance who ran the numbers for us said there's almost no return on investment in going from seventy to seventy-five wins, so they're like, 'Please, dear God, don't spend money unless you're ready to sort of get into the top half of the division in terms of wins.'"

Exactly how little the Astros spent in 2013 depends on how you want to calculate it, but the opening day roster was around $26 million. The Yankees, meanwhile, had a payroll of about $228 million, including a single player, Alex Rodriguez, whose $29 million salary exceeded the entirety of the Astros'. One Astros exec called the 2013 payroll "the puniest of puny," suggesting that when adjusted for inflation, it was the sport's lowest payroll in roughly thirty years.

By 2013, the team was now making a profit, successfully out of the red, according to Crane. "A lot of these teams are running deficits. In my opinion, that's not good business," he said. "One thing you'll learn about me, when I make a plan, I make a plan. We're not here to mislead people."

But just how much of a profit became a point of a contention.

*Forbes*, in so many words, suggested the 2013 Astros had rigged the system with the headline "Baseball's Worst Team Is the Most Profitable in History." The piece cited an estimated $99 million in operating income that season.

Crane was ticked by the *Forbes* piece and said he asked Major League Baseball to intervene with the outlet because "it was so far off base." *Forbes* put out another story, calling the first one erroneous, while noting the team was nonetheless making money.

"It was just the craziest deal I've ever seen in my life," Crane lamented. "I don't understand where people, fans, expect you to incur losses. . . . Listen, I didn't buy this team to cart money away. I bought this team to win. Period. Win. But I'll do it in a fiscally sound way."

Baseball teams have a few different revenue streams: tickets, hot dogs, local TV rights, national media money from networks like Fox and ESPN, and money from other teams. Revenue sharing between owners was established to keep parity among baseball's different markets, whereby the richest teams help prop up the others, much to the chagrin of the sport's largest earners.

For most seasons, exact numbers are difficult to verify unless they wind up in court documents. MLB teams do not publish their financial records, save for a team like Atlanta, which is owned by a publicly traded company.

Back then, Crane suggested back-of-the-napkin math. He said that every person who attended a game at Minute Maid Park was worth between $30 and $50, and suggested an average of $40. The Astros' listed attendance of 1.65 million in 2013, then, would have produced about $66 million. Now, those figures don't even include other revenues, like national and local TV money.

For comparison, court documents show that in 2010, the Astros took in $73.7 million from game receipts with about 2.3 million fans. (Publicly announced attendance figures in baseball are something of a misnomer, because they usually represent the number of tickets sold or distributed, not the number of people who actually come to games.)

That year, the Astros received $36 million from national broadcast deals and licensing, and another $27.9 million from local TV.

The rule of thumb Crane worked with was that if a team spends more than 50 percent of its total revenue on team payroll, give or take a few percentage points, it's likely to lose money. His Astros clearly weren't in danger of that.

When Crane took over the Astros, the league office and the head of the players' union, the Major League Baseball Players Association, were said to have had a conversation informally establishing that Crane would be given something of a grace period to spend on the team, a person with knowledge of that conversation said. The union has no direct control over ownership but does have a say in how teams spend their revenue-sharing dollars. The extremity of the 2013 payroll (and perhaps as well a turnover in leadership at the players' union that same year) ended that detente. The union publicly said it was monitoring the Astros, pointing to a couple of other low-spending franchises as well.

Teams like the Astros that tanked were very publicly taking themselves out of the marketplace for free agents, and anticompetitive behavior doesn't help grow player salaries.

"It's a very valued move to go get a top one or two or three draft picks by making sure your major league team is out of the market," said the sport's most famous player agent, Scott Boras. "So now we have a twenty-two-team league instead of a thirty-team league, and if organizations do that and they do it consistently, they've been rewarded for it.

"The model is to be noncompetitive for forty percent of a decade. And if that's the case, I don't think we want our fan bases in all the markets to know that. I think we want a different system. . . . While we want parity, certainly, we don't want a system where it is functionally beneficial for franchises to lose continually for a long period of time."

Draft position aside, one of the Astros' defenses for not spending was that they were directing money toward infrastructure and other improvements. "The upside of trying to squeeze out those extra three or four wins and spending an extra $10–20 million just didn't seem like a rational decision when we could invest that money in another farm-system team, more prospects, international signings, better staff, across the board," Luhnow said.

The Astros were also firm that they would, one day, spend on actual baseball players, when the team's younger players had emerged. Luhnow knew he would have no choice but to supplement the team through the market someday, because no team is entirely homegrown. "We'll have to stay in sequence with the way we're building up the team," Crane said. "We just don't want to spend money to be spending money. We want to make sure that fits into our formula. Not only for next year, but the next year. I doubt if you'll see any real long-term deals [heading into 2014], because we have so much coming through the system."

Yet, by stockpiling the farm system for years, Luhnow was giving himself every chance to avoid paying market price in the future, too, save for when absolutely necessary.

Another reason the Astros claimed they couldn't spend was still being litigated at the time of publishing.

○

Comcast SportsNet Houston, a regional sports network owned by the Astros, the Rockets, and Comcast, had launched in late 2012, the product of years of planning, well preceding Crane's arrival. George Postolos, the Astros president, was a driver of the project in his prior job as Rockets CEO, and the network was supposed to be something shiny and special.

"The idea was like, this is this huge part of this country that doesn't have this," said Steve Bunin, an ESPN anchor who opted out of his contract to join the new network. "ESPN can't give you enough Astros highlights and Rockets highlights and Texans highlights and make you happy, and the local affiliates only get two and a half minutes in their sportscasts. So this is like the great chance to do basically, regionalized, hyperfocused versions of *SportsCenter* and *Baseball Tonight* and *NFL Live*."

The business structure, however, was cumbersome. The Astros owned 46.5 percent of the station, followed by the Rockets at 31 percent, and Comcast at 22.5.

The network launched in time to carry Rockets games out of the gate, with Astros games waiting in the wings for the spring of 2013. Comcast had just merged with NBCUniversal and was the dominant cable carrier in Houston. That meant the new sports network, CSN Houston for short, was guaranteed to show up in all the Houston households that subscribed to Comcast, a strong position for the network.

Yet, even with that distribution, Comcast represented only about 40 percent of the Houston area's 2.2 million TV-watching households. A majority, then, would not be able to watch Astros and Rockets games unless CSN Houston could reach a deal with the other major providers in the area. So it was a question of price, of how much Crane and the other owners of the network would receive from the other distributors. Crane had expected $4.50 per subscriber.

As basketball season began, Rockets fans who didn't subscribe to Comcast for their television service were left in the dark, the start of an uproar from fans and media. But basketball fans weren't the only ones in trouble. Crane and the Astros were counting on large rights fees coming back from CSN Houston, including $56.6 million to be paid to the Astros in 2013. Local TV money is of great importance to teams. But that sum was predicated on the station gaining distribution with other carriers.

DirecTV was the most prominent holdout. "People take the same content, package it up, bid it up for three times the national average on a per-game basis and then try and stick it back to the other distributors in the geography. And I think that's very unfortunate," DirecTV CEO Mike White told the *Chronicle*. "We are taxing most of our customers who wouldn't be willing to pay for that content."

The situation was no better when baseball season rolled around. Crane doubled down just before Opening Day. "When we saw DirecTV, they said they had only lost a few customers," Crane said. "Well, when they lose a few thousand customers, guess what: they're going to pay that rate pretty quick, and everything is going to start running pretty smooth."

Bunin recalled the Rockets and Comcast being on the same page about reducing the asking price, with Crane in opposition.

"It was a little bit tough because we all knew that he was responsible for us not being widely distributed," Bunin said. "That's a pretty deflating feeling if you're doing good work and working hard, and only a third of the market can see you.

"At some point, we realized that this setup, the basic contractual framework, was going to be very hard to overcome. I don't know why they did it, but they had the three partners, and everyone essentially had a veto, everything had to be unanimous."

Houston's mayor eventually asked for a sit-down with the parties, trying to intervene. Crane, though, was never the type to be told what to do.

"Basically, there were two times where Comcast and the Rockets agreed, and Jim Crane said no," Bunin said. "So after the first time that happened, we were all like, 'Oh God, this is not gonna end well.' Or at least those of us who [had] been around the block, I think saw sort of the writing on the wall and started calling our agents and saying, 'How good is my contract?' And 'What happens if this goes under?'"

In ways small and large, Crane was brazen. Buying the Astros was a business move, a way to boost sales and prominence in his outside work. He would often bring clients and other connections to the stadium, which is to be expected. But in the midst of the action, the dugout was the players' domain exclusively. Crane didn't realize, or didn't care, that walking his guests during a game down the tunnel and up to the edge of the dugout was a bad idea.

Everything was Crane's, and Crane's way. He made a habit of landing his helicopter on one of the instructional baseball fields in Florida during spring training, which caused a stir, and at least one web headline, which Crane didn't like. "Jim was pissed and you know it was like—first of all, don't land your helicopter in the back field," one Astros contemporary recalled.

Crane used to tell people that he had a key to literally every door at the stadium. But to one high-ranking Astros executive, his pride lent itself to delusion, particularly with his insular inner circle of longtime associates. Crane's anger could come "so fast" if he was told he was wrong. "You cannot say something that is against what he says. If he says the sky is blue and it's raining, everybody nods," one executive said. "So there's a sense of, we're going to create our own world."

That held true in his approach to his TV network, too. One Astros higher-up laughed when they were first told what the price was that CSN Houston and, by extension, its partial owners, the Astros, were asking the other distributors to pay. The executive was convinced it would never work, because Crane had pelted the baseball world with a message that his team would be terrible for a long time. He was pushing a product strategy on the field that was incompatible to the distribution strategy.

"They just could not understand," the exec said. "They had gone out and said we're going to lose, and we're going to lose badly, and now will you pay us a premium so that you can watch us lose badly."

Postolos was a smart person, but colleagues could tell the TV wrangling was going terribly by how stressed he became. He would make a crack or two: "if this TV thing doesn't get fixed, it's somebody else's problem."

But it wasn't a joke. In May 2013, less than two years into his tenure as owner, Crane fired his team president. "This is Jim's management style," another Astros exec said. "If he doesn't believe you are the right person for the position of that time, regardless of what has transpired previously, he's going to find someone who he believes is the right person for the position."

With $56.6 million due to the team in 2013, the Astros returned 46 percent of the monthly payments for May and June to CSN Houston to keep the network solvent, Crane told the *Houston Chronicle*'s David Barron. Payments to the Astros for July, August, and September were not made on time. The debacle only added to the Astros' drive to spend next to no money on the roster.

As one Astros executive put it, "The TV issue was so omnipresent in everything we did.

"Because we had a bad team, we had no TV money. And because we had a bad team, no one was coming to games," they said. "So we had just no revenue. That, I think, amplified and accelerated what was already a strategy for the future, and it probably forced the organization to take an even more drastic approach."

In September 2013, as a third straight one-hundred-loss season wound down, the Astros suffered a new indignity: they played a game that recorded a 0.0 Nielsen rating. Barron noted it was the first time in Astros history, and possibly Major League Baseball history, "that an MLB game had no measurable viewership in its home market."

A few days later, the Astros were shocked when affiliates of Comcast filed for involuntary Chapter 11 bankruptcy against CSN Houston. Before the year was out, Crane turned around and sued the former owner of the team, Drayton McLane, for allegedly selling an asset that "they knew at the time to be overpriced and broken." Crane's group had paid more than $600 million for the team and its stake in the network, with the latter valued at $332 million.

The Astros, Rockets, and Comcast agreed to let Judge Lynn Hughes oversee mediation, although it was unfruitful. Eventually, CSN Houston would come out of bankruptcy in a different form, with a new name, altered ownership, and significantly less programming and staff. Of 141 employees, 96 were to be laid off in 2014, Barron reported, disrupting a slew of lives beyond just television viewers.

"There was a level of dysfunction and just pain that was especially galling here," Bunin said.

The employees knew the end was coming, and CSN Houston management brought roughly one hundred employees into the newsroom. They were sitting almost in silence during a delay, the time for gallows humor already passed. The network bosses began meeting with people in smaller groups of roughly ten—the producers, then the anchors, and the directors and so on.

"And they have ten envelopes, one envelope for each person, and in it will be a piece of paper that either says you're being kept or you're being let go," Bunin said. "So you march in there, and they've got these ten envelopes. And if I'm not mistaken, I'm pretty sure they said, 'If it's two pages, you're being kept. And if it's one page, you're being let go.' Well, in classic CSN Houston fashion, they had not made the fonts the proper size to limit it—everyone opened it up and had two pages. So all of us, for a split second were like, 'Oh my God, I'm the one they're going to keep.'

"So it was like one more fuck-you to take me through a breath of 'What?' And then you read the last line, your eyes start the last line, 'Thank you for your services.' . . . And then you got to march back into the newsroom and sort of eyeball everybody else and the seven or whatever groups who haven't gone marching in yet."

In a downtown Houston bar, the staff gathered for one final good-bye.

"It's a very hard thing," Bunin said. "It's in the news. . . . And when it's you, and you don't have a paycheck coming, and you can't just—there aren't just other networks. Many other industries, you can get another job. It may not be a great job, it may not be a job you want, maybe you have to move a little bit, maybe it's in the same town. You know, grocery store, hospital, auto shop—it's brutal no matter what. But there are other opportunities. Here, there's no opportunity. The four affiliates in town aren't going to hire you [just] because you worked at ESPN. There's no jobs in Houston for you."

Bunin, today, works as an anchor in Seattle.

"There wasn't enough millions for Crane," Bunin said. "You didn't have the marketing power and you tried to pretend you did and for you, you just lost money. But for us, we lost our livelihoods."

In 2019, McLane countersued Crane, alleging Houston's new ownership had "proceeded to intentionally and deliberately destroy the network, which it accomplished, in part, by 'tanking' the baseball team." In court, Crane submitted a declaration that "the ultimate failure of the network cannot fairly be attributed to poor team performance by the Astros or the Rockets or to any change in market conditions in the period from late 2010 to 2013 or 2014." He wrote as well that the Astros lost more than $85 million in rights fees from the debacle.

○

The 2013 season was rock bottom in Houston.

One of the enduring images was a headfirst dive by Jonathan Villar. Lunging for second base, the young Astros shortstop planted his face squarely in an opposing player's rear end.

Another memorable image was a photograph taken at Minute Maid Park of a vendor's tray of snow cones. The tray was sitting on the floor of an occupied bathroom stall. The vendor was fired.

In new manager Bo Porter's first season, the Astros lost their final fifteen games, finishing with a record worse than even the past two years' teams. In commemoration of the year, Luhnow took out a vanity license plate, GM 111, representing the final number of losses. Luhnow saw it as motivation, a reminder. No other franchise in the sport's history had amassed three straight hundred-loss years.

In the winter after the 2013 season, a new question about the team was posed on network television.

"The large valve used to control wellbore fluids on oil rigs is this 'preventer'; the Astros could have used one," read Alex Trebek on *Jeopardy!*

The correct answer: "What is a blowout preventer?"

The clue was odd, because no one in baseball really uses the term "blowout preventer." But the takeaway was obvious: the Astros had become the butt of the joke.

# 5

# THE ISLAND OF MISFIT TOYS

KEVIN GOLDSTEIN WORE JEANS ON HIS FORMAL VISIT, BECAUSE HE DIDN'T believe Jeff Luhnow would hire him, and either way, he wasn't going to pretend he was an Ivy League frat boy, or anyone else other than a baseball obsessive raised by Chicago punk rock. Goldstein, in his work for media outlets *Baseball America* and Baseball Prospectus, was an expert in all thirty teams' farm systems, and he had new ideas about how to structure pro scouting, the review of players who were already in the major league or minor leagues.

For Luhnow, that grounding proved more important than pants. The GM's penchant for outside expertise, groomed in his McKinsey days, had not waned.

Now, Goldstein's addition atop the pro scouting group, although outside the box, was something of a pledge to conventional scouting, to sticking human eyes on players. But Luhnow's bread and butter, what he knew would most separate the Astros, would be their analysis, their statistical capability—research and development. The Astros were behind the Cardinals as Luhnow and Sig Mejdal had left them, and for all of their grand plans to redesign the Astros' operations, nothing was more important than getting their analytics up to speed. This was Mejdal's department, and he had a nifty title, director of decision sciences, to go with it. Because better decision-making was the whole point.

But the mission wasn't merely to equip themselves with the most advanced information.

*Moneyball* had fanned the flames of the scouting versus statistics debate, effectively creating it. Even today, if you ask baseball executives which they value more, scouting or statistics, they'll usually give some variant of "You need to use both."

To this, the Astros would say, of course. But how?

At Mejdal's direction, the Astros poured greater energies into creating an objective way to combine all the information. A way to meld the objective numbers and the subjective scouting reports in a way that was, well, objective. "It's difficult for any individual person to weigh those two and do it in a way that is optimal. Our brains are limited," Luhnow said. "If there are ways to have a framework for how to balance the information, it's worth pursuing those ways.

"You can still choose to go against that decision, or you can choose to say, 'I believe the subjective information in this case more so than the objective, so this framework doesn't apply in this case,' and we do that sometimes still. But yeah, we've tried. It's hard. It's really hard. And it's not always correct. . . . It at least gives you a starting point that is based in logic and not emotion, and I think that's what we're looking for."

The terminology surrounding advanced statistics and metrics in baseball is muddled, and the same is true for the people who manage and produce those statistics. Two basic roles existed inside baseball R&D groups: analysts and developers, with some crossover between them.

If you have a dashboard that needs to be created, or want to automate and synchronize and cleanse data, that's usually the province of developers. These are often computer scientists, people with database expertise. The other world is that of the analyst, those who create the mathematical models to reveal the insights within the data—the actual analytics. These folks can be computer scientists as well, or experts in applied math and statistics or operations research.

At the Astros, the stats wonks were known as members of "the Nerd Cave," a moniker worn proudly by its participants, and sometimes wielded with derision by others inside the organization. One of their leaders, Mike Fast, is in the running for the most unheralded contributor to the Astros front office of the last decade.

Fast was a physicist and fell into the latter group, an analyst. For seventeen years, he worked as an engineer in semiconductors. Growing up as a Kansas City Royals fan in the Oklahoma panhandle, with a gentle accent to match, Fast didn't have games on TV every night, so he listened to the radio. He, like everyone else in this wave, was a Bill James reader, and had never imagined the game would hold a place for him.

Around 2007, MLB made a trove of data publicly available from a new system that tracked every pitch thrown in major league games, called PITCHf/x. When a sportscaster during a game would describe a sinker—a pitch that does just what you think as it reaches the plate, it dips downward—Fast now had a way to study it because of the tracking system. He could review the umpires who called balls and strikes and their missed calls. The advent of PITCHf/x meant Fast's physics training was newly applicable to the sport he loved, and it became an obsession.

He started to write for different publications, including Baseball Prospectus and the Hardball Times. One analysis he did brought attention from around the industry: a look at catcher framing, the importance of how a catcher receives the pitcher's throw. The most skilled catchers could, in essence, steal strikes, snagging the ball in a way that made marginal pitches that were not actually over the plate look otherwise to the umpire. Catching a low pitch with an upward motion, for example. The worst catchers, meanwhile, could inadvertently make a strike look like it had missed, hurting the team's chances.

The Pittsburgh Pirates talked to Fast about a job, but he didn't get an offer. Late in 2011, he actually got an interview with the Cardinals, with Mejdal and Chris Correa. Luhnow was right in the process of taking the GM job with the Astros. A few weeks later, Fast interviewed with Mejdal again, this time for a chance to come to Houston, and he jumped.

For the first year and a half or so in Houston, Fast's job under Mejdal was to build a new projection system, something that would predict how major and minor leaguers would fare in the future, a way of evaluating pro players. This model was separate from the other model the Astros would rely on in their earlier years, the one Mejdal built to discern the best amateur players in the draft.

More bodies were needed in research and development, too. Another analyst who had written for Baseball Prospectus—the same outlet that also carried Goldstein and Fast—Colin Wyers, was looking for a job. Wyers, who ran the revered publicly available projection system PECOTA over at Prospectus, told Fast he was applying for a gig with Cleveland, and asked for a reference. Fast was happy to provide one, but suggested Wyers talk to the Astros before deciding. Late in 2013, Wyers was on board in Houston, charged with making the model Fast had begun working on more robust.

Luhnow's core front office was so small at the beginning that most everyone had a hand in everything. Wyers, for example, would sometimes be involved in evaluating player health history, researching the history of players with similar types of injuries.

Everything that the Astros were putting together, the models, the data, needed to be housed in a way that was accessible, even user-friendly. Contract information, scouting reports, statistics common and proprietary—the Astros were intent on centralizing most every piece of baseball information their decision makers needed at one password-protected web address. When Luhnow made his twenty-three-page presentation to Crane, he included an outline of this proprietary database. In St. Louis, he had overseen construction of "Red Bird Dog," and the Astros needed their own system. A computer scientist they hired, Ryan Hallahan, started to build it. In a nod to Houston's NASA roots, they called it "Ground Control."

Baseball, like the rest of the business world, was entering the era of big data. "Even if you leave analytics out of it, there is a tremendous amount of information the decision makers want to see when they make their decision," Mejdal said. "What's happening in the baseball industry is not too different than what's happening in other industries.

"The amount of data available to make your decision is growing, if you want to use the term, exponentially. It's just growing significantly, and human capabilities are not growing significantly. The importance of assisting the human decision maker with decision aid is important in any field, and especially in a field that you can argue is a big data field."

At Luhnow's direction, Hallahan delivered features with great speed, and effectively. Goldstein in 2014 asked for a feature and expected it would take weeks. Hallahan did it in about five days.

"If you look at Hallahan's arc, he was hired in 2012, the Astros didn't have anything," a colleague said. "And he worked very quickly to develop a lot of things that people ended up relying on very heavily to do their jobs. He built pretty much everything from scratch in like a year and a half to two years."

And given the Astros' frugal approach, the cost savings of having Hallahan build the database in-house was significant.

"And a lot of people loved him for that," the colleague said. "The problem came that, well, how was he able to build everything in a year and a half? It's by cutting a lot of corners."

○

Mejdal and Elias had followed Luhnow from St. Louis to Houston, and they weren't the only ones. When he wasn't raiding Baseball Prospectus for the likes of Goldstein and Fast, Luhnow was dipping into the assembly of progressive thinkers he had recruited in St. Louis, creating a new tension between him and his former club. The Cardinals had made a mistake, a costly oversight, when they granted the Astros permission to hire Luhnow: they did not place any restriction on the number of Cardinals employees he could take to Houston.

A small migration began. Some Cardinals simply let their contracts expire so that they could join the Astros. Anyone who did so was within their rights, but it was an unusual move in the sport, and prompted suspicions that Luhnow had encouraged them to do so. In other cases, Luhnow directly asked permission to hire people away.

Baseball teams never have to grant another team permission to hire away someone under contract, unless their deal specifically calls for that allowance, but such a clause is exceedingly rare. Instead, the norm in the sport is to allow someone to interview and leave for a job if it's for a clear step up—and if no equivalent position is available internally. (Were it not for baseball's antitrust exemption, the restrictive nature of these contracts might be challenged in court.)

The Cardinals did not want to stand in the way of anyone's growth, but also did not want to see the organization they had built be whittled away. "We obviously were pleased at what we had built up," Cardinals president John Mozeliak said. "When all of a sudden you have a lot of employees that become flight risks, that's tough to manage."

Mejdal and Elias wound up in Luhnow's immediate inner circle in Houston, but Luhnow dotted the organization with transplants in other areas as well. A pair of forward-thinking minor league instructors, Jeff Albert and Doug White, were disciples of Luhnow's who did most of their work far from Minute Maid Park.

Albert only briefly played baseball in an independent league. He was writing online while finishing his master's, digging into video analysis of hitters' swings, when Luhnow found him in the Cardinals days. "He saw what I was doing and he just said, 'Hey, we don't have anybody that's doing that, this looks really interesting . . . let's see if we can make this work,'" Albert said. "I was like, 'Heck yeah, let's do it.'"

Luhnow's exit to Houston had a trickle-down effect on his followers. Albert "had a ton of power and persuasion with Luhnow" with the Cardinals, one fellow St. Louis émigré said, but once Luhnow was gone, Albert's own influence was diminished. Still, the Cardinals were not thrilled to see Albert leave. "Jeff Albert, even though I really don't think Jeff did anything—wink-winkish—the Cardinals were pissed about it," the colleague said.

Luhnow allegedly made overtures to others who did not ultimately bolt. Not everyone in St. Louis held Luhnow in the same high esteem, or frankly even trusted him.

Still others left St. Louis to join the Astros, and the Cardinals, eventually, had enough. The owner, Bill DeWitt Jr., reached out to say this had to stop. The teams reached a verbal understanding that Luhnow would stop poaching, and to the Cardinals' satisfaction, he did.

But they'll never make the same mistake again in St. Louis. Were he to leave today, Luhnow likely would be contractually barred from taking any other Cardinals for a period of two years.

"You look at how many people the Cardinals let go to one team in the offseason, and it's just like, fucking amazing," an Astros employee who did not come from the Cardinals said. "Like, who does that?

"The story I heard is that the Cardinals didn't think Jeff was going to get the Houston job, so they didn't expect a promise from him to not hire people. Which they would have done if they expected him to leave. And so Jeff just went ahead and raided the Cardinals for everybody that he wanted."

○

Most every day in Houston, Mejdal and Stephanie Wilka and others in Luhnow's inner circle would talk baseball endlessly. Even when Luhnow was not with them, they'd spend lunch near the stadium discussing random hypotheses on the backs of napkins. They wondered what impact advance scouting—the practice of sending scouts to evaluate another major league team shortly before the Astros played them— actually had over the course of a season.

Considering his entry as an outsider, Luhnow's network wasn't the deepest in baseball, but he had been around long enough now to have some connections. Wilka was a young Harvard-educated lawyer who dreamed of becoming a general manager herself. Her family was from St. Louis, and she had seen some of the publicity about Luhnow while he was in St. Louis and reached out. Wilka had a job with the Red Sox, and they stayed in touch over the years.

When she arrived in Houston, Wilka was doing the job of five people, by one colleague's estimate—a chief of staff, in a way. She helped prepare for that first June amateur draft, and then immediately switched gears to the July trade deadline and the rest of what awaited on the calendar.

Although Mejdal was spiritually at the core of all the Astros' innovation, Luhnow also needed an assistant general manager, a technical No. 2. He kept the incumbent on for most of 2012 before seeking his own choice. A young executive from New York City working for Cleveland came well recommended, and recommended by the right people. David Stearns, also a young Harvard grad, had worked for the commissioner's office in its labor relations department, impressing the league's top negotiators and actively aiding the construction of the new CBA. He knew the rules inside and out, and that included intimate knowledge of an area the Astros were focused on: the draft.

Add in Stearns's friendly connections to baseball's central office and other teams, and Stearns brought a background that Luhnow simply didn't have.

Despite the confidence Luhnow projected publicly, ultimately everyone in Houston was figuring it out as they went. At times, Stearns and the rest of the front office were just trying not to drown. Luhnow sometimes even reached out to old Cardinals connections for advice. One Cardinals executive thought that was an overstep, particularly when Luhnow asked for opinions about Carlos Correa going into the 2012 draft, although another executive thought the communication was reasonable.

"We had a general manager with a little bit of an unconventional background who didn't have a lot of the same training that most general managers in the industry have," one Astros colleague said. "And to some extent that's what made him so appealing to Jim, is that he was different and had a very different background than a lot of the candidates he was looking at." But in turn, a lot of responsibility wound up on others' plates, as well.

Wilka and Stearns, in particular, had experience with other teams, and were able to fill some of Luhnow's blind spots. They knew better where baseball convention would be valuable. Luhnow had some awareness of the limitations of his own knowledge, but his early staff also provided something of a guardrail. "I think he needed that balance," one Astros exec said. "And when he had it, it went well."

Luhnow was starting to gear his front office for the time when the Astros would, in fact, be a better team, when the prospects he was amassing through the draft would become big leaguers.

Although they were terrible in record in 2013, the Astros had some premier talent coming, even some that had already arrived at the major league level. One young star was a wizard of a batsman at a position that hasn't always produced a ton of offense, second base. Jose

Altuve had cost the Astros virtually nothing when he signed with the team out of Venezuela—$10,000 in a deal struck years before Luhnow arrived. In his younger days, some would call Altuve "enano," Spanish for dwarf and sometimes used derisively. But he had an uncanny ability to make contact, with lightning-quick wrists. He was fast, too, and could steal bases.

People constantly doubted Altuve because of his size, generously listed at five foot six, but he kept performing. When he was in the minor leagues, an opposing manager told his outfielders to come in and play shallow. "Let's go, you guys are out too deep, this guy's too short, he's not going to hit the ball too far away," the manager yelled. Altuve responded by ripping a pitch deep into the outfield for a hit, and he never stopped hitting.

Altuve was twenty-three in 2013, his second full season in the big leagues, and he was cheap. Teams can pay major league players whatever they want for a player's first three years in the major leagues, so long as it reaches the major league minimum, which in 2013 was $490,000. After a player's third year and, in some cases the second year, players become eligible for arbitration.

Arbitration-eligible players have a right to fight what the team offers them, and it's the first chance players have at the real money in baseball, the seven-figure salaries. The really big money typically comes once a player hits free agency, which takes six years to reach, and that's no easy length of time for a player to stay in the major leagues.

In other words, as a standout player nearing arbitration eligibility, Altuve was soon about to get a lot more expensive, a significant juncture for the player and team alike, particularly for a cost-conscious franchise like the Astros.

The arbitration process relies a lot on a comparison of a player's statistics at his position, as well as the number of times he's gone through the process. A second baseman who is eligible for arbitration for the first time is going to be compared to other second basemen who were also first-time eligible. The salaries typically increase every year a player goes through the process, up until they become a free agent after year six.

Luhnow, and some other executives in the sport as well, saw a huge opportunity with young players. The Astros could try to lock up some ahead of time at a savings to the team, with a contract that would also give the players greater security than they would normally find prior to becoming a free agent.

Altuve was one such candidate, and Luhnow started looking for a baseball economist, someone who could help the Astros with any long-term extensions, but also assist in valuations and contracts of any form.

"They liked the idea of someone with an investment banking background or an MBA," an Astros exec said. "At that time, the Astros had a basic projection system that Sig and Fast had built for them. It would tell you how many runs a player would produce each year into the future. But they didn't have any economic models to say which players are getting paid too much or too little given their projection, or what's the total asset value of different players."

○

On the shorter side, with a big grin and a full head of hair, Brandon Taubman grew up comfortably in Syosset, a hamlet in Long Island where the school system was strong and high achievement was standard. His father was a systems engineer, his mother an entrepreneur, and both of Taubman's brothers became lawyers. Trips to Shea Stadium, the old home of the New York Mets, were common when Taubman had time.

Ambitious and never leery of an argument, Taubman excelled at model United Nations debates and in math, punching his ticket to Cornell. Those math skills and, of course, the chance to someday make a lot of money, drew Taubman to finance. He became an investment banker, working in equity derivatives, and was at Barclays when Luhnow's help-wanted ad went live.

At its essence, Taubman's day job was to figure out what things are worth. Derivatives in their simplest form are contracts that get their value from the value of something else, like an underlying asset, and Taubman used them to help Barclays make money.

Although successful, Taubman was starting to grow disillusioned.

He graduated from college during the subprime mortgage crisis, and his first employer, Ernst & Young, provided an up-close glimpse of the crumble of the financial world. Barclays had poached Taubman from Ernst & Young, one of the Big Four accounting firms. Ernst & Young had done some consulting for AIG, whose collapse was at the center of the market's crash in 2008.

At Barclays, one of the projects Taubman directly worked on was pricing the collateralized debt obligations, or CDOs, of Lehman Brothers, which had also collapsed. Later, a different division of Barclays than Taubman's was caught in a major scandal over the manipulation of interest rates, culminating in a $450 million fine and the exit of the company's CEO in the summer of 2012.

Between the industry's scandals and realities of his own work, Taubman was starting to sour, dreaming of another path. He loved the fantasy baseball leagues he played with friends, where the annual buy-in to participate kept going up and up. A new offshoot of fantasy baseball also provided a different allure. Daily fantasy sports, a variant involving wagers on a nightly basis, offered a chance to make money—particularly for someone skilled at valuing things.

Although math was his forte, Taubman was really a hybrid. He was oriented toward strategy. By most standards, he wasn't a computer scientist. Mike Fast's technical ability, for example, was far superior. But Taubman taught himself different programming languages to the point of proficiency. To beat the competition in daily fantasy, Taubman began building a database of baseball data, and from there, projections of what players would do on a per-game, rate basis. He pulled data from third-party websites that offered pricing of players on a given day: Altuve, for example, could cost a daily fantasy player ten dollars one day out of a fixed, fictional budget. The websites Taubman was reading gave their own recommendations of a player's worth.

Then Taubman layered in the daily conditional data, like the match-ups between different players. He did his own study on weather, in fact, and concluded that the environment was not a good predictor of performance, save for one thing: in more humid settings, fewer runs were scored. Wind only mattered when it was particularly strong, blowing in from the outfield, shortening the distance a batted ball would go. None of his findings were counterintuitive, but the importance of humidity stood out more than he expected.

Taubman would make daily adjustments if a player got injured, and at the end of it all, the system would spit out a recommended roster that should perform better than any other. Taubman spent most of his time in head-to-head formats, his roster versus another individual's. He was winning close to 60 percent of the time, enough so that he effectively made it a small side business: $20,000 or so one year, another $32,000 or so the next.

The first interview Taubman landed in baseball was not with the Astros, but with the Red Sox, who sought an intern who could eventually become a full-time analyst. To the Red Sox, Taubman was detectably a Wall Street type, but ultimately fine in his interview. But they were seeking someone who was more traditionally trained as an analyst.

When Taubman did his study on the weather, he decided to reach out to some analysts already working in baseball. One of them, Chris Correa of the Cardinals, struck up a conversation with Taubman. Correa told him the Cardinals would consider Taubman for a position as soon as one opened up, but Correa noted to him that the Astros were hiring right then. Taubman was unaware.

Taubman, who was making six figures in investment banking, had never been to Texas before his job interview. He read up on Luhnow and Mejdal and Elias. He grew inspired by the idea of building a sustainable pipeline of players and then being religious about letting those players walk in free agency when they no longer became cost-effective assets.

In 2013, for $49,000 a year, Taubman joined the Astros, reporting to the assistant GM, Stearns.

"Most of the people that worked for the Astros at that time were the fucking Island of Misfit Toys," one Astros exec said. "Most of us could not have gotten a job in baseball elsewhere. No other team is going to hire Kevin Goldstein to run their pro scouting team operation. What other team was going to hire Brandon Taubman or [fellow early Luhnow hire] Bill Firkus anywhere? Not that these were bad people to have in those jobs, like, I think the results speak for themselves. But they weren't baseball people. They weren't made in the industry. There were clubs that had some guys like that, but filling a whole front office with those sort of guys was unheard-of and really caused a lot of problems around the industry with our reputation."

Taubman's first project was to create an underwriting model to understand the expected value of multiyear extensions. Some work had been done online in that space, but the standards in the industry were mostly reliant on shorthand rules of thumb.

In a parallel to Taubman's finance world, baseball players too can have options in their contract: a team option, player option, or mutual option to exercise an additional year with a team at a certain price. A four-year deal, for example, can have a club option for an additional $5 million tacked on to the end of it. Taubman built a model for the Astros to price options that was more like the one commonly used in his past life, a Black-Scholes model.

More than a player option or mutual option—the latter a design where both parties have to agree to exercise it—club options were already known to be favorable to teams. One of the insights produced by Taubman's project was that if the club paid just a bit more in annual salary, and in exchange, they could tack on additional club options, the advantage to the team could be huge.

Another of Taubman's first tasks was working on Altuve's contract extension. The second baseman in 2013 agreed to a deal that guaranteed him a total of $12.5 million for the 2014–17 seasons.

Had Altuve not taken the contract, he would have been in line to become a free agent after the 2017 season. But his new deal also included two club options for the Astros, for the 2018 season at a clip of $6 million, and 2019 at $6.5 million. These were bargain rates for the team, such that if Altuve continued to perform well, or even improve, he would hit the open market two years later, and two years older, than he would have otherwise.

Just before Altuve took the deal, he had switched agencies, leaving the game's most famous rep, Scott Boras. "If he would have asked me, 'Would you have signed that contract?'" Boras said the following year. "Just like I would have told him before, that's not what All-Star players get paid. But players have different reasons for signing contracts and doing things, and clubs have very right reasons on their part for offering such things."

In July 2013, when Altuve's deal was being finalized, the Astros happened to be in Luhnow's old city, St. Louis. Luhnow and Altuve met alone over omelets at the Westin to hash out final details.

"He and I met for breakfast and worked through all the outstanding issues," Luhnow said. "Did the whole thing in Spanish. . . . We'd gone back and forth a little bit. We were both there in St. Louis and decided to get together and just see where we would figure it out. And we figured it all out there.

"It was one of those situations where the player was motivated, and he approached us, and we started to put together a couple of different ideas. I can't remember exactly who talked to who first. But it was clear from the beginning that he was interested. And you know, he used to have Boras Corp. represent him. He switched agencies."

Naturally, Altuve's motivations were centered on the early delivery of cash—he would be a multimillionaire now instead of having to wait and risk injury.

But a player's family's needs and upbringing matter, too. Altuve came from a middle-class background in Venezuela, which in 2013 was on the verge of economic collapse. "Now you can help your family," Altuve said. "You're giving a better life for them."

"At the time, we knew it was a really good deal anyway, but obviously it ended up being by far and away a better deal for the club than we expected at the time," one Astros exec said. "We thought there was like $10 or $15 million in surplus value in that deal. And there ended up being $70 or $80 million in surplus value, five or six times what we thought."

# 6

## RADICAL WAYS

THE GROUP OF PLAYERS THAT WOULD LEAD THE ASTROS OUT OF THE ABYSS was starting to knock on the door, and one of the expected early arrivers presented a problem.

The son of a gymnast and eager-eyed, George Springer sometimes did backflips on the field for fun. He was the prize of the 2011 draft, the last before Jeff Luhnow and the new regime took over, and Springer had put together a wondrous season in 2013 between the two highest levels of the minor leagues: a .303 batting average with 37 home runs and 45 stolen bases. The combination of 40 homers and 40 steals is a benchmark in the sport, something few players have ever done, warranting its own moniker: a 40–40 season. He wasn't yet playing at the game's highest level, but he was making a strong case he was ready.

Given how awful the 2013 Astros were, Springer was easily better than most of the major league roster. On that basis alone, he deserved a promotion immediately. He wasn't too young: at age twenty-three, he was actually a few months older than Jose Altuve, who debuted in the majors in 2011. A player like Springer would have made the 2013 Astros a little less torturous to watch.

But the front office had two large reasons to keep Springer in the minor leagues. The first was, in spite of all the positives, a question of performance that left the nascent baseball ops group split.

Springer struck out a ton in 2013, 161 times, a suggestion he needed to improve at recognizing pitches and making decisions to swing before facing the world's best pitching. Strikeouts have become acceptable in the majors if they come with a lot of power and walks, but for players in the minors, they are often a harbinger of future struggles. The Astros' projection model for pro players, built by Mike Fast at Sig Mejdal's direction, hated high-strikeout players. Springer's projection was bleak: he would last maybe two or three years, with minimal contribution.

What, though, if the model was wrong? Fast and Mejdal were on opposite ends of the debate, their first significant split, and not close to the last. Mejdal, the ex-blackjack dealer, vehemently believed in relying on the model, for the model represented the odds.

"There was a real organizational debate over what should be done with George," one executive said. "The Astros front office was very factional. And different factions were always pushing for different things. And so I think that was a case where there were some people that wanted George to stay down longer, and there were some people that wanted him up right away because they were just tired of losing; they wanted our best outfield out there.

"He was either going to be a huge piece of the championship team, which is what he ended up being, or there was a view among some people that he was like striking out over a quarter of his plate appearances against shitty pitching. And they're like, 'Kids with that profile don't project well.' So you know, he's worthless, we might as well get something back for him now while we can."

Late in 2013, the majority of Springer's career had still been spent at the lower levels of the minors. Every plate appearance was modeling Springer to players of similar lower-level minor league experience.

Fast was starting to more deeply consider what it meant to be data-driven at all: How are you picking your data, and how are you framing your questions? Dubious of his own model, he dug into some underlying numbers: Springer's strike zone judgment, how hard he hit the ball, his foot speed. He found a player who was very obviously different from the others that his own model likened to Springer, and he believed the model was comparing him to the wrong population. Springer, as he saw it, really belonged to a group of athletic players with defensive value and a strong ability to assess pitches, yet the model wasn't looking at him that way.

As a group, the Astros front office understood that any new information outside the model was potentially perilous. Mejdal, in particular, had a very high bar to clear for new information to be worked into the model, or worse, for it to be considered as supplementary outside the model. Mejdal didn't believe that Fast or the group could confidently say they were evaluating the new context well enough. The projection system, Mejdal would say, has a thousand comparisons in it, so why would I look at the ten comps presented outside the system?

With Fast and Mejdal split, Luhnow asked Brandon Taubman to put together a study, one of many such assignments Luhnow would give his new valuation expert. Taubman sided with Fast, and was to make a presentation to owner Jim Crane about his findings. The study included the other motivation for the Astros to keep Springer in the minor leagues: service time. The clock.

When a player arrives in the big leagues, a countdown starts on their march toward paydays in arbitration, and eventually, free agency. The presentation to Crane, called "Springer call-up cost analysis," included three scenarios: a call-up in August 2013, in late April 2014, or in June 2014.

The first choice meant that Springer would become a free agent after the 2019 season. The latter two promised Springer would be with the Astros for another year, through at least 2020. The last date added some sweetener, too: it would ensure Springer would not become one of the few players to hit arbitration eligibility early, keeping his cost lower.

Now, the Astros were not the first team to factor in a player's clock. The rules clearly incentivized teams to wait, and the players' union agreed to those rules. But teams also tend not to publicly say they're debating a promotion for service-time reasons because it could theoretically cost them millions of dollars. The players' union can, and has, filed grievances alleging teams acted in bad faith over a player's clock, but such a case is very difficult to prove absent hard evidence.

Now, if the Astros could sign Springer to a long-term deal just as they had with Jose Altuve? Then Springer's pay schedule would be locked in, and the clock wouldn't matter as much. Yet locking up Springer would be odd, because teams rarely give long-term contracts to players who have never been to the majors before.

In September 2013, the Astros offered Springer a deal that would guarantee him $7.6 million with a total potential to make $23 million over seven years.

Signing bonus: $1 million
2014: $4 million
2015: $1 million
2016: $1 million
2017: $600,000 with escalators up to $3 million
2018: $3 million club option
2019: $4 million club option
2020: $6 million club option

The proposal, however, was heavily influenced by the projection model. Those salary figures were not reflective of the potential superstar ceiling the Astros knew Springer could hit. "We ended up too anchored toward Sig's number when we made a pretty shitty offer," one member of the brain trust said.

Springer and his agent, Greg Genske, didn't want to sell away their upside, not for such a lowball offer. So Luhnow decided to make the conversation more intimate. He allegedly brought Springer to Houston on the premise, explained to both the player and some staff, that Springer was in town for an eye exam. And without Springer's agent present, Luhnow tried to sell his budding star on the offer. Springer, youthful and energetic but also a little bro-ish, asked one Astros staffer playfully, "Are you going to pay me a bazillion dollars?" one witness recalled.

People connected to Springer were furious at the so-called eye exam, and in retrospect, some members of the Astros front office acknowledge how bad an idea it was. Attempting to isolate a player from his agent in talks is a no-no, but at least some of the junior members of the front office were simply unaware of the norms. "We wanted to make sure like the communication around it was good, so we had George come to the office," an exec said. "Greg wasn't there, so that was one of the things that upset Greg, and knowing more about how things work now, I don't blame him." Luhnow should have known, but it also might have been a calculated risk, with the potential to save the Astros many millions.

Springer declined the offer. At the start of the next season, Luhnow left him in the minor leagues on Opening Day—even though Springer would have already been in the majors had he accepted the contract. The union considered filing a service-time manipulation grievance against the Astros, but didn't.

"Springer should have made our club," said the Astros' bench coach in 2014, Dave Trembley, the second-in-command to the field manager. "There's no question."

Luhnow wound up promoting Springer two weeks into the season, the middle scenario that the front office presented to Crane. That two-week wait guaranteed Springer would be a member of the Astros for an additional year, through 2020, rather than after 2019.

For the future of their roster, the Astros had acted shrewdly. But for player relations, which could also affect the future of their roster, they had made a mistake. After the so-called eye exam, the Astros had provided reason for one their best talents to look at the organization skeptically, before he had ever set foot in the big leagues.

During spring training, vendors often visit teams to sell players high-end wares, including suits. Springer was being fitted one day when Trembley ran into him.

"It was late, six o'clock, I'm working out, getting done, and I'm leaving, and Springer's out there in the hall and he's getting fitted," Trembley said. "And he looked at me and he says, 'What do you think, Dave?' And I go, 'You know what's going on.' He goes, 'I ain't gonna make the club.'

"But he said, 'But when I get a chance to get 'em, I'm gonna get 'em.' He was talking about money. He said, 'When I get a chance to get 'em, I'm gonna get 'em. And I'm going to get 'em good.'

"The players knew. The players know. There was always a feeling there of, you know, you're there, do the best you can—but be careful what you say. Be careful what you say. 'Cause there was spinning it in the media. Luhnow was spinning it in the media.

"There was always a feeling that it wasn't quite aboveboard. There was something else going on. They weren't being totally honest."

The attempt to sign Springer was just one piece of a larger puzzle. The Altuve extension had emboldened Luhnow to direct Taubman to construct a flurry of similar offers for young players, including Jason Castro, Matt Dominguez, Robbie Grossman, Jon Singleton, and, eventually, Dallas Keuchel and even prospect Carlos Correa.

Castro's offer was dated March 9, a $12 million guarantee with the potential to make $30 million. Grossman's was dated March 10, a $7 million guarantee with the potential to make $23.5 million. Both players declined.

The scattershot approach was purposeful and, in fact, targeted. The Astros knew that some of the deals, had they been accepted, likely would have worked out poorly. "The idea of the strategy was that it would be OK to go bust on thirty to forty percent, which is like an alarmingly high number, because the surplus value on the ones that do work out more than compensates for the losses," an Astros exec said. "It's a venture capitalist sort of approach. You take a handful of big bets instead of making a multitude more of small, safe bets."

Purely from a cost standpoint, the plan was new and ingenious. Yet, early in the 2014 season, no other players had taken the bait. Players and their agents were also starting to fume, because some of the contracts came with implicit pressures: take a team-friendly deal, and you can be promoted to the big leagues. Or take a deal, and you'll stay on the major league roster if you're already there. But if you didn't? Well, who knows what will happen?

One of them did eventually bite. Jon Singleton, a power-hitting prospect, was not yet in the big leagues when he accepted a contract in the middle of the 2014 season. He was immediately promoted upon signing. The deal guaranteed him $10 million for five years, with club options for three additional years—pushing back his potential free agency by two years.

Singleton and his agency were criticized heavily for the contract, on the belief it would cut off Singleton's potential earnings. But the agency knew Singleton well, better than the team and public did, and knew that his future in the sport was more tenuous beyond the ever-present risks of injury and poor performance. Singleton had personal issues the Astros were aware of, but only to an extent. The team was still willing to gamble on him because of their dedication to the math.

One Astros employee noted that the front office didn't ask opinions of those who worked closely with Singleton on the ground, and that the message they would have received would have been to stay away.

In spring of 2014, prior to accepting the offer, Singleton had told Associated Press reporter Kristie Rieken that he was an addict. "I know that I enjoy smoking weed, I enjoy being high, and I can't block that out of my mind that I enjoy that," he said. "So I have to work against that." Singleton acknowledged to Rieken his reliance on alcohol, as well. Baseball, even more so back then, did not provide the most supportive environment for players with addiction problems to recover, sometimes treating substance use punitively. Marijuana use, even for those who used more casually than Singleton, led to suspensions in the minor leagues until only recently.

But once a player arrived in the major leagues, a more player-friendly system, as bargained by the union, protected them. The union back then did not represent most minor league players.

Once Singleton had agreed to the deal, he flew to Houston for his physical. About an hour before the contract signing, Luhnow called Singleton's agency to alert them to a problem: Singleton allegedly had tested positive for THC.

"Well, I think we have a bigger problem," one of Singleton's representatives shot back.

Luhnow asked why.

"You just drug tested a forty-man-roster player without probable cause," the agent said.

Any player you see in the major leagues has to be part of what's known as the forty-man roster. But some players, like Singleton was at the time, are on that roster while still playing in the minor leagues. So Singleton was one of the small group of minor league players who were active members of the major league union, and covered under the more player-friendly drug testing rules afforded to big leaguers. Those rules prohibit drug testing without cause.

Potentially violating a player's collectively bargained rights was no small matter. The agent believed Luhnow was trying to get a better deal leveraging the drug test. Luhnow was told he had two choices: move forward with the deal, or scrap the whole thing, and that he had twenty minutes to make up his mind.

If Luhnow called off the deal, a grievance from the union likely would have followed. He needed only five minutes to reach an answer: the deal would go ahead as agreed to.

Singleton didn't last with the Astros for the length of the contract, his substance use continuing. Years later, he was back in the minor leagues with the Astros and off the forty-man roster, fully a minor league player again, and subject to minor league testing and discipline. Singleton again tested positive for a substance that was not publicly identified, leaving him with a one-hundred-game suspension in 2018. Likely concerned primarily about his investment, Luhnow allegedly tried to leverage the later failed drug test to void the rest of the money Singleton was owed. Singleton and the Astros are said to have ended up with a settlement to part ways, and it wasn't until the 2022 season that Singleton latched on with a big-league organization again, joining the Milwaukee Brewers, where a couple of former Astros executives had migrated.

○

Luhnow's rebuild in 2014 was entering its third full year, and contracts weren't the only area where the Astros were implementing their brand. To the taste of some of the brain trust, the pace of change actually wasn't fast enough. Yet relative to the rest of baseball, this was breakneck.

Luhnow described two ways to make change. "One is to be on the bleeding edge. And so, for example, a business example, setting up retail distribution in China," he said. "You're on the bleeding edge there because the way products get delivered to consumers in China is not like it is in the States. So if a Walmart or a Target or somebody goes into China, and they want to set up a distribution, they're going to have to forge through the forest and cut down the trees and figure out how to do it. That's called the bleeding edge. True innovation happens that way.

"I would consider in Major League Baseball, the Rays are an example of a team that have done that. The A's to a certain extent are an example of a team that has done that. Where they have done something so unique, but it's not without risk. But they're doing that because there's a reward on the other side.

"The second way to do it is to be a fast follower, and once you see evidence that something is working, then you follow quickly. You learn from the first movers' mistakes or what he did right and you fast follow."

I agreed late in the summer of 2013 to take a job covering the Astros for the *Houston Chronicle*. Before I arrived, I told a player agent, someone who counted a relative nobody on the Astros' roster as a client, of my new role, which hadn't yet begun. Their response to me was immediate and memorable: something weird was going on in Houston, they said. Something was off about the way that franchise was doing things.

Over that winter and into the 2014 season, I heard that same sentiment many times over. What quickly became clear was that for all their smarts, the Astros were not creating a lot of buy-in or trust among different stakeholders.

Not all points of contention were off the field. The Astros were using the defensive shift very frequently, a strategy that statistically made a ton of sense and grew in usage league-wide afterward. But their pitchers, at the time, were having a lot of trouble believing in it.

The shift moves fielders into spots where the numbers show batters usually hit the ball. But the shift's gains are easier to see over a span of time, rather than on a nightly basis. Sometimes, batted balls that would have been outs under a normal alignment become hits, a mental challenge for pitchers. "There was times when during games, the second baseman on a weak ground ball would go through, and those guys would just come in the dugout, be pissed," Trembley said.

Bo Porter, the manager, and the coaches had to smooth it over.

The Astros weren't the first team to shift, but their usage of it had increased dramatically year over year. This was an area where the Astros were fast followers, Luhnow pointed out.

In the minor leagues, a couple of changes were afoot. There was a rumor that the Astros were telling hitters not to swing, but to take walks, which would be an over-the-top recommendation. The reality was a little different.

"Telling guys, when you're in a count 3–2, 2–2, to still focus your strike zone smaller than the actual strike zone, and focus on good pitches to hit," an executive said. "Swing at strikes, but if it's a close pitch, take it, because the numbers were showing us that long term, umpires are calling more balls than strikes. And that was all they were saying. . . . It probably got misconstrued a little bit."

Luhnow also reprised something he had started with the Cardinals, the use of tandem, or piggyback, pitchers. Starting pitchers would be used differently than they were in most other organizations, beginning a game one day but entering later in the game in another. It was a challenge to routine that prompted some pitchers to worry about their arm health. "My whole life has been on a five-day rotation and that's all it was, that's all it's been," said one of their young prospects, Mike Foltynewicz. "Throwing in a piggyback system and throwing on one more day of rest, I couldn't tell you what the issue was, but I definitely was a little sore."

Foltynewicz wasn't the only one who felt uncomfortable.

After drafting Carlos Correa with the first overall pick in 2012, the Astros took a college pitcher in 2013 in the same position in the draft, right-hander Mark Appel out of Stanford, a consensus blue-chip prospect if there ever was one. But after he signed with the Astros for a $6.35 million bonus in 2013, his career started to go sideways almost immediately.

Prior to the 2014 season, Appel underwent an emergency appendectomy. He didn't think much of the procedure until doctors, years later, asked him about it, when they found he had essentially no ability to control or activate his lower abdominal. Heading into 2014, his rehab from the appendectomy was nonexistent. He said he had been told it would heal on its own.

Whether the appendectomy started the chain of events that followed or not, more trouble was on the way, and the tandem system threw Appel for a loop.

"The piggyback system was really, really difficult on me," Appel said. "I'm not saying that critical of anyone or anyone who made that organizational decision. But for me, it was really tough.

"I don't know if it was the piggyback system or not, but there was something that happened that caused some compensation [in my throwing motion], and my elbow started struggling. And when my elbow starts struggling, I started changing the way I throw, and that starts affecting my shoulder."

The Astros in 2014 also sent Appel to a minor league team that played in a stadium where hitters thrive because of the desert air, a mistake, an executive admitted after the fact. Appel should have been able to overcome that challenge on its own, but it likely compounded his struggle.

Appel's agent, Scott Boras, called the tandem system "physically and mentally very disruptive for Mark." Boras represented Lance McCullers Jr., as well, and reached out to Luhnow to ask for adjustments to be made for his clients. Boras felt the Astros were more accommodating for McCullers than for Appel.

Being a top prospect in Houston in this era wasn't the easiest job. High draft picks always have pressure, but because Luhnow was so loudly touting the draft and the future as the centerpiece of his work—and because Appel happened to have Houston roots—the spotlight was beating down on Appel intensely.

"The expectation was like, 'Oh, Mark will be helping out the Astros maybe by the end of 2014, if not early 2015,'" Appel said. "And so I'm like, 'I don't have time to get hurt. I need to get my innings in, I need to get my reps in, I can't throw 80 innings in a season and then be expected to throw 250 the next year.' So that was something I was just kind of unprepared for, because for whatever reason, I stayed really, really healthy in college, and I had a lot of games where I was over 120 pitches in college, and like it never bothered me. And then, you know, I started throwing in the Astros' org."

A project began: fixing Mark Appel. And the Astros front office would later come to be convinced his woes were not their fault.

○

Even if pitching in a tandem, or playing behind the shift, were mental matters that players could relearn, they're creatures of routine. Baseball is famously a game of failure, and its participants are full of sensitivities and idiosyncrasies. The task was not as simple as telling players, "Do this, we swear it'll make you better," particularly not in those days.

All that Luhnow was undertaking, both the off-field and on-field maneuvering, came against a backdrop of losing, and that doesn't do much for credibility. The firings had been jarring to some inside and outside the club, as well. It was a bad scene, prompting some players, agents, and baseball staff—including old-school types who were predisposed to dislike Luhnow—to complain.

The long-term contract pursuits were front and center. The approach had irked people. "Players are people, but the Astros view them purely as property that can be evaluated through a computer program or a rigid set of criteria," a player agent said. "They plug players into it to see what makes sense from a development or contractual perspective, and it does not engender a lot of goodwill in the player or agent community.

"They wield service time like a sword and basically tell a player, 'This is what you are worth to us, take it or leave it.'"

Said Luhnow: "No one's forcing anybody to sign any contracts in this game."

But players were ticked, too.

"They are definitely the outcast of Major League Baseball right now, and it's kind of frustrating for everyone else to have to watch it," said Bud Norris, a pitcher who was with the Astros in 2013 but had moved on to another team. "When you talk to agents, when you talk to other players, and you talk amongst the league, yeah, there's going to be some opinions about it, and they're not always pretty."

On their own, some of the individual gripes faced reasonable counterarguments. Shifting would help in the long run, and most people, at least outside of the clubhouse, knew that.

But whether each complaint was totally rational or irrational was to see the trees, rather than the forest. The collective sentiment was the problem. People didn't like how the Astros were handling them in a variety of ways. The front office's adherence to the numbers across the board was a turnoff. Too many in the industry thought the Astros were dehumanizing the sport and the players.

Say Luhnow's front office had already become the smartest anywhere. What good were their ideas if they didn't know how to make people believe in them? If the players and agents didn't trust them?

"I don't think anybody's happy. I'm not," an Astros player said. "They just take out the human element of baseball. It's hard to play for a GM who just sees you as a number instead of a person. Jeff is experimenting with all of us."

The Astros weren't the only organization living and breathing analytics, but they had been very loud about their adoption. Their plan also might have been the most extreme, owing in part to their belief that the advantage lay in the speed of adoption. "The trend is going toward sheer statistical-driven analysis," said Jed Lowrie, a player who spent time with the Astros in different stints. "Baseball is kind of going through this tectonic shift, and there are people out there banging on tables saying, 'This is not the way the game's supposed to be played or evaluated.' But from a business standpoint, I get it.

"It is a purely statistical analysis. I think you can't have that approach and expect to have good personal relations. That seems like a hard balance to strike, when you're judging someone strictly on numbers and nothing else, and I'm not talking about whether it's a good guy or a bad guy. But there are certain intangibles, and the perception is the numbers are trying to drive out [the importance of] those intangibles."

Luhnow and Mejdal had lived through resistance with the Cardinals, albeit without responsibility as broad as theirs in Houston. Their success in St. Louis following the revolt of the Cardinals' old guard only hardened their resolve in Houston. They knew negative reactions would arise again, and they believed that most had to be ignored. Mejdal's position was long established: change is hard.

Baseball isn't an easy sport for leadership communication, no matter the circumstances. The minor league staffs all work remotely; same with scouts, save for rare exceptions. But even within that context, Luhnow's greatest weakness was his communication outside his inner circle.

"I don't think that he sat and thought, How do I get everybody to buy in?" one Astros exec said. "He was thinking, How do I build the best operating structures? How do I build the best system to win a World Series?"

Luhnow and Crane had both been criticized in the media before, and each time, had plowed forward. When I newly brought them questions about their industry perception in 2014, their tolerance to hear others' criticisms was low, to say the least.

"I've been in this business longer than you have," Luhnow said. "I have family who are journalists that have been around way longer than you have." He appeared to be referring in part to his brother, who works at the *Wall Street Journal*, and to his ex-wife, a former television reporter. "You make your choices," he said to me.

The owner, meanwhile, threatened my access.

"I'm going to be in this town a long time," Crane said. "And I'm not going anywhere. And anything negative on our team, affects the team, affects the players, affects the people, affects the fans, affects the city, affects me.

"I'll be very reluctant to continue to visit with you if we continue to get negative information on the team, because I don't think it does us any good."

Crane said that both he and Luhnow treat people how they want to be treated. Crane, too, pointed to his other businesses. "Check my track record, it's pretty good," Crane said. "Everything I've done's turned around."

In our first conversation about the criticisms, Luhnow was adamant that there was no link between the different endeavors the team was undertaking: that the shift and contract negotiations and tandem pitching in the minor leagues had no shared thread. In a follow-up discussion, he was calmer.

"No question, you have to get feedback from everybody," Luhnow said. "But you also have to realize, we're not running for election, we're not trying to get votes. This is an industry where only the best survive. It's an up-or-out industry. People are going to get released. People are going to not have the playing time they want. People are not going to get promoted the way they want. People aren't going to be in the role that they want, and there's going to be a lot of complaining by definition. And we understand that. You have to sort through that to get the kernels of truth that you really need to help you achieve your goals.

"We're trying to win big-league games, and we're trying to produce major league players in the minor leagues. So if those two results are occurring, that's predominantly what we care about. Now, of course, anytime you've got human beings involved, whether they're coaches or players or trainers or anybody, fans, you want to understand how they're impacted by whatever it is you're trying to do."

In May, the *Houston Chronicle* published my piece with the headline "Radical Methods Paint Astros as 'Outcast.'" It centered on one question: How much criticism should be inherent to the Astros' process and how much should signal trouble?

"If it starts to affect us in a meaningful way, that we can't sign players or players quit, or players don't give us their best effort, then we'll have to address it," went Luhnow's answer. "But as of now, that hasn't happened."

If Luhnow believed he was right, he would push forward.

"One of Jeff's great qualities as a leader, and potentially also something that got him in trouble, is he really doesn't care what people think of him," one Astros exec said. "You want to talk about thick skin? He has incredibly thick skin and he does not care what people think about him."

How, then, would Luhnow know when he was wrong, or if he had gone too far? A group so comfortable challenging everyone else's beliefs was, ironically, not keen to hear concerns about their own. He felt like "these problems aren't real problems," another lieutenant said.

The antidote to the complaints was actually quite simple, in Luhnow's mind: the Astros needed to win. Winning, he believed, would fix everything.

"Perception will change when we succeed," Luhnow said. "When we win a division, all that perception will turn from negative to positive. That's how it works. You think if Oakland didn't have success—how many people hated Moneyball, the idea of Moneyball? But Oakland has proven over and over again how successful they are, by being creative, by being innovative. So they're heroes."

O

In many ways, the 2014 season became a crash course in crisis management. Initially, Luhnow thought one of the first disasters might have been owed to a photo in the *Houston Chronicle*.

During spring training, I wrote a feature story explaining Ground Control, the team's database. The piece considered the risk involved with putting all that information in digital form, accessible on the web. "We have done what we need to do to minimize information leaking," Luhnow said. "If someone leaves, they're allowed to take what's called the residual intellectual property with them, which is anything they remember in their head. They're not allowed to take anything beyond that. There are ways to protect yourself by making sure that people have access to the data that they only need to make the decisions in the area."

The story went live on the *Chronicle*'s website the night of March 8. The next morning, I got a call from Luhnow, who was anxious, if not a little panicked. The team had allowed a *Chronicle* photographer to shoot photos of Ryan Hallahan, the architect of the database, next to his computer monitor at the Astros' office. If you zoomed in on the image, you could see what was a very basic URL: groundcontrol.astros .com.

People were trying to get into the system, Luhnow said, and my editors agreed to remove the photo from the web. The Astros quickly changed the URL and made other moves to bolster their system, actions they would have done well to take ahead of time.

What Luhnow did not know is that the system had already been breached long ago. Starting no later than March 2013, a Cardinals executive had been logging into Ground Control and the Astros' email systems.

Chris Correa—the same Chris Correa who had sent Taubman the

Astros' way—had gained access to the Astros' proprietary information.

Correa, at the time, was a rising star in the Cardinals' front office. He had an undergraduate degree in cognitive science and a master's in psychology. "Obviously, I thought the world of him: I promoted him to scouting director," Cardinals president John Mozeliak said. "And he was always someone that was evolving and growing, and as far as like the team I had put together, he was one of the key members on it."

Correa's first connection to the Cardinals had been through Mejdal, helping Mejdal to prepare college data and analytics for the draft. He worked closely with both Luhnow and Mejdal, and took personally the possibility that when that duo had left the Cardinals, they brought Cardinals' proprietary information with them. He was suspicious, skeptical. It had taken the Cardinals years to build up their analytics prowess, thanks to his sweat and many others'—why, and how, should the Astros be able to re-create it so quickly?

Correa knew the password Mejdal had used in St. Louis. Mejdal was said not to have meaningfully, if at all, changed it since his St. Louis days, a major failure of password hygiene. Armed with that knowledge, Correa logged into different Astros systems, both Ground Control and email. He set out to learn what, if anything, the Astros had stolen from the Cardinals.

The day after the story ran explaining Ground Control's existence, the Astros reset all the passwords to the system. The following day, March 10, Correa logged into Mejdal's email and found an email attachment that had a new default password for all users, and the new URL for Ground Control. He kept going, illegally. But the Astros had no hint yet as to who was infiltrating their system.

Ground Control was a repository for trade notes: what other teams were asking for in exchange for certain players, what discussions had taken place. A reporter had obtained a store of the Astros' trade notes and informed the Astros of it. "A journalist had it, sent it to Jeff and said, 'I want you to know that I have this, not gonna run it because I don't think it's right for me to run it. This clearly is not something

I should have. But I want you to know out of courtesy that it's out there,'" an Astros exec recalled. "The guy said they got this from an anonymous email address, and I don't know who this is coming from. But it certainly appears either stolen, or not something that you would want out there. So we immediately alerted MLB security; they began an investigation on this. We thought what had happened was the *Chronicle* ran a story on Ground Control.

"We had no idea how internal conversations were ending up on public internet sites. We had no idea how that was happening. We thought we had a pretty secure system."

Not every media outlet was so deferential. About a month later, in June, the same trove of information made its way to Deadspin. "Leaked: 10 Months of the Houston Astros' Internal Trade Talks," went the headline. For the first time, the public knew the Astros had been breached.

The story was embarrassing on multiple levels. The Astros were so confident in their methods, yet hadn't been able to protect confidential trade talks. "I feel bad about that," Luhnow said. "I've been on the phone with other teams expressing my apology and letting them know what happened. That's about all I can do at this point."

Details of how the Astros valued their own players were also uncomfortable for the players themselves. Players are often mentioned in trade rumors through the course of their careers, but the possibility of having to switch cities and teams is nonetheless an added mental burden.

Some of the actual trade conversations were also laughable, with the Astros making lopsided requests for other teams' players.

Luhnow said some of the conversations were inaccurate, although he offered no specifics or further proof. One deal discussed, a trade for Rockies outfielder Dexter Fowler, had already happened.

According to Deadspin, the trade notes had been posted at Anon bin.com, a site where users anonymously shared information that had been hacked or leaked. But the Astros still were in the dark as to who would break into their systems.

"We were one of the more active teams in the trade market the last couple years," Luhnow said when asked why the Astros were targeted. "Maybe that had something to do with it. I really don't have an idea."

The FBI was now in charge of finding out.

○

In June 2014, less than a week before Deadspin published the Ground Control notes, *Sports Illustrated* revealed it gave the Astros their famed cover treatment. Diminished since then by layoffs and an ownership change, the magazine was still considered the industry standard back then.

Luhnow granted journalist Ben Reiter particularly high access to the front office, including during the amateur draft in June. The piece was laudatory of the front office's direction, and received a lot of attention for the cover that came with it. George Springer was batting, with a prediction printed: "Your 2017 World Series Champs."

Although Luhnow did exhibit a rare ability to ignore outside perception, he also strove to bend it in his favor when he could, and in this way, he did actually care what others thought of him. As it had been in St. Louis, Luhnow's approach to the media was often selective and almost always self-serving. "He'd talk to the *Wall Street Journal* and he'd talk to the *New York Times*," one Astros lieutenant said. "He wasn't talking to strictly baseball writers. He would talk to kind of broader audiences."

Dave Trembley, the bench coach, put it more bluntly: "Jeff hated the press."

But for the Astros, even curated, positive publicity wasn't always positive. Although Houston fans ate up the *SI* story, the piece was not well received inside baseball, including inside pockets of the Astros, because it came off as gloating and self-aggrandizing at a time when the Astros had not actually accomplished anything. It also ran counter to the Astros' otherwise intense and sometimes over-the-top efforts to keep their front-office work private.

"It rubbed a lot of people the wrong way," said Alex Jacobs, who was in just his second year as a pro scout with the Astros in 2014. "I remember having a conversation with Kevin [Goldstein] about it. Like, why are we telling everybody our secrets?

"Why was that necessary? Why give Ben Reiter that opportunity to write about our draft process? . . . Because they wanted the attention, they wanted to reinvent the wheel."

Luhnow granted access to another major publication, *Bloomberg Businessweek*, where Joshua Green, a prominent political reporter, wrote a more measured feature that didn't receive as much attention, and then that was it for a time. Jim Crane ordered a soft gag order on Luhnow's public chatter. "That *SI* article did not endear Sig and Jeff and Elias to the rest of the baseball industry in a lot of ways," an Astros colleague said.

"At the time, they've been taking so much heat for two and a half years, because they were the Dis-Astros, the Laugh-stros," Reiter later told reporter Bradford Davis, then of the *New York Daily News*, about the access Luhnow gave him. "People thought these guys were, you know, tanking and embarrassing the game. I think that they were ready to open up a little bit and show the world what they were doing and the best way to do that was through me and *SI*."

○

The June draft would be the last of three straight when the Astros picked first overall, their reward for losing. They were getting one more first overall pick to add to the other two, Carlos Correa (2012) and Mark Appel (2013).

This year, the Astros would go for a category of pitcher that was not considered the most reliable atop the draft: a high schooler.

Growing up in the San Diego area, Brady Aiken had turned himself into a baseball machine by the time he reached high school, showing the kind of dedication to the sport that has become required for players to stand out in a youth landscape that is growing ever more competitive and costly. Five a.m. wake-ups, hitting the gym, playing on travel ball teams at an expense of time and money were all part of the formula. Prospect development and youth baseball had already become their own cottage industry, and Aiken dominated the circuit.

The Aikens were sensitive to any suggestion that Brady had specialized too early. He indeed went to the gym at an early age, but Aiken's trainer said he didn't start lifting weights until he was fifteen. "We mainly did it for agility," said his father, Jim Aiken. "In soccer, we were working with him on speed and agility, and that's what we did. . . . I read some things, that, 'Boy oh boy, he's been going to a trainer since he was ten.'

"My son didn't really start lifting weights until he was in high school."

Aiken's makeup, a broad term typically encompassing character and poise and work ethic, was considered particularly strong. Altogether, he had done everything he could to put himself in position to be the top overall pick, with a fastball in the low to mid-90s and excellent control, the ability to throw the ball where he wanted. "This is the most advanced high school pitcher I've ever seen in my entire career," Luhnow said on draft day. "He has command like I've never seen before."

In most cases, and particularly with the No. 1 overall pick in the draft, teams and players reach a verbal understanding of a signing bonus ahead of time. The Astros' planned deal with Aiken was for $6.5 million, a savings of about $1.4 million compared to the money allotted for the pick, $7,922,100.

Aiken, like all prominent players, had a player agent working with him. At this time, the NCAA had a silly rule that forbade players from fully employing an agent, lest the player endanger their NCAA eligibility. So agents were instead known as "advisors." But the distinction was meaningless window dressing.

Casey Close, a premier agent whose most famous client was Derek Jeter, worked with Aiken. Another of Close's clients, high school right-hander Jacob Nix, was also drafted by the Astros in 2014, in the fifth round.

In effect, the $1.4 million saved from Aiken's deal was earmarked for Nix, who was getting an above-slot deal. Nix's spot in the draft was valued at $370,500, but the bonus he agreed to with the Astros was $1.5 million.

But deals aren't finalized until players pass physical exams. In baseball, drafted players do not have to be looked at by a team doctor until after they are drafted.

For everything Aiken had done to prepare for the sport, what he could not control was the anatomy of his elbow. The Astros found that Aiken's throwing elbow created an abnormally high-risk profile, because of a "cut-and-dry issue," as one person with knowledge of the evaluation said.

The ulnar collateral ligament, which is connected to the upper arm on one side and the forearm on the other, undergoes extreme stress in the act of throwing. Often, pitchers' UCLs are at least somewhat damaged from regular use. But Aiken's elbow was said to be anatomically different. "He may have some" of a UCL, "but not much," the person said.

The crux of the concern was not only the possibility Aiken might need to replace the ligament. That procedure, known as Tommy John surgery, is common enough, an epidemic in the sport in its own right, but one that players can recover from after about a year's time.

But the Astros feared that even with surgery, Aiken wouldn't bounce back well because of the structure of his elbow.

"They drill holes in your bone and tie, tether the new ligament on to these holes," one person with knowledge of the diagnosis said, describing the process of a Tommy John operation. "He didn't have the space to do that. He was going to be a real artwork type of surgery."

One Astros executive recalled an estimated 80 percent chance Aiken's elbow would blow out within a year.

Second opinions were gathered on both sides, although the Astros, to one employee, were a little too gung ho. Luhnow in 2013 had hired a medical risk manager and analyst with a finance background, Bill Firkus, who was not himself a doctor.

"They wanted another doctor to look at his files," said Nate Lucero, the Astros' head trainer in 2014. "And they wanted it done immediately. And I was like, 'Well, I don't know how you're going to get that done, you can FedEx it and stuff, but you better get all your HIPAA papers signed. . . . He's not the one who's seeking that advice. It's you guys. You better get some HIPAA papers signed by Aiken.'"

Lucero was concerned about protecting Aiken's medical privacy as Firkus tried to arrange for a second opinion.

"Why don't we just Skype [the doctor]? Or why don't we just let him do a GoToMeeting and he can look at your computer?" Lucero recalled Firkus saying.

"I said, 'No, you're not doing this shit on my computer,'" Lucero said. "I didn't let them get on my computer and the doctors weren't there yet, and that was Firkus trying to get that done, I was like, 'No, you're not going to do a GoToMeeting on my computer and let a random doctor look at his files and me lose everything I've ever worked for. . . .' He didn't know anything about HIPAA."

Most physicals do not produce major red flags or a desire to restructure a deal. Nix passed his.

The problem was that to sign Nix without incurring a huge penalty in baseball's bonus-pool system—the setup the Astros had navigated masterfully in 2012 when they drafted Carlos Correa—the Astros had to actually sign Aiken.

Having Nix go for his physical before the Aiken deal wrapped up proved a major procedural error.

"They brought 'em both out together," an Astros exec said of the timing of the exams. "We should have done them one at a time. We just never thought of this crazy scenario happening. Because [Nix] came in, his family was there, actually took his physical, and we didn't sign him after."

The calendar had flipped from June into July, and draft signings had to be completed by the middle of the month. HIPAA made it virtually impossible for the Astros to say much publicly.

The Astros knew well what the sport's rules allowed them to do, and their procedure became a cost-benefit analysis. If they offered Aiken at least 40 percent of his slot value and he declined, the Astros would get a compensatory pick one spot later in the following year's draft—No. 2 overall.

The Astros tried to estimate the chance of Aiken's successful recovery, and whether there would be any impairment to performance. They thought the pick was worth about $100 million, because it was measured not by Aiken's signing bonus, but by the opportunity cost attached to a first overall pick. But the front office's valuation put Aiken, in light of the diagnosis, as a $40 million player over time, someone that they would not have drafted in such a high position.

"I remember one day, Jeff texts at like seven o'clock in the morning, he's like, 'Get to work early today, we're talking about the Aiken thing, there's some shit there,'" an exec remembered. Elias, Mejdal, Taubman, and the executive the Astros had hired to oversee their medical efforts, Firkus, went around the room giving their opinions.

Taubman and Mejdal said the Astros should offer the minimum amount to get the compensatory pick a year later if Aiken didn't sign, no more. Elias and Firkus were in favor of a discounted offer above that amount.

"Bill's attitude was basically we should make an honest effort to get this guy at something close to the pre-evaluation offer," a colleague said. "I think Jeff thought that was soft."

The Astros made Aiken that minimum offer, at $3,168,840. Now, if Aiken accepted that deal, there would be a new wrinkle: the Astros would have considerably more money to play with, because they'd still have his full allotment of more than $7.9 million that could be distributed to other players.

In other words: at that price, they could sign Aiken and Nix and still have money left over. So they reached out to their twenty-first-round pick, pitcher Mac Marshall, who they previously thought wouldn't be signable.

"So we're looking at this and going, 'OK, this guy might take the 3.1 at the last second,'" an Astros exec said. "So we're like, 'Fuck, what do we do?' And so we went to the kid that we had randomly taken in the twenty-first round for shits and giggles: we might end up with extra money here."

But to Aiken's camp and to the players' union, the maneuver only fueled the idea the Astros were trying to squeeze Aiken for all they could, trying to leverage an extra player out of the ordeal. Through Aiken's injury, they could land a player they otherwise would not have had money to sign. Those in Aiken's corner saw a pitcher who was healthy, as he was still able to pitch.

All through the second opinions, the Astros never wavered in their belief that the elbow was a gigantic risk. But the Astros' reputation and Luhnow's bedside manner were actively working against him and the team.

With just days to go until the signing deadline, the agent working with Aiken, Casey Close, who very rarely speaks publicly, blasted the Astros. "We are extremely disappointed that Major League Baseball is allowing the Astros to conduct business in this manner with a complete disregard for the rules governing the draft and the twenty-nine other clubs who have followed those same rules," Close told Ken Rosenthal, then of Fox Sports.

The executive director of the union, Tony Clark, jumped in, too: "Our hope here going forward is that what we think has happened, didn't happen," he said, calling it "manipulation."

Until this episode, Jim Crane had largely let Luhnow run baseball ops on his own, but the developing debacle drew his attention. "Jim was getting frustrated and felt that Jeff should have been making more of an effort to sign Aiken," an Astros exec said.

Unbeknownst to nearly everyone at the time, Crane and a baseball dignitary who was working for the Astros, Hall of Fame pitcher Nolan Ryan, flew out to meet with Aiken's family. The family was "being real staunch, there's nothing wrong with him," an Astros exec said. "Jim and Nolan said it was weird." The full, original offer was said to be the only one Aiken's family wanted.

When the signing deadline arrived on July 18, the major league team was in Chicago while Luhnow was in Mexico. Elias was out scouting, so Taubman and Firkus were primarily manning the situation. Taubman was to speak with Close if the agent called.

"Bill was on standby because he was the representative or surrogate for all the medical information, and Jeff was gone. Jeff was in the air during all of this," a colleague remembered.

Said another executive: "Jeff was negotiating from fucking Mexico. I'm like, how really invested are we in this kid?"

Although Luhnow's visit to Mexico had been preplanned, people in the front office were annoyed. Firkus and Taubman both felt the situation was BS, that with their combined year and a half or so of experience working for the team and so much media attention, they shouldn't have been left alone. "It's the sort of thing where if shit hits the fan, you don't go," a member of the inner circle said. "It's not like this was a once-in-five-year anniversary trip for Jeff. He went to Mexico like three times a year."

Close didn't bite, and the Astros did not sign Aiken or Nix. Firkus and Taubman went out after the signing deadline passed to a nearby steakhouse for a drink.

To that point, I had never heard Luhnow quite so rattled as when he called me after the afternoon deadline passed. He made a point of noting to me that he had called me first, before any other outlet.

"We tried to engage the other side, Casey Close, three times today," Luhnow said within minutes of the deadline passing. "Never received a counter. Really, they just never engaged, for whatever reason, there was no interest. There just didn't appear to be interest to sign on their side.

"We did nothing unethical. We did nothing disingenuous. We tried to sign good players at the appropriate values and that's all we ever do with the draft."

There was one wrinkle. On the final day, Crane had directed the front office to raise the offer to Aiken from the minimum amount necessary to $5 million.

"Jeff would not have done that on his own," an Astros exec said. "That was one instance where Jim got involved and I think Jim was frustrated with the onslaught of poor publicity. He got involved and wanted to make it go away." Luhnow was ticked off, an executive said, because it was the first time he felt like Crane had gone over his head.

Crane was said to have agreed to elevate the offer mostly for PR purposes, but in a way, it backfired. If the Astros believed that Aiken could still be worth $5 million—worth something more than the minimum offer they left on the table for so long—then why wouldn't they have offered it to him sooner? It only added to the perception that the Astros were trying to take advantage of the medical process, attempting to play hardball while two kids' careers hung in the balance.

"Today, two young men should be one step closer to realizing their dreams of becoming major league ballplayers," Clark, the union head, said the day of the signing deadline. "Because of the actions of the Houston Astros, they are not."

Within a week, the union filed a grievance on behalf of Nix. He and the Astros reached a six-figure settlement to resolve the grievance. Nix wound up with the San Diego Padres, where he made the big leagues in 2018.

Literally everyone involved was unhappy. But proof that the Astros or Aiken's crew had made the proper evaluation of the youngster's elbow was not going to be easy to come by, because the debacle was centered on risk.

Say Aiken went on to a tremendous career and stayed perfectly healthy—that wouldn't have necessarily proven the Astros wrong. It could have meant that Aiken had effectively beaten the odds as the Astros saw them. The same held true in the opposite direction. If Aiken subsequently got hurt, it could be because of a new injury he suffered, not necessarily because the Astros had read his elbow properly. (Nix, for example, underwent Tommy John surgery in 2021.)

One potential sequence of events, though, stood out as potential validation for the Astros.

"The closest scenario that would match what we know of the Astros' concern for Aiken is if he does not recover well from the operation," I wrote for the *Chronicle* in 2015. And that's what came to pass. Aiken not only needed Tommy John surgery right away in 2015, but even once he started his pro career with Cleveland, he never was the same. He left the sport without advancing beyond the low levels of the minor leagues.

Aiken received $2.5 million as the seventeenth overall pick with Cleveland in 2015, far less money than he would have made had he taken the Astros' $5 million. In hindsight, were Aiken and his family too stubborn, refusing to believe what the medicals showed? Did Aiken's agent think he should sign the Astros' final-day, $5 million offer, only to be overruled by the family, or did Close actually advise against it?

"The idea that Jeff is mistreating this high school guy is, well, it's fiction, and it's not as interesting as the real story of a delusional father and agent," an Astros exec said.

"You're sitting there during the Aiken drama, and you know, like, the kid's physical's a ticking time bomb," another executive said. "And you just keep getting pounded anyways. And you're like, 'Well, they are out to get us.' It felt that way."

Aiken and his family may have turned the Astros down on principle. Either way, a question of the Astros' tact throughout the process lingered. If the Astros nailed the medical evaluation, and it seems they did, did they handle Aiken and Nix and the entire delicate affair as well as they could have? In the other direction, the dubious read is that Close and Aiken could have been attempting to leverage the distrust that they knew the industry held for the Astros.

Yet, it seems more likely that Aiken and company, as well as the players' union, were genuinely leery of the way the Astros did business. The Astros had already created a reputation for themselves that eliminated the benefit of the doubt, even in a situation where they might have otherwise deserved it.

# 7

## THE COUP

WHEN HE GOT TO THE ASTROS, BENCH COACH DAVE TREMBLEY GOT SOME dope on his new GM, Jeff Luhnow, from an old friend in the sport and now a colleague, instructor Dan Radison. Radison was one of Luhnow's St. Louis imports to Houston.

"'Let me tell you something,'" Trembley recalled of Radison's words, "'this guy is the most coldhearted person I ever met. If he had to fire his mother, he'd fire his mother.'"

At one of the first meetings Trembley attended, Luhnow declared he wanted to change the way the game was played. Quickly, Trembley found he didn't believe in his new boss's MO. To him, the way Luhnow and his cohorts walked around resembled FBI agents: besuited men strolling down to batting practice from left field, where the Astros' offices are at Minute Maid Park. "As soon as you saw those two guys coming," Trembley said, "it was like someone pulled a curtain, and it was complete silence."

Trembley's boss, Bo Porter, didn't arrive in Houston blindly. Porter knew what a rebuild would mean. But after all the other drama of 2014, Porter's relationship with Luhnow was starting to spiral over issues that, for Porter, centered on communication and transparency. Luhnow and the front office would often second-guess his moves, not unlike what his predecessor, Brad Mills, experienced. The front office would send down suggested lineups that Porter didn't have to use. Yet, if he went against the grain, he would often be in for an unpleasant conversation.

"They used to give us these projection sheets," one member of the coaching staff said. "So the projection sheets basically would match up our bullpen with the opposing teams' batting lineup and bench players. Which are good metrics. Because it's telling you who you have that's a good matchup for the other team and vice versa, right? So green means go, red means stop, just like traffic signs. So we go to play, I'll use the Red Sox for example. We've got eight guys in our bullpen. All eight guys, straight away across all [the listed Red Sox hitters], is all red.

"Meaning, we don't have one pitcher in our bullpen that, as their analytics will put it, is a good matchup.

"Put the names in a fucking hat."

Now, Porter was not a perfect manager. Some players felt his door was too often closed, that he wasn't the leader he thought he was. In spring training, he would hold team-building exercises—winning team serves the other ice cream—that prompted eye rolls and appeared better fit for Little League. Same for a *Wheel of Fortune*–like flywheel he brought into the clubhouse with words like "desire" and "commitment" as possible landing spots.

But Porter and Luhnow were increasingly operating in different worlds.

For all of the hoopla around the fruits of tanking, the Brady Aiken saga was proof that the draft could be quite rocky. The disappointing progress of the Astros' prior top pick, Mark Appel, was also proof.

Appel, the righty out of Stanford, was struggling in the minor leagues, and the Astros were trying everything they could to get him on track. In late July, that included bringing Appel into Houston to throw in front of Astros staff, while the major league season was ongoing.

Porter had no idea that the front office planned to host Appel at Minute Maid Park for this purpose. The manager was driving to the stadium when he got a phone call telling him he needed to arrive quickly, because players were angry. Jarred Cosart, a starting pitcher for the big-league team, was scheduled to throw a practice session that morning at the stadium, at the same location Appel was, in the bullpen. "He was told he had to wait until Appel was done because Appel was late," an Astros staffer said. "Appel was supposed to come before anybody else was going to get there. But he was late."

Major league players don't like interruptions in their schedules. But more germane, in their minds, was the pecking order, the privilege of earned stripes. Some big leaguers were angry that a golden-boy minor leaguer was unexpectedly using their bullpen in the middle of the season. Four players, including Cosart, confronted Porter, whose response was that he had no idea why Appel was in town. Luhnow, in turn, told Porter he needed Porter's support.

Porter felt he could have backed Luhnow, had he actually been told the bullpen session was happening in the first place. He might have even attended the throwing session himself, had he been invited.

Luhnow ordered Porter to get his players under control, so Porter told some core figures the situation never should have happened, and that he didn't want anyone else to discuss it publicly. The issue seemed to be quieting.

A day or so later, a player came into Porter's office and closed the door.

"Do you know this general manager, he's pulling people in the back to corroborate a story about saying it's OK that Mark Appel was here, and that the players didn't have a problem with it? And asking us to go tell the reporter that?" went the message.

Porter was livid. Within days, Cosart was traded. Luhnow did not keep Porter in the loop on the trade discussions, and come August, Porter was winging it half the time in his daily pregame media sessions, because Luhnow wasn't keeping him informed.

In just his second season managing the Astros, the manager was on borrowed time.

"Bo ate it," Trembley said. "He just wanted to put the best players out there. He'd get in arguments with Luhnow all the time, we don't have the best players on the field. And that caused a lot of problems. A lot of problems.

"Some of the things that Bo did I think carried over and the players saw it. . . . Because he has a football background, becomes very agitated, and did some things probably that later on he wishes he didn't as far as his emotions."

Porter was in regular communication with the Astros' relatively new president, Reid Ryan, the son of the famed Astros pitcher Nolan Ryan. Reid had replaced George Postolos as president in 2013, and Nolan was working for the team as well.

The younger Ryan's position was watered down compared to Postolos's role. He didn't have oversight of baseball operations, which was solely Luhnow's baby. Now, Ryan was not an elite strategist, but he wasn't brought in to be one. He was genial, adept at shaking hands, and could draw on a deep network of relationships inside the sport. He was, in short, a suitable face of the organization. Crane wanted a softer touch on the business side, a liaison to the community, and Ryan came from a family of baseball royalty.

But all those qualities made him water to Luhnow's oil.

"When I got there in 2013, Bo had already been hired, Jim had already hired Jeff, and there was a plan going on," Ryan said. "I had really the goal of, outside the four walls of Minute Maid Park, telling the story of what we were going to do inside the walls of Minute Maid Park. And I used a lot of my personal credibility from growing up, to go out and tell people that trusted me and trusted my family that, 'Hey, this is the plan, and this is why we think it's going to be successful.' And so whenever you come in as a new guy, your first job is to try to build relationships, sort of with everybody in the organization."

That included forging a good relationship with Porter. Both men were naturally outgoing. But what exactly happened between Porter, Ryan, and Crane in late 2014 is still contested.

A large number of people in Luhnow's inner circle all offer variants of the same story: that Porter went to the owner to get Luhnow fired, and that Ryan was backing Porter. That after the Aiken debacle in the middle of 2014, Porter smelled blood in the water, and went for the kill.

"I do know that Bo was trying to get Jeff fired," one lieutenant said. "I think at times Reid had a significant degree of interest in becoming the general manager of the team. And like, perhaps saw this as an avenue to doing that."

Multiple baseball operations executives said that for a day or two, Luhnow was genuinely worried that he was about to be axed.

"Bo and Reid basically went and they said, 'We gotta fire Jeff,' and Reid proposed himself as general manager. And Jim went to Jeff, and said, 'I want to talk with you tomorrow morning at six a.m.,'" one colleague recalled. "Jeff thought he was going to get fired. He really freaked out.

"Jeff got called in to Jim's office to actually be told by Jim what had happened the day prior, that Reid came in and tried to get Jeff fired."

It was a war that Porter could not win. Crane backed his GM, the architect of his plan, and Luhnow fired Porter before the season was over.

Porter and Ryan both denied the attempted coup. Ryan said that it was "completely not true."

"As I grew into the job, I came in in May of '13, you know I started to sense a tension with Bo, towards the plan," Ryan said. "As we got into 2014, I really felt like Bo was trying to spin me, and trying to influence what I thought by becoming more demonstrative in his beliefs of what was right or wrong on the field. And so at that point I went to Jim and I just said, 'Look, Jim, not my area, but I'm just telling you what I see, I think you have a problem with Bo, and it doesn't appear to be working out.' And I actually agreed with Jim that I thought he needed to be replaced."

Said Porter: "No, I did not try to get Jeff Luhnow fired. No, I did not go to Jim Crane trying to get Jeff Luhnow fired. Any conversation that I may have had, whether it was in passing, with Jim Crane, it was related to, how do we make this work? We need to improve the line of communication. My problem with Jeff Luhnow was the line of communication.

"I never knew anything about Reid going to Jim Crane, trying to get Jeff fired. Reid and I, the conversations that I had with Reid, were centered around: there needs to be a line of communication. We all have a job to do. And we can't do our job without understanding organization structure, what's going on. And it puts me in a bad spot as the manager when there is no communication. Anyone who's telling you I tried to get Jeff Luhnow fired, they're lying. I'm just going to say it plain and bluntly."

Trembley and others on the coaching staff were fired, too, as is common in a managerial change.

When Trembley arrived at the office after his dismissal, David Stearns met him downstairs. Trembley, in a universal sentiment, thought very highly of Stearns. As they were heading up, Stearns asked what went wrong. "I'll tell you what went wrong here," Trembley said. "There was no trust at all."

The same was true of Ryan and Luhnow's relationship, which would never be the same. Luhnow admonished Ryan afterward.

"Now having the support of Jim, I think it gave him the balls to like go to Reid and say like, 'Fuck off,' basically," a member of the inner circle said.

"Reid Ryan got his hand slapped," Trembley said. "Luhnow basically told Reid, 'You mind your own fucking business.' . . . Reid said, 'Dave, I gotta be careful, you won't be seeing me around here that much, and I gotta watch what I say.'

"Luhnow hated him."

Moving forward, Luhnow did not want his inner circle dealing with Ryan when avoidable. At the winter meetings, when the Astros were discussing player moves in their hotel suite, someone would run over and cover up a whiteboard with the baseball moves under consideration when Ryan entered the room. "It was like, so fucking awkward," recalled one person who saw that happen. "But this was the dynamic between Reid and Jeff, where Reid was relentlessly trying to be included, and Jeff was relentlessly trying to shut him out in a way that made things awkward for everybody else."

When the Astros made a trade late in 2015, Luhnow is said to have purposely told Ryan the wrong player that was being included in the deal, on the suspicion that Ryan would leak the information. Indeed, a player who was not in the final trade was reported by multiple outlets to be included. "You sometimes wonder, how does that happen?" a colleague explained. "Is it a game of telephone? And probably most of the time it is. But in this case it was Jeff fucking with Reid, and to prove that he leaked shit, as was already suspected. And then Jeff nicknamed him 'the sieve.'"

(However, reporting out of both Houston and Philadelphia at the time suggested the trade was actually modified from its original form, rather than having been erroneously reported.)

Ryan denied that he ever leaked information. "Human beings have emotions and human beings end up spinning their own narrative that fits what they're trying to do, and most of the time, that's from a self-preservationist standpoint," Ryan said.

O

Throughout this madness, Luhnow's hiring practices in the front office had created some auxiliary benefits. One was a high level of loyalty. Many people he brought in had not worked in baseball before and might not have ever had the chance, otherwise. Those folks had no experience with other clubs, no context for the sport more broadly, and ultimately understood it was Luhnow's way or the highway.

"I just did what Jeff said and wanted," one staffer said. "So if he wanted Reid shut out, I never told Reid anything ever, and I basically didn't trust him. I was taught not to trust Reid because Reid would try to get us all fired and Reid wanted Jeff's job and blah blah blah."

The way Luhnow constructed his office also had something of a PR benefit. The Astros, probably more than any other team, made themselves the public flag carriers for the analytics movement post-*Moneyball*. They had hired away media members who were at the forefront of the new age, and who still had friends in the media.

The scouting versus statistics debate, fraught as it was and is, was still raging, and an oversimplified protectionism had set in. To some in the media, any story that reported something negative about the Astros was treated as tantamount to attacking the overall movement and its practitioners.

In 2014, Keith Law took a question in a mailbag for ESPN. "Is Jim Crane anywhere near as upset with Jeff Luhnow as the media seems to be?" Law is a prominent writer who once worked at Prospectus, and had also once interviewed for a job with Luhnow's Astros.

"It's not even 'the media,'" Law wrote back. "It's the *Houston Chronicle*. Their coverage of the Appel controversy was one of the strangest things I've seen, a single media outlet going all-in on the local team when no one else agreed with their point of view. I don't know a single baseball scout or executive who told me the Astros did something wrong."

The Appel story was accurately reported by my *Chronicle* colleague, Jose de Jesus Ortiz. The fight over a minor leaguer appearing at a major league stadium on its face could appear silly—or as one Astros exec put it, "the dumbest possible thing to fight over."

Indeed, not every player was on edge about it. "The majority of us thought it was more comical than anything," said reliever Chad Qualls. "It just showed the top-round-pick privilege. We understood that. I didn't think it was a big deal."

But the incident was nonetheless significant inside the hallways of Minute Maid Park. What some on the outside did not know, or did not seek to know, is how broken the relationship between the manager and GM already was, and the underlying issues that the Appel incident exacerbated.

As one Astros executive put it, "We had some crazy shit going on in 2014."

And to end the year, Luhnow was embarking on a search for a new field manager, his second personal selection. Very often, GMs don't get the chance to hire a third before they're on the hot seat themselves. Luhnow's next move would be crucial.

"When you stop and think about it," Trembley said, "Bo was probably a guy they hired—he was an African American, he was real positive. They knew they tanked it on purpose for three years. They let him come in here and get beat up, and when it's time to win, we'll get who we want."

○

Just as the Astros were searching for their new dugout leader, a major transition was also under way in baseball's central office. Bud Selig, the commissioner of the sport since the early 1990s, had long been threatening to retire, and the 2014 season was to be his last. His successor, Rob Manfred, was a management-side labor lawyer, a graduate of Cornell's Industrial and Labor Relations School and Harvard Law School, and Selig's right-hand man.

Smart and aggressive, Manfred was savvy to the internal politics of the sport, currying favor with Selig for years. After he was pulled into the league office full-time in the 1990s, Manfred became the lead negotiator for the owners, where one of his chief responsibilities was managing Selig's response to the sport's steroid era.

Selig said he first started to regard performance-enhancing drugs, or PEDS, seriously in the middle of 1998, when reporter Steve Wilstein of the Associated Press spotted a bottle of androstenedione in slugger Mark McGwire's locker, and wrote a story about it. That substance, which boosts testosterone levels, was technically legal, both in the country's law and the sport, although it had already been banned in the NFL, NCAA, and the Olympics. In 2005, McGwire took the Fifth in Congress, before half a decade later admitting he used PEDs. Sammy Sosa, who had combined with McGwire for a famed chase of Babe Ruth's single-season home run record in 1998, was later reported to have tested positive, but has always denied using performance enhancers.

Just how much PEDs impact a player's success is still debated. Undeniable, though, was the heavy public pressure on both players and owners to clean up the game. PEDs were billed as a public health issue, one where children could be inspired to use potentially harmful substances at young ages as they sought to emulate their baseball heroes. In the late 1990s, the sport did not have standard drug testing for PEDs.

"PEDs are illegal. We're getting pressure from Congress, the clubs were being threatened if they didn't do something with the loss of the antitrust exemption," recalled Gene Orza, one of the top lawyers for the players' union at the time. "We were being threatened, if we didn't do something, with the loss of free agency by making it a nonmandatory subject of bargaining with revision of the National Labor Relations Act. So there was a lot of pressure being put on us in Congress."

The players' union was well known to be the strongest in sports, and labor fights in baseball had historically been bitter. But regardless of the labor climate leading up to the PED furor in the late 1990s, the union was never going to quickly and easily allow sweeping drug tests, or big punishments. A testing policy was agreed to in 2002 and actual testing began in 2003, a trial year of sorts, where if enough positives were registered, a fuller program would begin. There were enough.

The introduction of testing and escalating punishments hardly quieted the clamor. Barry Bonds, who in 2001 had broken McGwire's three-year-old home run record, was investigated by the feds for his receipt of a substance called "the clear," a designer PED produced by Bay Area Laboratory Co-operative, or BALCO. Reporters Mark Fainaru-Wada and Lance Williams at the *San Francisco Chronicle* owned the story.

Health concerns were also hitting home: a pitcher for the Baltimore Orioles, Steve Bechler, died during spring training of 2003. His use of ephedra was ruled a contributor to his death, which the medical examiner ultimately attributed to heatstroke.

Filleted publicly, Selig ordered an independent investigation, conducted by former senator George Mitchell and published in 2007.

"Frequently," Orza said, MLB's investigations serve public relations interests. "The Mitchell commission, for sure. . . . A lot of investigations are unwelcome, but they're forced by public outcry. There are very few investigations undertaken *sua sponte*. What I mean by that: of their own accord, let's investigate this. People complain about the time of games: let's establish a commission to look into time of game. If nobody complained about it, and said, 'Gee, we wish the games would be longer, we're having so much fun,' then they wouldn't have had a time-of-game commission."

Likely, no one on the management side of the sport had or has a deeper understanding as to how the steroids era evolved than Manfred himself. He explained to Congress how the availability of PEDs on the internet and in countries outside the US was a problem almost too large to be an issue a private employer could tackle on its own.

"He was the point person, but he was taking his marching orders from, I'm sure, the executive council and Selig," Orza said. "But yes, it was him. He was the PED guy. He helped write the agreement, he helped administering it."

Manfred developed an intimate understanding of how the problem arose in the first place: the nature of players and competitors, of what could and did move players to cheat.

Players are almost always hyper-driven. Few make it to the elite level of the major leagues without a superior sense of motivation, an insatiable desire to improve. Players are in an environment where success, fame, and, ultimately, money are potential rewards for PED use—be it for direct effects on performance, or in physical recovery, helping players potentially heal faster and feel more energetic. In their book, *Game of Shadows*, the *San Francisco Chronicle* reporters Fainaru-Wada and Williams traced Bonds's use of PEDs to jealousy over the success of McGwire and Sosa.

The late Ken Caminiti, a slugging third baseman who played fifteen years in the major leagues and won the 1996 National League Most Valuable Player award, had helped open the floodgates to the topic in 2002, in a famous interview with *Sports Illustrated*'s Tom Verducci.

"It's no secret what's going on in baseball," Caminiti, who coincidentally spent the bulk of his career with the Astros, told *SI*. "At least half the guys are using steroids. They talk about it. They joke about it with each other. The guys who want to protect themselves or their image by lying have that right. Me? I'm at the point in my career where I've done just about every bad thing you can do. I try to walk with my head up. I don't have to hold my tongue. I don't want to hurt teammates or friends. But I've got nothing to hide."

"If a young player were to ask me what to do," Caminiti continued, "I'm not going to tell him it's bad. Look at all the money in the game: You have a chance to set your family up, to get your daughter into a better school. . . . So I can't say, 'Don't do it,' not when the guy next to you is as big as a house and he's going to take your job and make the money."

Rule-breaking in sports carries certain provincial nuances, and compared to real-world settings when people skirt the rules, typically lower stakes. But cheating has at least some crossover with corruption in business settings.

The first thing that Peter Rodriguez, dean of Rice University's business school in Houston, usually tells people is that corruption is everywhere, but it's not the same everywhere.

"Everywhere you go," he said, "there's some market for influence. In a third-world nation that is just grappling with its initial time in democracy, you might go straight to the top, and there are a lot of payments to those in power. And you sort of have this big, explicit, or at least not hidden, top-down corruption that we're all familiar with. That's something that's common.

"You also have corruption that's sort of embedded in the society in the way that it becomes the norm. It's viewed as just the cost of do-ing business. . . . In fact, in a lot of places, India's a good example, it's legal in some ways. It's the Foreign Corrupt Practices Act. You could give a tax deduction to payments in countries where it was appropri-ate to pay what they would call a 'facilitating payment,' which means you do need to make a payment to someone who doesn't have the explicit authority to receive it, to give you something. But it's right, and it's fair. And that really boils down to countries deciding: there's a lot of red tape, and you can either choose the sort of fast lane, or the slow lane."

Rodriguez's research, which has often centered on corruption in developing and autocratic countries, showed that choosing the fast lane rather than the slow lane doesn't typically create much damage. An example would be an application to get a driver's license, where the applicant legitimately meets the necessary criteria but is being held up by a bureaucrat exploring or leveraging their power. If the bureaucrat is paid off, the outcome—the license is granted—is not unwarranted. "You may think it feels bad, it's the wrong way, but at the end of the day, does it cause any damage?" Rodriguez said. "If it's really just 'I'm paying for something that I deserve, I'm just trying to get it quicker or avoid all of the unnecessary steps,' well, then the outcome is an out-come that was just to begin with. You just chose a means to get it that was unsavory, or in another environment, wouldn't be good.

"What really gets bad," Rodriguez continued, "is something dif-ferent about corruption, and that's when people are able to achieve an outcome they actually don't merit."

Like paying off someone to win a government contract when the service provider is not actually offering the best deal for the government. "Explicitly, that's the abuse of public power for private gain which is the classic definition of corruption. It's not just a moral issue, it's like you're abusing the power. So in that sense, that's a little like sports, too. When you have people who don't deserve to win a competition, win a competition, you feel like something is wrong."

Steroids proliferated in part for that very reason: players felt their peers were succeeding when they should not have because of the use of PEDs. "The argument that you so often hear, 'Everybody's doing it,' is a remarkably common justification for unethical behavior in sports," said Max Bazerman, a Harvard Business School professor who studies the psychology of unethical behavior. "And it may or may not be accurate."

To prevent cheating in these environments, where the allure of breaking the rules is endemic, Rodriguez said business leaders have to speak openly and candidly about the environment they're operating in. Training can be delivered to employees and managers. "You typically have this, kind of usually not terribly effective training, which is, 'These are the rules, don't violate the rules in a way that anybody's going to know about it, especially.' Or 'These are the rules, don't do this.'

"But what you need instead from upper management is a candid acknowledgment of the situation, and explicit guidance. So for example, a lot of managers will say, 'Well, I didn't figure I had to tell people not to break the law.' And the answer is 'Yeah, you pretty much do.'"

The conversations look different depending on what tier or group of employees is involved. A talk with players, Bazerman said, would be centered on how to act morally. At a team level, it could be about changing incentives. "But it may be that it has to come at the highest level, regulatory form, and that would be the commissioner's office," Bazerman said. "But there's no great evidence that the commissioner's office has ever been a particularly good source for ethicality, either.

"We had this kind of steroids scandal that went on for years and years and years," he continued. "The owners were sort of fine and happy with all of that until they couldn't avoid the problem anymore because the media went after that, and then the owners, rather than stepping up and taking responsibility for it, essentially questioned players for taking steroids in order to be competitive, said, 'Look at the bad Barry Bonds,' or 'Look at the bad, you can pick the player.' They looked at the bad apple, rather than the systematic structure that was created that even encouraged it."

A decade after MLB had begun testing and two years before his commissionership would begin, Manfred was at the center of MLB's handling of another PED controversy. Before his retirement, Selig's last chance to show just how tough he could be on PEDs (or not) came during the Biogenesis scandal.

MLB controversially purchased records from a Florida anti-aging clinic called Biogenesis of America in efforts to suspend more than a dozen players, including Yankees star Alex Rodriguez. Eddie Dominguez, a former member of MLB's Department of Investigations, later published a book, called *Baseball Cop*, detailing the depths and darkness of MLB's investigative work. Manfred, when talking to his investigators, would refer to Selig as "Al from Milwaukee," Dominguez wrote. (Selig once owned the Milwaukee Brewers.)

"Al from Milwaukee doesn't give a fuck about seventeen players," Manfred said, according to Dominguez. "He wants fucking Alex Rodriguez."

Manfred's pursuit of Rodriguez was a spectacle and a debacle, immortalized in a documentary called *Screwball*. The Biogenesis fallout, including accusations that MLB itself had played dirty, prompted Manfred in 2014 to fire several members of its Department of Investigations, the head investigator among them. In its first iteration, DOI was run by ex-cops. Now they were attorneys.

O

When he took over as commissioner in 2015, Manfred set out to chart a different course than Selig. Efficiency-minded, he restructured the league office, which Selig had allowed to operate in fiefdoms and, in some pockets, grow bloated. Manfred pulled in some outside help, signing up McKinsey & Company to help him consolidate. "He laid off a ton of people, some painfully," said one league executive who departed voluntarily. "There were a lot of hurt feelings."

"Whenever you have change at the top of an organization, you're more likely to take a look at the alignment of the organization, the way it functions, and make changes that you think could streamline the organization and make it more effective," Manfred said. "I don't think in any of them it was about head-chopping for me. It was about making sure that we were organized in a way that allowed us to do the best job for the clubs. And [doing] the best job in terms of dealing with the people that we generate revenue from.

"Instead of 'I'm interested in pursuing the agenda of my fiefdom'— your word—'I'm interested in pursuing the agenda of the organization as a whole.'"

Just as the Astros had an agent of change at the top, MLB did, too. Manfred's modernization efforts were to go beyond the structure of the league office. He wanted to consolidate more of the sport, and the revenue generators inside the industry, under the MLB umbrella, an initiative dubbed "One Baseball." In a letter to fans he wrote in 2015, he also outlined two goals: bringing more people into the sport, and modernizing the game on the field.

Modernizing meant catching up technologically. Baseball in 2008 had instituted a limited use of video instant replay, to determine whether a batter had actually hit a home run in instances where, say, the ball might have gone foul. But compared to the NFL, where referees on the field could review many types of plays with video, MLB looked left behind: How could the sport not equip its umpires with access to the instant replays that fans already watched on telecasts?

Manfred led the charge to institute an expanded replay system for the 2014 season. As part of the new project, teams were provided league-sanctioned access to video feeds to help them make decisions on what plays to challenge or not challenge. "Last season's expanded instant replay improved the game's quality and addressed concerns shared by fans and players," Manfred wrote in that 2015 letter to fans. "We made a dramatic change without altering the game's fundamentals. I look forward to tapping into the power of technology to consider additional advancements."

The new commissioner, the veteran of the PED wars, had no idea what he was tapping into.

# 8

# VALIDATION

HOUSTON WAS NO LONGER THE WORST CLUB IN BASEBALL, THE THREE-year streak of ignominy over. For all the chaos in 2014, the team on the field had improved. Heck, the 'Stros weren't even the worst team in the five-team American League West, finishing in fourth place, at 70–92.

Jose Altuve took a huge step forward, leading the majors in batting average at .341. Lefty Dallas Keuchel wasn't the hardest thrower, but notably possessed both a strong sinking fastball and strong beard. He finished with 200 innings thrown, the benchmark for durability and consistency.

George Springer's debut season included 20 home runs in just 78 games, although the front office still wasn't totally sold on him. Different trade offers come in all the time that the public never hears about, even for players who are unlikely to be moved. But once Springer was in the majors, the internal debate surrounding him had not quieted. One Astros executive remembered trade talks with the Seattle Mariners, who were shopping a promising pitcher, Taijuan Walker. The Astros discussed it, but didn't bite.

One move the Astros had made prior to the 2014 season became a banner acquisition for the young front office. The Astros grabbed a relatively unknown pitcher who had spent a little time in the majors, Collin McHugh, off waivers, baseball's version of the scrap heap. Mike

Fast led the push to snag him, with pro scouting director Kevin Goldstein supportive as well. Looking at McHugh's pitching data, Fast saw a very good curveball and overall mix of pitches, as well as a pitcher who had simply had bad luck. He also thought McHugh had a way to encourage better luck moving forward.

McHugh didn't stand out enough to make the Astros out of spring training. When he was called up from the minors in the first month of play, the new Astros pitching coach, Brent Strom, met with McHugh to go over a novel approach. Strom was a former big-league pitcher himself, but he was open-minded, a talkative and intelligent man, who, despite the leanings of most baseball people in their sixties, was very much on board with Luhnow's plans. Luhnow had hired Strom back in the St. Louis days on the minor league side, with the *New Yorker* cartoonist as their conduit.

"I was very happy in St. Louis," Strom said. "I worked with young pitchers, the team was having success. Everything was good, and then Jeff called and he basically asked me, quite frankly, he says, 'Wouldn't you like to see what you know, if it'll work at the major league level?' And that's what kind of intrigued me to do this."

The front office recommended to Strom that McHugh stop throwing his two-seam fastball, which had sinking action, to right-handed hitters. McHugh had most recently been in the Colorado Rockies organization, and because the Rockies play in the thin air of Denver, which creates a poor environment for pitchers, McHugh had a greater incentive to keep the ball on the ground. But now, the Astros believed McHugh could have more success if he pitched up in the zone with his straight fastball, the four-seamer, instead.

Cerebral, McHugh was better known for his blogging than his strikeout ability when he made his debut with the team. Importantly, in the meeting with Strom before his start, McHugh was willing to listen to what the Astros were selling. He was rewarded right out of the gate, striking out twelve in that first outing.

"He's a different guy than I saw in spring," Strom said that April. "I didn't know much about him. He was sinking everything."

McHugh established himself as a mainstay in the rotation going into 2015, a new weapon, one the Astros had plucked out of relative obscurity and then helped finely tune. For the front office, the lesson was clear: players are not just fixed assets.

Once he was on the inside, the Astros were able to better ascertain why McHugh's curveball was so effective: in part, because of its spin rate. The front office was increasingly geared toward technological innovations, new ways to gather information about the granular movements of players and the baseball itself. The Moneyball revolution had been largely built around rethinking information already available. The trick now was to find more and better information than everyone else, and then find ways to apply it—and in many cases teach it—before the other guys did.

In the St. Louis days, Sig Mejdal had become the first person to throw a pitch on a major league mound that was measured by TrackMan, a radar system that provides detailed readouts of each pitch's attributes, including its spin rate (measured in RPMs) as well as pitch speed, how far it moved, and the pitcher's release point. The standard tracking system in baseball that all teams had access to, PITCHf/x, provided some of that information already. But TrackMan's ability to track spin rate provided a new trove.

TrackMan was founded in 2003 to make radar tools for golfers. When it expanded to baseball five years later, Luhnow and Mejdal were all over it, and during installation of the system at St. Louis's Busch Stadium, the most athletic person around was Mejdal, so he gave it a whirl. Back then, no other major league team had installed the contraption, which looks like a pizza box and is usually attached somewhere behind home plate, off the field of play.

The Astros would do a lot more with the data than the Cardinals did in that time, though.

TrackMan applications grew to become a team effort, with Fast and Taubman taking cracks. The Astros broke down the data by handedness: the difference between righty and lefty hitters, and righty and lefty pitchers. Fast, the most technically skilled of the group, did a lot of the heavy lifting.

Quickly, in combination with TrackMan, pitching prospect Mark

Appel became another flashpoint. Appel, the first-round pick in 2013 out of Stanford, threw hard, in the mid-90s, yet hitters had no trouble squaring up his fastball.

Appel's struggles had contributed to a front-office feeling that greater changes in player development and scouting were needed. He had been turned off by the tandem pitching system in the minors and hampered by injuries, but the front office had also come to view Appel as stubborn. He was deeply religious, which made some in the industry, both in Houston and out, question his commitment to the game. It's likely that many of those questions were unfair.

But true to form, the front office felt the most relevant truth about Appel could be found in the numbers, and specifically, numbers they didn't have when they drafted him.

TrackMan wasn't yet a mainstay at every college event when the Astros took Appel. But once the Astros got him in their pipeline, they were able to record many more readings on him, and concluded his fastball was lacking.

Mejdal had built an early model off the data, combining the attributes of each pitch to describe how likely it is to perform. One of the takeaways was dubbed "the tongue," for the look of an early U-shaped visualization that showed how horizontal break and vertical break interplayed with a pitch's effectiveness.

"His fastball was the quintessential bad TrackMan fastball," an Astros exec said of Appel, "and the reason why is because it has equal parts rise and run, or equal parts vertical break and horizontal break. And in TrackMan-attribute terms, and what we learned through the research, is that the more a fastball had extreme hopping action, or extreme tailing action, the more unique it was and the more unique the pitch is, the less it's being seen, the harder it is for a hitter to do contact or do damage against.

"The other main tenet of our research learning is that the more tail you have on your fastball, the more of a platoon split it has," the executive said, meaning the pitch has a different level of effectiveness depending on whether the hitter is lefty or righty. "So guys with heavy sinking fastballs tend to have more of a platoon split. Guys with a riding fastball tend to have less of a platoon split. So Mark Appel had this very average two-seam fastball, equal parts rise and run, and putting aside the fact that he could throw harder than average, it was the exact sort of fastball that we spent the next four years trying to avoid in basically every pitcher we went out and acquired, or the pitchers we worked to develop internally."

TrackMan wasn't just a tool of revisionist history. The Astros wanted to try to show Appel ways he could improve by engineering his fastball, and he was one of many players who would receive that advice as the Astros started to use technology more directly as a coaching tool.

But Appel was getting very mixed messages: the front office would say one thing, his minor league coaches another. The minor league staffers and the front office were not in lockstep, and to the front office, the Appel experience would underscore the danger of that.

Appel felt jerked around, and when Taubman personally went to meet with him in the minors, Appel didn't want to talk to him. Appel even "chewed out" Taubman at one point, an executive said.

"If we knew everything we knew about him at the end, would we still have drafted him where we did? I don't think so," an exec said. "He wasn't the player he thought he was, [but] the player development process wasn't supporting him. Like the coaches—you put him at Double-A and you hear one thing from a pitching coach, you send him back down to High-A and the High-A pitching coach was on a completely different page. That's one critique you hear a lot about the Astros or about modern player development with organizations in general . . . that they take away autonomy from coaches, and I think there's some truth to that.

"But at the same time, I don't think people appreciate how autonomy for coaches can really fuck up a player if they're not getting consistent messaging on the right way to go about things. And I think that's a lot of what fucked up Mark Appel, is just our coaches."

Appel, though, believed his health was the largest problem—not his fastball.

"If you judge me on that," Appel said of the TrackMan data, "you would have said, 'Well, how did Mark have any success at Stanford, if this is what he was working with?' I'd be the first to tell you, I knew that something was categorically different about how my body was feeling, even in that first year.

"Man, there'd be days in 2014, 2015, and 2016 where I'd wake up, and I couldn't bend my elbow past ninety degrees. It was swollen, it was painful, and then like two days later, I could fully straighten my arm."

The Astros traded away Appel after the 2015 season. It was that trade where Luhnow, allegedly, told Reid Ryan the incorrect name of a different player involved.

○

Across the board, players and the sport were becoming inundated with technology, video in particular. Staff, for example, would now more commonly record practice sessions on video for later review, allowing players and coaches to check on different angles of swings and pitches. The introduction of expanded instant replay by the commissioner's office in 2014 also required all thirty teams to dedicate staff to in-game video review.

During games, club employees would have to quickly look at replays, and then, using a phone that ran directly to the dugout, advise the field manager whether to challenge an umpire's call on the field. For hours at a time, and sometimes whole games, the staff in the video room might not spring into action. But when a questionable call was made, they had to get an answer to the dugout, ideally, in ten to fifteen seconds.

In 2014, the Astros' video coordinator was a holdover from the prior baseball ops administration in his final year with the team, Jim Summers, an ex–Green Beret who once worked as jet-setting publisher Malcolm Forbes Sr.'s bodyguard. Approaching sixty, Summers was paired in the Astros' video room with a much younger baseball operations staffer, another holdover from the old administration, and one of the few whom Luhnow had taken a particular liking to, Pete Putila.

Tall and affable, Putila was a survivor of the purge. He had started as an intern with the Astros in 2011, and had showed enough chops and open-mindedness that he caught Luhnow's attention. He manned the replay system on the road in 2014.

The Astros had spent between $300,000 and $400,000 to upgrade their video system heading into the 2014 season. Seven new cameras provided 360-degree views of batters, in high definition.

"There's a software that takes all of the fifteen camera angles," Putila said. "It allows you to configure the formats and everything and play them at the same time and play them frame by frame."

Looking to tape was also becoming more valuable in another endeavor: advance scouting, the act of reviewing an opponent's tendencies and strengths and weaknesses ahead of time. Luhnow had hired a young scout, Tom Koch-Weser, away from the Seattle Mariners, a division rival. When he joined the team, he introduced himself to then bench coach Dave Trembley in spring training.

"Dave, I just need to tell you, you gotta be careful with your signs," Trembley recalled Koch-Weser saying.

On a baseball field, information is constantly communicated in code via hand and body signals.

On offense, a coach or a manager in the dugout signals the team's third-base coach, who relays the play to the hitter and to runners on base. It might be a command for the hitter to take a pitch, or for the runner to steal a base.

Another set of signs are used nonstop throughout the game while a team is playing the field: those from the catcher to the pitcher. Catchers, working in a crouch, tell the pitchers what to throw by flashing their fingers in front of their crotch. Traditionally, one finger pointed downward means fastball, and two means curveball.

Theoretically, were a camera to be trained on the catcher or a coach, then a team could later go back and review those signs to use in a future game.

Now, if players steal signs with their eyes and wits, it's totally fair game. But at that time, once electronics got involved, it would be a question of usage. It would be illegal to use the information in real time. For knowledge in a future game, though, as a scouting tool? Ostensibly legal, but to some, at least a little shady.

Not everyone was aware the practice was growing, or even happening. When Koch-Weser warned Trembley that Seattle had captured some signs he had given, Trembley was confused.

"What are you talking about?"

"We played you guys eighteen times last year," Koch-Weser said. "We had all the signs."

"How'd you have that?" Trembley asked Koch-Weser.

"We had a camera on Bo [Porter] and then on [coach] Eduardo Pérez, and then when the games were over, we went in and we deciphered 'em," Koch-Weser said. "We figured out what the signs were."

"You had a camera on that?" Trembley asked.

"We had 'em all," Koch-Weser said. "I would be careful this year, because that's what's happening."

O

For the 2015 season, Luhnow landed the manager he wanted most.

A.J. Hinch represented a complete package, because he knew how front offices and dugouts worked alike. He was highly charming, something of a media darling, and he was intelligent, the conduit Luhnow needed between the players and upper management. The first time Luhnow pursued Hinch, back when the Astros hired Bo Porter, Hinch didn't want to risk further blemishing his managerial record. Now, though, the team was turning around.

Hinch had always been earmarked for greatness. Six foot one with a warm outreach, Hinch was a prototype, the all-American boy from the heartland who was not only smart, but a gifted athlete. In baseball he was a catcher, and for his high school football team in Midwest City, Oklahoma, the quarterback. At sixteen he was offered the choice to have a car or a batting cage to practice hitting with. He chose the latter.

Years later, on his first date with the woman who would marry him, Hinch declared he would someday go to the big leagues. Erin, who taught ballet, asked what the big leagues were.

In the early 1990s, when he went to Stanford to play baseball, Hinch was as well-known as any young ballplayer could be before the internet boom, making the cover of industry bible *Baseball America*.

He debuted in the big leagues in 1998, the starting catcher on Opening Day at the Coliseum in Oakland. But his hitting never took off. The way big-league pitchers could make pitches move, their sliders, kept his production in check. He spent parts of eight seasons in the majors, a career to be proud of on its face, but one short of the expectations Hinch's talent had created.

"I've always viewed the playing part of my career as disappointing to myself," Hinch said. "I have really high standards and really big beliefs in trying to excel. Part of that is just who I am. Part of that is just how I was taught. Part of that is what I learned at Stanford."

Driven, Hinch has to be in a sort of perpetual motion, rarely comfortable without a task to fulfill. On a family outing to the beach, he couldn't just sit for much more than twenty minutes. "He's like, 'OK, what are we going to do? Let's play Frisbee,'" Erin said. "He likes being there, but he's not very good at relaxing. Maybe he doesn't need to be. His relaxing is just more of a beach walk. He would just never come in and lie down on the couch.

"If the TV's on, it's because he's doing work or something else."

With his playing days behind him, Hinch started on a new path: the front office. He went to the Arizona Diamondbacks and became farm director, in the same time period when Jeff Luhnow held an equivalent role for the Cardinals. One time when they crossed paths, Hinch and a few other colleagues went the extra mile to make Luhnow, the outsider, feel welcome.

"We were like, 'Come here, Jeff,'" Hinch said. "'Come have a beer with us.'"

In 2009, the Diamondbacks fired their field manager, Bob Melvin, who was better liked by players than by his front office. And in Melvin's place was Hinch, who had never been a coach or manager previously. At the age of thirty-four, he became by far the youngest manager in the big leagues, in a job where experience had traditionally been prized. "I thought I could do anything," Hinch said. "Even at thirty-four years old and plopping into a major league dugout."

In many ways, Hinch's hire in Arizona was ahead of its time. In the next decade, it became trendy for teams to bring on young ex-players who hadn't managed before. But back in 2009, the sport and its players weren't ready yet. Hinch didn't last through the entirety of his second season.

"Any manager who is taking over a team midflight and a team with flaws always has something stacked against him," said a front-office colleague of Hinch's from Arizona, Jerry Dipoto, now the president of baseball operations for the Seattle Mariners. "It's a tough scenario in which to thrive, but in that moment in time, it wasn't very well received. It wasn't very well received in the media or with the public, the fans. And in some context, the veteran players in the clubhouse."

Hinch went back to the front office with the San Diego Padres, where he continued to rise, and at one point was effectively the team's de facto GM. Hinch could have kept going as an executive, perhaps becoming a full-time GM, if that had been what he wanted. But he still had something to prove elsewhere.

He kept his eye on the field, and in 2013 interviewed to be manager of the Chicago Cubs. When Luhnow brought Hinch to Houston for an interview, he asked Hinch if he was all in. The question, Hinch felt, came from a good place, considering his front-office exploits.

Naturally, his goal was to win a World Series. "And everybody says that when they're in this game," Hinch said. "But I've always also—when I've visualized myself celebrating—been in a baseball uniform."

○

The Astros lost four of their first ten games to open the 2015 season before rattling off a 21–7 run. Right away, they had stormed to first place in the American League West. This campaign was supposed to bring improvement, but the Astros weren't supposed to be division-title contenders. Not yet.

Luhnow had made some shrewd, low-dollar adds that were paying off. An outfielder, Colby Rasmus, whom Luhnow had once drafted in St. Louis, went on to hit 25 home runs. Another pickup, the burly and bearded Evan Gattis, would hit 27. His journey in baseball is among the most unique: substance abuse in high school preceded an exit from junior college. He took jobs as a janitor and a valet before sleepless days and nights in search of spiritual enlightenment led him back, eventually, to baseball.

Lefty Dallas Keuchel's growth was immense coming off a breakout 2014 season. He was so good, in fact, that he won the 2015 American League's Cy Young Award, the greatest annual honor a pitcher can receive. Collin McHugh, in his second season in Houston, was also stellar, forming a one-two punch with Keuchel.

The farm system, that vaunted machine Luhnow had spent years building, was now starting to show its fruits. A confident curveball artist, Lance McCullers Jr.—the pitcher the Astros were able to snag with some smooth maneuvering of the 2012 draft bonus system—came up in May. He wore Batman logos on his shoes the day of his debut, a bold move for a rookie, and one that technically at the time wasn't allowed. Baseball had arcane rules restricting what players wore. But McCullers, like many of the young Astros, had a swagger.

Swagger, though, isn't always welcome in locker rooms. Baseball clubhouses have long-held pecking orders, where older players enforce clubhouse rules. Young guys carry the beer for veterans, traditionally. Across the sport, the dynamic has somewhat loosened up over time, and for the better as societal attitudes toward anything that could be considered hazing have changed. But no matter the generation, some semblance of order in the clubhouse is probably necessary within a group of well-paid, sometimes immature young players. And the means of enforcement can vary.

One time, when the rookie McCullers didn't follow dress code while traveling, Luke Gregerson and some veterans cut up McCullers's pants into a speedo, and made McCullers walk into the team hotel with the newly fashioned speedo on. Gregerson was respected, though, not only for his age, but his smarts. He was constantly doing crossword puzzles, and likely would have been a lawyer had he not been a ballplayer.

At the time, Houston was an odd place for veterans to play.

"[Crane] never owned a team before," said veteran reliever Pat Neshek, who, like Gregerson, was new to the team for 2015. "Everybody's position in that organization was like the first time they were doing it. A lot of us would be shitty with them [the staff] and be like, 'Hey, we need to change this shit.' A lot of times, it did change.

"You would just see many faces that you were like, 'Who the hell are these people?'" Neshek said, naming Brandon Taubman.

In June, on a Sunday afternoon in Toronto, the Astros had made the kind of blunder that plagued them in years past. In the final inning, shortstop Jonathan Villar went to field a routine pop-up when he bumped into a Blue Jays baserunner. The ball fell, and the Astros lost by one run.

The Astros' flight out of Toronto was delayed. Hinch grabbed a bottle of wine and went to the back of the plane, where the players were. It was quiet, and nobody was having any fun, until Hinch announced that Carlos Correa, the first overall pick from 2012, was joining the major league team.

"The plane went nuts," one person on the flight said. Now the Astros had help.

This was the infusion of a young superstar on an already talented roster. "He came in with this little fedora hat," Neshek remembered. Correa would continue to make trips to hat shops on the road.

The timing of Correa's call-up had been preplanned. The front office had waited just long enough on the calendar to make sure that Correa would not become eligible to enter the arbitration process after three years, rather than two. (The Astros had already tried, back in 2014, to get Correa to sign a long-term extension as a minor leaguer, on a guaranteed $30 million deal, and it went nowhere.)

Right when Correa was promoted, the 2015 draft was going. Luhnow and scouting director Mike Elias used the compensation pick they had received from the Brady Aiken debacle—the No. 2 overall selection—on a kid out of Louisiana State University, Alex Bregman. Springer joked with Correa that the Astros had just drafted his replacement.

Springer hit 13 home runs in the first half, and his postgame presence was almost as important. He was the hype man, arranging for dance music and a smoke machine in the clubhouse after victories.

"For a young guy, it was weird to see, but he would get the whole clubhouse amped and pumped, he would put the music on," Neshek said. "And even me, I'd be kind of like, 'Eh, I'm not feeling it today,' but he would try to get everybody hyped. He was kind of the positive guy. He did a really good job with that. We had a lot of good young guys. It was kind of one of those situations where you knew the guys were going to be superstars, and you were wondering how they were going to keep us all together."

The Astros' early success was underscored by multiple selections to the midseason All-Star Game: Keuchel and Altuve. Hinch went, too, the group growing together. But the team needed more firepower for the second half.

The trade deadline was at the end of July, and it presented a conundrum for Luhnow and Sig Mejdal. To add players who could help the Astros in the near term, the front office would have to give up prospects, players with years of club control who could blossom into excellent players. The Astros weren't favorites yet, however. They weren't in a position where they could dramatically tilt the odds in their favor with a reasonable trade. Yet, to let the trade deadline pass without help would send a terrible message to the players already on board, to the coaches, and to the fans. "Hopefully, we can get an arm and a bat, and make a run at this thing," Keuchel said.

The most rational move for asset building would have been to do nothing. And doing nothing would have been the wrong move in every other way. Luhnow, to his credit, realized as much. He traded for a pair of starting pitchers, Scott Kazmir and Mike Fiers, who slotted right away into the rotation. He also picked up an outfielder, Carlos Gómez. Fiers would throw a no-hitter that season, going nine innings without allowing the opposing team a hit, a rare accomplishment for pitchers.

"It was another way of showing support to a team that had worked its ass off all year to be relevant again, for the first time in a long time," one member of the team said. "Two-fifths of our rotation was acquired at the deadline. We had to do it to have relevance."

The Astros couldn't hold first place, though. The Texas Rangers, their geographic rival based in Arlington, Texas, just outside Dallas, took the division, and the Astros barely made the playoffs at all. In mid-September, the Astros played a four-game series in Arlington that left Hinch about as angry as he ever was in his time with the Astros. Houston lost all four games. After one of them, Hinch busted a towel dispenser in the visiting manager's office.

Instead of moving directly into the first round of the postseason, the Astros advanced to a one-game playoff, a "wild card" play-in game. Keuchel, a cool customer, marched into the Bronx and held down the game's most famous franchise, the New York Yankees, in an upset. "Keuchel was like the man that year," Neshek said. "That was the biggest story."

The core of the Astros had never sniffed the postseason before, and now the group was headed to the American League Division Series.

"Guys are like, 'Oh man, what's it like?'" Neshek said. "Maybe it was Springer or somebody, and they would ask, 'What's it like to be in the playoffs? Man, I would love to play in the playoffs one day!' And I had a few games. You would tell 'em, and then you think how cool it would be if we ever did that. And by the end of the year we're celebrating in Yankee Stadium, which was pretty unbelievable."

The Astros looked like they would win the following round, too, going up two games to one in the best-of-five series opposite the Kansas City Royals. Starting with a key moment late in Game 4 in Houston, when a ball shot by shortstop Carlos Correa that he most often would have corralled, the Royals stormed back. The series moved back to Kansas City for a winner-take-all Game 5, and the Astros were done. They had lost to a worthy opponent, at least: the Royals went on to win the World Series.

In all, the year had been a resounding success. With a new manager and the farm system starting to show its fruits, Luhnow's plan was starting to produce exactly what he said it someday would: results, even if they came at a cost. Josh Hader, one of the young pitchers Luhnow gave up at the trade deadline, would later go on to become an All-Star.

"I do think that the short-term gains often appear very attractive and will lead to decisions being made that are potentially suboptimal for the long term or even the medium term, and quite frankly, we did it last year with the Kazmir trade," Luhnow said the next spring. "That was not done for job preservation. That was done to try and help this team achieve a milestone that would propel us even further.

"That continuum always exists."

Luhnow's vanity license plate was no longer GM 111. He switched to OCTOBB, a reminder of the month that hosts baseball's postseason, where Luhnow wanted his team to be playing every year. He even added some orange tires into the mix to represent Astros colors, from the high-performance wheel company run by one of his brothers.

The Astros' surprising playoff berth also stirred up lingering resentment. An Astros team built around Altuve, Keuchel, and Springer—with catcher Jason Castro, another former first-round pick of Houston's—was a team heavily reliant on players whom Luhnow inherited.

For years, Luhnow trashed what his predecessor Ed Wade and company had left him.

"You got to remember, we had not only an underperforming poor record at the big-league level, we had one of the worst farm systems in baseball," Luhnow said in spring training 2014. "That combination of factors, there are not too many teams that have started from that point. You could argue it's equivalent to an expansion team or potentially even worse, because you've got some inherent things that are negative rather than positive."

Even prior to the playoff run, the old administration didn't take Luhnow's framing well.

"I think for people to say it was the worst farm system in baseball is not true," the former team president, Tal Smith, said in 2014. "How did it go from being the worst to being the best? It hasn't been just because of the drafts of 2012 and 2013.

"I just think there have been a lot of comments . . . by people that just looked at the Astros' terrible win-loss record in 2010, '11 and '12 and '13 and then cast it all upon a very poor, or a terrible farm system that was the result of the previous general manager and scouting director, and I don't think that was fair at all."

O

When the Astros arrived in New York for the wild card game against the Yankees, pitching coach Brent Strom had asked the pitchers and catchers to change their signs. "I didn't pitch in that game, but they wanted us to go through that like the days before with the catcher," Neshek said.

Strom and bullpen coach Craig Bjornson had thought the Yankees were stealing signs. The suspicion was that the Yanks had positioned someone in center field to wave a towel as a means of relaying what pitches were coming to Yankees' hitters. Many hitters love to know what type of pitch is coming, if they can. A colleague said that Pete Putila was sent out to investigate.

The Astros didn't figure it out then, but the Yankees had, indeed, been up to something that season.

For all of time, players have known that if a runner reaches second base, the catcher's signs are in danger of being intercepted. A runner on second has a direct line of sight to the catcher, and the fingers he's throwing down.

If the runner can pick up the code, he can tell his teammate who is batting what's coming with a small movement. Maybe a hand to the helmet means fastball.

For all of time, too, it had been legal to do this, and encouraged. As a defense, catchers often used a more complex set of signs when someone reached base, particularly second base. They might put down three or more signs before a pitch was delivered. The pitcher would have advance knowledge of which sign in the sequence actually matters. Colloquially, then, if an opposing team has learned "the sequence," that means they know the indicator—which sign was determinant.

But what baseball's rules had long prohibited was the use of electronic equipment to aid the theft.

Telecasts had been available in clubhouses and locker rooms for decades. Every once in a while, a player or a staff member could pick up a sequence by watching on TV. If that information made its way to the dugout, and to runners on base, a hitter could have an advantage—so long as the pitcher hadn't changed the code in the meantime. But using the telecast in the clubhouse to break the code was uncommon enough to be ignored.

By the early aughts, tech advancements were producing other possibilities.

"When I was with the Twins, we used to have [video] in the Metrodome right behind our dugout, which was like on the field," Neshek said. "It was just a laptop with all the shit, but it was live, like you watched it live. It was right there, and that was in '06, so we had that stuff. It was kind of a concern, where you would like hear stories about guys when they needed to get [a sign] would yell."

But the Twins didn't use that video to decipher signs, Neshek said.

"I didn't notice it in Minnesota, but there were whispers [about others]," he said. "You would hear it your whole career, it was something—they had the technology in '06 to do it. The thing was like, who did it?"

The landscape had radically changed by 2015. The still nascent replay system in baseball that Bud Selig and Rob Manfred ushered in for the prior season, and the video rooms that every team staffed in support of that system, were fertile ground for an ulterior usage. With myriad camera angles available for instant replay in a centralized spot, players or staff could sit, watch, and try to pick up the signs being used.

This wouldn't be an act of advance scouting, but an attempt to gain an edge inside the very same game. The information would go back to the dugout, and when a runner got to second base, they'd know the catcher's code.

The Yankees started using their video room to decode signs no later than 2015. The Yanks were a seasoned team, with veterans who knew how to find advantages. Those rooms are often positioned near the team's dugout, making them easily accessible for hitters and pitchers alike during a game.

"I'm just telling you from a broad perspective, living it, it didn't feel that wrong," said a Yankees player. "It was there for everyone, that's all.

"If I could figure out the signs from the telecast, I was not going to hold on to that information. I was going to share that with whomever."

Indeed, if it could help win an extra game or two, why wouldn't the players give it a go?

"Whatever is available to teams, they're going to take advantage of it," a different 2015 Yankee said. "Major League Baseball knows that. If you have this technology that's available to where you have twenty cameras on the field, cameras that can look at signs, I mean, it doesn't take a rocket scientist to see, 'Oh, if I'm in the video room and I see the guys' signs.'"

Baseball's electronic sign-stealing era was under way.

# 9

# BASHFUL AND THE BULLDOG

WITH THE ASTROS' FIRST TASTE OF SUCCESS CAME A SECTARIAN PULL.

In the midst of the postseason push in September 2015, the team suffered a major loss in leadership. David Stearns, the lone assistant general manager to Jeff Luhnow, left to go run a team of his own, the Milwaukee Brewers. Just thirty years old, Stearns had always been presumed to be on the path to become general manager, perhaps once the Astros' turnaround was completed. The opportunity might have come earlier than expected, and his exit shifted the makeup of the Astros' front office at a crucial time. Stearns's temperament and approach made him extraordinarily well liked, a glue guy. He would talk to A.J. Hinch after virtually every game.

"Huge deal," an Astros staffer said. "Huge deal. [Mike] Elias was there, but was not at anywhere close to the major league team. [Brandon] Taubman was an understudy of Stearns. And then [Mike] Fast and Sig [Mejdal] were in the research room and [Kevin] Goldstein was in Chicago. There wasn't anybody else. And the farm director was Quinton McCracken at the time; he was gone. Jeff was going to change that."

Another member of the early brain trust, Stephanie Wilka, had already moved out of baseball operations into a counsel position for the club, one she thought could advance her career more quickly. A little more than a year later, she would leave the organization entirely, joining the San Diego Padres.

Without Wilka and Stearns, baseball ops was growing smaller and more insular. In one sense, Stearns was different than the rest of the group. His resume and prior work in the sport with the commissioner's office and other teams put him apart from the overall character of the Island of Misfit Toys. "He had the smell of success on him from the second he walked into Houston," an Astros colleague said. "Great guy, I wish him well, and I'm glad he's got a chance to do well for himself in Milwaukee. But he was not like the rest of us. If shit didn't work in Houston, none of the rest of us were going to work in baseball ever again. He was going to go to the commissioner's office for a year and be fine."

Luhnow did not run out and replace Stearns with an outsider, nor did he make a promotion to fill the role, either. For 2016, the Astros technically had no assistant GM.

"If you look at the tenure of the Astros under Jeff Luhnow, what you see very little of is poaching successful baseball executives from other organizations, bringing in other people's good people and giving them jobs," an executive said. "The Astros sort of built the front office the way they built the roster in the early years. Where it was sort of like the Collin McHugh acquisition: like, what can we get off the waiver wires to fill in a front office?"

Luhnow's desire to keep the Astros' budgets lean did not stop with travel budgets or the player payrolls at the start of the rebuild. Even the salaries of his closest confidants were subject to the same approach. Astros staff were to ideally earn in the second quartile of the sport, below the 50 percent mark for their positions.

Every year, Luhnow would have to make a presentation to Jim Crane and the team's other part owners. And every year, Luhnow's favorite part was showing them where the Astros ranked relative to other teams across the different areas of operation. "The pitch to ownership was always like, 'We're good or great in all of those areas and I'm like twenty-eighth of thirty on the cost list,'" an Astros employee said. "And ownership fucking ate that stuff up. Jeff was really good and didn't cost money relative to other GMs and that was Jeff's staying power. That was his resiliency, that even if he was cutthroat and business-oriented or whatever, here, you have one of the smartest GMs in the game, and he's cheap. Owners didn't know he's working his people eighty, ninety hours a week. They saw a successful team and a low budget."

Keeping salaries down while simultaneously keeping an open assistant GM job worked hand in hand for one of Luhnow's goals: continually pushing his people. Jockeying to replace Stearns began. Goldstein was interested, and so too was the most obvious candidate, Taubman. Goldstein and Taubman were opposites to begin with, the former the ex–punk rock aficionado with an earring, the other the ex-banker. Taubman, hungry, had already rubbed plenty of people the wrong way.

"He came from that cutthroat, Wall Street, who-wears-better-shoes type of atmosphere," said scout Alex Jacobs, one of Taubman's friends in the organization. "He was curious, he didn't know much about the game, but he learned a lot to the point where he moves mountains in a way. He's very smart, he wants to do everything himself. He's difficult letting other people do work.

"Keeps a lot of things close to the chest, almost to a fault. There's one time I was playing with the TrackMan on the back field, and I showed him a snapshot of one of my pitches on the TrackMan, and he flipped out. He's like, 'You shouldn't see this.'

"There was a proprietary map that they were afraid I was going to put on Instagram or something. They were very paranoid about the information. I mean, this isn't Brandon alone. This is everyone in the front office."

Taubman, who got a bump to a director-level title after Stearns left, had become Luhnow and Crane's special projects manager, a drop-in reviewer of whatever issue was pressing. The valuation expert had quickly shown himself sharp and capable. Two of Taubman's earliest projects were looking over the Astros' research and development and player development departments—core areas. In R&D, Taubman quickly realized the Astros needed to make an even bigger push.

But for Luhnow, spending took some convincing. "Jeff always had this rule, he would call it the ten percent rule," an Astros exec said. "'If you're asking me for ten percent more, tell me what ten percent needs to go.' . . . He always talked about getting the first kill. He wanted all of the managers to be willing to fire their worst performers."

Player development featured its own set of conflicts, despite how well the Astros' farm teams were performing. Sig Mejdal had created a color-coded system to let the front office know when a minor league player was ready to be promoted to another level: green was go, and there were different shades. Different shades of red, meanwhile, suggested a demotion. It was called the pressure-to-promote tool. "It had pretty colors and it basically worked and aligned with the intuitions of Jeff and others, for the most part," a front-office member said. "But then it became a mature enough process where Jeff was curious about its legitimacy."

McCracken, Luhnow's farm director, and Mejdal were not seeing eye to eye. Mejdal was "very value-driven, he just relied on the numbers and he didn't really care as much about the opinions of the player development staff," a colleague said. There were monthly calls with player development staff, including minor league coaches. Afterward in smaller conversations, Mejdal would sometimes mock the old-school coaches who had been on the other end of the call. "Oh yeah, big boy down there in Lancaster just hit one out to left field," he would say in a rumbling voice, mocking what coaches had said about a player.

Mejdal didn't actually care about "big boy" hitting one out, because he could see home runs in the box score. He wanted to know about a player's underlying growth.

McCracken, meanwhile, had misgivings about the changes the Astros were making to farm system personnel. Over time, Luhnow had let the vast majority go, because he was not going to wait any longer to synchronize views and approaches. The coaches had to do what the front office wanted, lest Mark Appel Part Two arise.

Nonetheless, that amounted to the firing of people whom McCracken was loyal to, people who might have done all they reasonably could to keep their jobs.

Said an executive: "Q basically told Jeff, 'I'm not doing it. I'm not firing these guys. I'm not going to do it.'"

McCracken was moved out of the farm director role in October

2015 and eventually left the organization. Allen Rowin, a holdover from the Ed Wade administration, was named farm director, but Luhnow was keeping the seat warm for Pete Putila, who would take over a year later.

For 2016, the Astros had a new role in the minor leagues: development coaches. Mostly younger, analytical-minded folks who could implement what the bosses wanted. "We started bringing in development coaches who were outrageously inadequate, or nontraditional, in their resumes, and players started gravitating towards them, and then they did just fine, and then eventually all the staff was replaced over the course of five years," one executive said.

Over time, though, others felt the Astros minor leaguers weren't getting the fundamental instruction they needed. "I get these guys are smart and driven and all that kind of stuff, but they don't know how to teach a bunt play," complained one of the more veteran minor league coaches. "Yes, they're great outside-the-box thinkers, but they don't know what's inside the fucking box."

In his floating assignments, Taubman had also studied the worth of taking out insurance on players, a practice in baseball that's known to exist but is rarely publicized. According to an Astros executive, eventually, the Astros would start to insure some of their best players at premiums of typically $2–4 million per year to hedge against injury. (Jose Altuve, and later, Justin Verlander and Charlie Morton, were some of the names over time that the Astros took out policies on, the executive said.)

Crane at one point even had Taubman check the work of the revenue team, on the business side: Did this executive's ticket revenue plan make sense, or was another's dynamic pricing model a better bet? These arrangements, not too dissimilar to having an outside management consultant drop in, left Taubman in inherently awkward positions. He was asked to stick his hand into departments that were not titularly his.

Mejdal, for example, ran the Astros' R&D department at the time Taubman did his review.

"None of this is perfectly healthy," one Astros exec said. "It's not like we had a really transparent, inclusive decisions-making process. . . .

It was more like Jeff told Sig, 'Brandon is going to look into your area. You have these resource requests. I want to make sure he agrees with it.'"

In Luhnow's structure, conflict was central, and rifts were growing as the start-up began to mature. "Jeff did like when his people argued with each other," one exec said. "I think what he really wanted was to use the phrase 'radical transparency,' this Ray Dalio concept, that anyone at any level can challenge another person with evidence on their side." "Any level" is a stretch, because Luhnow could easily shut out many voices outside of the circle. But inside the front office, the environment was both collaborative and lacking in clear boundaries.

Taubman had worked closely with Stearns and Luhnow, and the young analyst knew what made Luhnow tick. It was clear to most of the Astros' brain trust what Luhnow valued, and what he did not. Taubman and the rest knew it was their job, almost exclusively, to deliver that to him.

O

The same week that Stearns left, Taubman headed up a massive presentation to the core of the front office, a PowerPoint of well over one hundred slides with contributions from Mejdal and Fast and others. "Other people definitely contributed, Fast in particular," one executive said. "He was bashful, and Brandon the bulldog."

With one playoff appearance under the team's belt, Taubman addressed every corner of baseball operations in a proposed blueprint for the Astros as they entered the next stage.

The Astros' advantage in the draft, that gold mine of cheap talent, was shrinking. Taubman did a study showing that the industry was getting better at recognizing talent. The Cardinals of 2005–11, in the time Luhnow and Mejdal ran the draft, were almost 20 percent more effective than other teams in the same span. The gap now, however, was closing. The statistics that other teams had previously overlooked were now widely understood, which meant teams were taking better players earlier in the draft.

At one point during the presentation, according to an executive who was present, a reference was made to internal draft valuations the Cardinals had made during Luhnow and Mejdal's time with the team. It was a look back at how the Cardinals had ranked players ahead of different drafts, based purely on what those players had done statistically prior to the draft.

In 2006, the Cardinals considered first baseman Allen Craig to be the seventh-best player in the draft, based on his statistics. They snagged him in the eighth round that year.

Pitcher P. J. Walters was the sixth best that same year, and the Cards grabbed him in the eleventh round, after hundreds of picks had been made.

In 2009, the Cardinals considered first baseman Matt Adams the seventeenth-best overall statistically, and the Cardinals selected him all the way in the twenty-third round.

A pitcher the Cardinals did not draft in 2007, Josh Collmenter, was the nineteenth best overall, as the Cardinals saw him. He went to the Diamondbacks in the fifteenth round.

Although club draft projections, years after the fact, aren't the most valuable pieces of information, this was the kind of information that likely never should have made it into an Astros presentation years after Luhnow and Mejdal left St. Louis.

TrackMan's proliferation was helping to shrink the Astros' advantage. From 2013 to 2015, usage of the radar system jumped both around the league and throughout the Houston organization. In 2013, the Astros carried TrackMan in only the majors and Triple-A. By 2015, the Astros had a unit at every level of the minors, and it was Houston's understanding that every major league franchise had at least one unit. But, because the Astros were an early adopter, they had access to more data than most teams over time, even as other teams got on board—an advantage in sample size when running studies.

Teams could also buy some data exclusively. The Rays made an arrangement to have a TrackMan unit installed at a top college, the University of California, Los Angeles, which would not feed the general pool of TrackMan data. The Astros followed suit. "Not only did we go from partial consumer of TrackMan to the most aggressive of TrackMan in all of baseball, but we actually did a private deal with TrackMan where we financed the installation of the TrackMan unit at Vanderbilt," an Astros executive said. "And the agreement was, we'll pay for it, and we'll teach you how it works, and we'll get this data exclusively. And it was an awesome deal for us."

Major League Baseball eventually stepped in and halted the practice, at least in part for fear it was a violation of NCAA compensation rules, where college programs are not to accept money from major league teams. But the Astros were said to have received multiple seasons' worth of data out of their Vanderbilt unit. They also at one point paid TrackMan a premium not to sell international data to other teams, an executive with knowledge of the deal said.

Taubman was spearheading this arms race in an unregulated market, convincing Luhnow and Crane that tech was an area to spend more aggressively in, and he was helping keep the Astros ahead. The Astros even tried to get a TrackMan unit into Cuba, where the Astros had hired an analyst who also worked with one of the Cuban teams, the Industriales, based in Havana. The commissioner's office, multiple Astros employees said, squashed the effort for concerns over how the US Office of Foreign Assets Control would view it. "Trackman went to MLB and that's the point where MLB said, no, you can't do this," one Astros employee said.

Very early on, an executive said, the Astros had thought about trying to buy TrackMan outright. They decided not to because part of its value was tied to its availability in different stadiums, creating the pool of data.

But the Astros' overall TrackMan advantage, separate of the draft, was eroding, Taubman told the group. The Astros had six analysts in R&D in 2015. Taubman wanted the Astros to spend more to pursue people with doctorates and PhDs because the future of the club would be reliant on their work processing information from TrackMan and other sources.

Meanwhile, the international market, by Taubman's calculations, was an area where the Astros had not been aggressive enough. Uncertainty with international amateur players, most of them from Latin American countries, was high. Many do not pan out as big-league players. But teams at that time had no cap on how much they could spend internationally. Even if one viewed the international market like a lottery, the return could be so high and the cost was low enough that the Astros would still be wise to buy more scratch-offs, Taubman believed.

A part of the presentation that Mejdal authored covered John Kotter's vision of change management. Mejdal was a fan of Kotter, who had described eight ways organizations fail in change programs. "Sig felt we should be embracing those tenets more than we were," a colleague said.

But the piece of the meeting that was perhaps the most ominous—and in a way, also the most ahead of its time—was on pro scouting, the scouts who review players who are already playing professionally.

Taubman determined that pro scouts weren't creating much of a discernible advantage. He measured two forms of evaluation: One was the way the Astros valued players based on statistics. The other was how the team viewed players when those statistics were combined with preference lists compiled by scouts. The advantage of mixing in scouting information was about 2 percent better, Taubman found.

The human eye was no longer as valuable as it once had been. TrackMan and other tools could do what traditional scouts did—provide insight on performance—but in many cases, better. "At some point in recent history, a fucking box up on the awning of the press box is doing a better job covering the majors and minors than scouts can," an Astros executive said, a reference to TrackMan.

Taubman and Luhnow had the same vision for pro scouting, but Luhnow actually wanted to move more slowly. Perhaps feeling the pressure of the criticism he had taken, Luhnow was leery of the conflict any quick action would cause.

"Do it slowly, fire three people at a time," an executive said of Luhnow's stance. "He had this five-year outlook where over the course of time we'd like get the head count and the expense down."

Taubman didn't outright want to fire everyone. But he did want to move quickly, and was interested in teaching scouts who were willing and capable of learning the new approach.

Luhnow, Mejdal, Fast, Putila, and Elias were on hand for the presentation. One person who was not invited, an executive said, was

Goldstein—the one who oversaw pro scouting. The subject matter was obviously touchy, but Goldstein also did not live in Houston.

Taubman and Goldstein constantly butted heads. An older pro scout on Goldstein's staff, Hank Allen, had started his major league playing career in 1966. But he was making a low six-figure salary, one executive said, and the Astros were paying additional money to put him on the road. (By contrast, Taubman was not yet making six figures in Houston.)

"He was in the DC area, this scout followed only two teams. Kevin had coverage determined by team," an executive said. The Nationals played in Washington and the Orioles in nearby Baltimore. "It was like, what sense does it make for this guy to spend fifty percent of his time covering the Nationals, when we have good info [through other means]? So, this was a point of contention."

In all, the Taubman-led presentation would be a loose map the team would follow in the coming years. It was, in a way, his coming-out party. The ideas, not solely his, were smart but controversial.

"The culture wasn't noticeable until the end of 2015," said Jacobs, one of the Astros' pro scouts. "I can pinpoint exactly when."

Jacobs was sitting in a conference room at the training complex in Kissimmee at the end of the 2015 season when he said his boss, Goldstein, got an email from Luhnow asking for a one-, three-, and five-year plan for pro scouting. Luhnow had asked for such plans before, and from other departments as well, but this email had stood out to Goldstein.

"He knew. He pretty much said to me that the staffs are going to be much smaller," Jacobs said. "That's when I realized that things were going to get interesting."

Jacobs heard that, at the end of the 2015 season, another team, the Miami Marlins, called for permission to hire him away. The Astros didn't have to grant the Marlins permission to talk to him, but Jacobs said his bosses didn't immediately alert him to the request. Technically, they were not required to do so. But the working standard in the sport, which seems to be eroding over time, is that if a better opportunity exists elsewhere that the current employ cannot match, the team would grant permission for the employee to interview.

"At first, I wasn't really told the truth, and then eventually the truth was told to me that the Marlins called," Jacobs said. "Then they didn't give me permission to talk. I got a very modest raise, which was good. I got a good raise. And then things started to get weird. When we had meetings in Kissimmee in spring training, and then Jeff would say our jobs are pretty much going to be like pointless in a couple years, or be different in a few years. In front of everyone, the entire department: 'You guys might not have jobs in a few years.' And quite frankly, he was probably right. Houston saw the future of pro scouting before anyone else really did."

○

The Astros' push for innovation was touching every corner of the operation, including one that is rarely discussed publicly, the team's medical staff. The athletic trainers and strength and conditioning staff sit under that umbrella.

After the Brady Aiken saga, the Astros had a smaller public dustup over a player's health heading into the 2015 season. Ryan Vogelsong, a free agent pitcher, had an agreement to join the Astros, but the team balked at his medicals. "I made a visit to Houston and met with A.J. Hinch—the manager—and the staff, the training staff, and I took a physical. Just as the process went along here, I really wasn't comfortable with what was going on," Vogelsong said.

Medical disputes with free agents happen with other teams, too, but Vogelsong's camp were skeptical of the assessment and the personnel making it.

Around the time Luhnow hired Taubman, he had hired a medical risk manager and analyst, Bill Firkus, from a group of about 250 applicants. The pool of job seekers included surgeons, but Luhnow's selection was not a doctor. "He did stay at a Holiday Inn Express," Luhnow joked. Firkus, instead, was an MBA who had worked in health care investment banking and medical sales marketing, the type of business background that always resonated with Luhnow.

Injury prevention was a huge area of opportunity. "The research is ongoing, and the carrot is so big. If you're able to reduce injuries or increase performance, the value's so great that there's always going to be a lot of work done in this area," Luhnow said. "But it is a very difficult area to study, because you have limited subjects and you can't do experiments with the subjects. And they're real-life human beings out there under real-life conditions."

Sports medicine is an expansive world, and much of Firkus's job was prioritizing and figuring out what projects the Astros should pursue. This was not in itself a new endeavor. Technically, Firkus was not the Astros' medical director. Every team has a head doctor, and for the Astros, that's Dr. David Lintner, who was affiliated with Houston Methodist and had been working with the club since 2000.

Lintner, for example, had studied shoulder surgery for pitchers, repairs to the labrum. But Lintner had other responsibilities, and Firkus was hired to review studies on a full-time basis. Team doctors often have responsibilities away from the club.

A couple of other teams carried positions that were similar to Firkus's but had filled them with certified athletic trainers—licensed professionals who, although they are not doctors, have bona fide credentials to work directly with athletes. Luhnow, forever the outside-the-box thinker, obviously didn't think that background was necessary for someone in an office job.

"I think I'm the only nontrainer to have a similar role like this," Firkus said. "I knew the cardiovascular space really well, just because I had lived that for three years. So I felt comfortable telling Jeff and the rest of the medical team, 'Look, I am not a doctor. But I've proven that I can learn a medical space, and I'll work as hard as I can to do so on the sports medicine side.'"

The same problems the Astros encountered with their coaching staffs in the push for synergy started to plague the Astros on the medical side.

Nate Lucero had been inside the Astros organization since 1993, and with the major league team since 2007, rising to head athletic trainer—the lead respondent when a player gets injured on the field.

Firkus, Lucero said, "had no, I guess you could say, court awareness."

"He'd come in and try to show me something he found on Google or whatever it may be, and I said, 'Man, this is not the time to do that, brother. This is the time that we're trying to get ready for a game,'" Lucero said.

Like Bo Porter, Lucero found Luhnow's communication void to be problematic. Luhnow, to Lucero and others, was "extremely arrogant."

"He was unapproachable most of the time," Lucero said. "Not only my phone calls, but the field manager's phone calls when we were trying to get a hold of him. Then turning around and telling you that you were bad at communication."

Lucero at one point made a Twitter account because he believed it would be a quicker way to find out what was going on with the Astros than to be told directly.

"I remember we're in Oakland one time, and he made a comment to me about me needing to be more vocal and to communicate with him better, and I said, 'Jeff, I tried calling you. I emailed you. I texted you. I do everything possible. I call David Stearns ninety-nine percent of the time because I know he'll answer.'

"And he turned around, he said, 'Yeah, I guess I gotta get better at that.' And that day we were in Oakland, and we were standing right by BP [batting practice], and I was like, this guy's going to let me go, because [he's] probably thinking insubordination, because I'm challenging him a little bit."

Lucero was right: Luhnow let him go after the 2015 season. The turnover on the medical staff that offseason might have impacted at least one player.

"There was a time where there was like no trainer for a month. I didn't really know what to do," reliever Pat Neshek said.

Neshek had suffered a hairline fracture in his foot in spring training of 2015 but was able to pitch on it during the season. "So all season they were like, 'You don't have to run all year, we just need you to pitch,'" Neshek said. "Well, then by the end of, it was probably August, the thing was just throbbing, and [a coach] came up to me, and he was like, 'Hey, we're looking at your chart from last year with your stride, and your stride is like, six inches shorter.' And I'm like, 'Yeah, it's probably because I have a broken foot.'

"I was supposed to have a bunch of shit done at the end of the season. And that got kind of lost in the shuffle."

When the new head trainer arrived, he asked Neshek how his foot was. When Neshek said it was broken, he was sent to the hospital for X-rays.

"And the foot doctor down in Florida was like, 'Dude, you got a full break, this thing needs to have surgery and [a piece of bone must] come out immediately, you shouldn't be walking on this thing,'" Neshek said. "I was just expecting to fly in and fly out that same day."

A picture of the bone removed from Neshek's foot circulated the next spring training, and besides being gross, it looked to be about an inch in diameter.

Even some of the new staff that Luhnow was bringing in, not just the so-called old guard, were starting to question the Astros' plans.

Although Luhnow had said publicly that he didn't believe in experimenting on players, privately Luhnow had told staff that he viewed the minor leagues as laboratories.

"There was about ten to fifteen of us in the room and we were talking about different types of shoulder programs and arm care," said James Ready, a newly hired major league athletic trainer. "And some people that were, I'd like to say, on the 'good' side, wanted to try some other stuff than what we were doing. And basically our doctor—the doctors, the head medical professionals, some of them were in the room—said, 'We don't agree with this. Ethically, we can't put somebody at risk.' Like that's our job to protect the athlete, not try stuff out on them. And then at the end of the meeting it came down to—Jeff and Bill even said it at the time—'Well, we're going to try to figure out a way to do this anyway.'

"That was kind of like the first one where I'm like, 'Huh?'"

Dr. Lintner put the kibosh on certain things with finality, Astros staffers said. But Luhnow and Firkus continued to push for other elements. An Astros staffer recalled that a group of players who were going to be released anyway were told toward the end of spring training that they were goners. But, if they wanted to stick around and try out some experimental training methods—methods the staff was said to have felt more comfortable with compared to some others—they were welcome to do so.

Not every initiative provided disagreement, and some worked out well. But the front office's approach left staffers leery. "Jeff and the front office there wanted yes-men," Ready said. "They wanted people there that would agree and do what they ask for, and if you had differences of opinion, they weren't exactly the biggest fan of you because of that."

One oddity that multiple Astros employees pointed to: the X-ray machine that was installed to measure the hands of players in the Dominican Republic.

"For the most part when it came to our athletic training budget, we had enough money," Ready said. "There was certain times we'd want certain things, it'd be like, 'No, let's spend here.' We brought in an X-ray machine to put down in the Dominican to take pictures of their hands to see how big we think they're going to be. And I'm like, 'Is that $50,000, $80,000 machine better spent elsewhere, to help out a minor league team?'"

One Astros executive said the machine was used so that Astros could better tell what age players were, because Mejdal "knew a guy who claimed he could tell what age you really were based off your hand X-rays, because of the way certain bones developed."

○

In 2014, the Astros had let go of a player they should not have. Outfielder J. D. Martinez, prior to that season, had not been a very good major league player. But he always had high potential as a hitter, and in the winter leading into that campaign, he entirely rebuilt his swing mechanics. He told the team this, too. In spring training, the Astros barely played Martinez and then released him. The Detroit Tigers picked him up, and he rewarded them with a combined sixty-one home runs over the 2014–15 seasons.

The decision to cut Martinez had contributed to some of the rift between Bo Porter and Jeff Luhnow. Whose fault was it that Martinez had gotten very little playing time in spring training? Both blamed the other, but the front office was in the greater position of power, and was rarely afraid to impose its will.

Now, Mike Fast of the R&D department had been squarely in the camp that Martinez was not a good player. His model had told him so.

And as Martinez bashed long balls for the Tigers, Fast realized he had been very, very wrong. How did this happen? he wondered. Until he could figure out why his model had missed on Martinez, he felt like the Astros' entire method of evaluating players was lacking.

The model to that point had accounted for any short-term fluctuation as random, suggesting that a player would regress to their past average performance. But what if a player had meaningfully changed, or blossomed?

The Astros had all these new technological tools at their disposal, information streams pouring in. Martinez, even before his swing rebuild, had hit the ball as hard in 2013 as almost any player in the Astros organization. But the Astros didn't have a lot of data to work with when Martinez was cut. More technology could have helped. A swing sensor attached to a hitter's bat—something that could measure swing speed and launch angle—was just arriving in the sport, but not in time to influence the Martinez decision.

Now, in the 2015–16 offseason, granular performance information could be better quantified. How the Astros would use it was at the center of the team's future.

With Stearns gone, Luhnow made another major change. Mejdal's time running the Astros' R&D department, decision sciences as it was known then, was over. Fast was in charge.

Luhnow believed that Mejdal, his longtime friend, could help in a different area: implementation. Change management was becoming more of a focus, if a little late. But other issues led Luhnow to remove his buddy from atop the department.

For one, Mejdal and Fast saw the world differently. "Mike and Sig were not getting along. They had different ideologies about how research and development should work," a colleague said. "Mike was as valuable, and in the eyes of some people, more valuable, than Sig, even though Sig was Mike's boss and more senior and had been with Jeff longer."

Mejdal was also aware that he simply wasn't as technically skilled as the army of people entering the workforce every year. His experience and knowledge would always be worth something, but his technical skills wouldn't keep his window open forever. Mejdal, too, didn't want to live in Houston, but rather wanted to be with his family in North Carolina.

Speed was an operational goal in the early years. Everything had to be built quickly, including the actual models in R&D. The result was an R&D department waist-deep in technical debt.

"For all R&D shops, there's this technical debt question: What's the trade-off between doing things more slowly, but with less technical debt, with less issues that you'll need to fix in the future?" one executive said. "Sig was like the master of the MVP [minimally viable product], the master of getting done something that's simple and helpful. But the drawback of his approach is that often whatever he would create had issues that would fester. And that's what technical debt is. And so Sig was four years into running R&D at the Astros, and some of those technical debt issues were starting to manifest themselves.

"One, for example, is that for the amateur draft projection system, the code was in such terrible shape, and like no one understood it. So when it came time to iterate on that model, it became much more difficult. So we had all this anticipation and effort on the draft front to continue to outperform there, but it was becoming increasingly harder. And one example is with TrackMan: How do we get the TrackMan data into the projection systems, so we can understand how a college pitcher's TrackMan changes how we forecast his future career? Sig couldn't solve that problem, because the code base was such a mess. And so that was frustrating for Jeff, to have this powerful data set that, in the minors and majors for pro players, we were starting to have a lot of success with, and the trips [some in the front office were] taking to affiliates to talk about that stuff. And we just couldn't get [the draft] up to speed with what we were doing in other departments."

Two factions were rising over a major philosophical dispute. On one side was Luhnow and Mejdal, who were highly skeptical of information outside the projection model. If the trick was to follow the odds, and the model interpreted the odds, relying on information outside the model was perilous.

On the other side was an emerging and often like-minded trio: Fast, Taubman, and the former intern who survived Luhnow's purging, Pete Putila of the player-development group. They were more inclined to use new information streams, even if they had yet to be worked into the model. "This information is valuable, and we gotta use it. Even if we can't necessarily put it into a projection, we can help our players get better with this, we can use it in the draft to make smarter decisions," an executive said. Together, the three would power much of the Astros' success moving forward, the innovations in technology, and the synergy the Astros would grow in their farm system as the major league team turned the corner.

Putila led the charge to add one new tool in particular, slow-motion video. High-speed cameras, however, were traditionally incredibly expensive, and expensive wasn't the Astros' thing. So Putila went on a mission to find a cheaper option. Taubman got involved, and they found a company through Kickstarter, the online crowdfunding platform, called Edgertronic. "Are you frustrated that access to professional-grade, high-speed video cameras is limited to big-budget shows on the Discovery Channel?" went the Kickstarter ad. "Do you dream of having the frame rate and resolution of a truly professional camera sitting on your tripod?"

Putila, in fact, did. Taubman tried to negotiate an exclusive with the company, so that the Astros could be the only team to buy the cameras, which didn't happen. The work with the cameras was clunky at first in 2015, but by 2016 there was some structure around it.

When Dallas Keuchel was struggling that year, the Astros were able to use the camera's frame-by-frame ability to help him identify what was wrong. Edgertronics were not just a scouting tool, but a coaching tool, producing 400 frames to even 1,000 frames per second.

Leading up to the 2016 June draft, Taubman accompanied Mike Elias, the amateur scouting director, on a trip to San Antonio to see a high schooler projected to be selected early, Forrest Whitley. The sample size was woefully small at thirty to forty pitches. But the Edgertronic footage allowed the Astros to determine some of the same information they would have gleaned from TrackMan, which high schoolers weren't exposed to as often as college players. Edgertronic cameras were more portable than TrackMan systems.

Using video game development software, the Astros determined the spin and the speed of the baseball and the axis from the footage.

"It would show the baseball rotating on the screen," an employee said. "And what you could do with that is, if you sat there playing with the numbers enough while watching video, you could get the two to line up. You could say, 'OK, that's his spin rate.' And so that's how we know . . . Forrest Whitley's spin rate."

His spin was desirable, too. The team still was leery of taking high school players near the top of the draft, "because there's never data to support it," an exec said. "But now finally we had some data points, even in small samples."

Fast and Taubman wanted to believe in the data, and the Astros had a little bit of TrackMan info on Whitley separately already, which helped convince Mejdal. They drafted Whitley with their first-round pick in 2016. But the tension was still brewing.

Although Fast was now technically the head of R&D, Mejdal still had some sway over the direction of the draft model. Fast would try to make changes and would get his wrist slapped.

"He was still in Jeff's ear second-guessing everything Mike wanted to do," a colleague said. "That was an incredibly unhealthy dynamic that I think led to a lot of the problems that you see in the organization. Not just that particular situation, but that you had people [who] were willing to enter into that sort of a dynamic. Like, if Sig's not the guy, he's not the guy. Get rid of him. If Sig is the guy, don't promote somebody else to his old job and then keep him around without a portfolio."

A few months after Fast had taken over as director, he gave Luhnow an assessment of the department and its needs. He believed that the Astros' software stack was in need of repair, but he wasn't sure what to do with it.

"Do you want me to bring in consultants?" Luhnow asked.

Fast said he didn't think it was a question that required the help of consultants, at least not right now. To bring in management consultants to evaluate baseball operations was unheard-of in the sport, but that had never been a deterrent for Luhnow.

Luhnow, in fact, had stayed in touch with his old consulting network. One night in Houston, he wound up at a social event with Sanjay Kalavar, the managing partner of the Houston office of McKinsey & Company.

# 10

# IN THE CAN

IN THE SUMMER OF 2015, THE *NEW YORK TIMES* REPORTED THAT THE FBI was honing in on the culprit who had hacked into the Astros' computer systems. For the first time, the public learned something shocking: the hack was believed to have originated inside the St. Louis Cardinals organization. In July, the Cardinals announced they had fired Chris Correa, their amateur scouting director.

A week into 2016, the Astros had their vindication. Correa, the former colleague of Jeff Luhnow and Sig Mejdal in St. Louis, was sentenced to forty-six months in prison.

It's not every day that a baseball employee gets sent to a federal penitentiary, but the Astros were embarrassed and seemed out for blood.

"MLB and the FBI investigated heavily," a Cardinals executive said, "I think somewhat at the behest of the Astros, who were adamant that this be treated as a federal crime, not as a rogue employee. It could have been handled differently, I think. But it seemed like the Astros were adamant that it not be."

The feds had their own interests, as well.

"One of the purposes of prosecuting and convicting criminal cases is deterrence, to prevent other people from engaging in similar conduct," a former prosecutor and outside observer, Peter Toren, said in 2015. "In a case like this, that has widespread press, the government is going to look at it as having meaningful deterrent value."

Correa hadn't merely peeked at Astros' trade notes and player evaluations when he shouldn't have been. He violated the 1986 Computer Fraud and Abuse Act, which makes it a criminal offense to access a computer without authorization and obtain information that affects interstate commerce. In other words, an act of corporate espionage.

"The significance has to be taken in context with computer crime in general," Ken Magidson, US attorney for the Southern District of Texas, said shortly after Correa's guilty plea. "We're trying to demonstrate when we get information through federal investigative agencies that show that crimes are committed—and I mean that are provable beyond a reasonable doubt that show felonies are being committed—that this office will take action. And that's what we did in this case. We tried not to view it through the context of our national pastime or Major League Baseball, but this is a serious intrusion of a legitimate business enterprise."

In front of Judge Lynn Hughes, on January 8, Correa pleaded guilty to five counts of illegally accessing the Astros' systems, both their email system and Ground Control, the database with all the player information.

One could say that Correa had hacked the Astros, but "hacking" can also be suggestive of someone hunched over a computer in a darkly lit room, banging away at a keyboard for hours to gain access. Correa's effort wasn't quite so complicated or intensive. A professional hacker, for one, might not have been caught as quickly or easily. But all around, a lack of sophistication was at play: both in Correa's illegal entries, and the Astros' security practices.

"From a breach perspective, attribution is hard, because they have a lot of ways to cover their tracks," Tim De Block, an information security professional in South Carolina and Astros fan, said at the time. "It's kind of telling that the FBI was able to identify the Cardinals as the organization that had the unauthorized access."

Regardless, it was a crime, and Correa had indeed made some effort to cover his tracks by using publicly available software in an attempt to mask his location, his identity, and the device he was using, Assistant US Attorney Michael Chu said in federal court.

In the end, the Astros were certainly victims, legally and otherwise. But they also could have made their data considerably more secure. "Our security practices were abysmal around Ground Control," an Astros employee said. "We didn't have anything really. Like, our software development was so bad."

Their public position was different, though.

"I think we were prepared," Luhnow said in 2014. "We had security in place, and when you're talking about criminals, we just never know if we have enough."

Considering the confidence Luhnow had projected in the team's technological advances, and the lengths the Astros went to in other ways to keep their work secret, the hacking produced a clear irony.

Before joining McKinsey, Luhnow had worked for the company that makes Gore-Tex.

"Nobody knows how to make Gore-Tex fabric," an Astros colleague said. "They keep the actual specifics of how to make it locked in a room somewhere, and if you need access to the formula and you go through a security checkpoint, and you sign in a logbook, you leave your phone at the door so you can't take pictures.

"We were never that bad, and obviously our security practices fell well short of our paranoia, but that was always sort of the mindset: we had this secret sauce, and we need to do everything short of paying our employees well or making them feel valued or doing good at cybersecurity to keep those secrets from being spilled out to the world. Like, they wanted to do stuff to limit who can print things, so there weren't extra copies lying around of our advance reports. Meanwhile, Ground Control gets broken into."

Prior to Correa's guilty plea, Luhnow did an interview with Ben Reiter at *Sports Illustrated* in which Luhnow said it was "absolutely false" that the hacking owed to his failure to change passwords.

"I absolutely know about password hygiene and best practices," Luhnow told Reiter in what was billed as an exclusive interview. "I'm certainly aware of how important passwords are, as well as of the importance of keeping them updated. A lot of my job in baseball, as it was in high tech, is to make sure that intellectual property is protected. I take that seriously and hold myself and those who work for me to a very high standard."

The answer seemed carefully worded, and was relayed without discernment. The problem with Luhnow's answer, of course, is that just because he may have known about password hygiene, did not necessarily mean he or his group had effectively practiced it.

"Dealing with financial institutions and Fortune 500 organizations, we see the gamut of what people believe are good passwords," said Tom DeSot, an outside observer and the chief information officer of Digital Defense, an information security company, in 2015. "And a lot of times, what one person feels is a strong password is actually fairly easily guessable."

Chu said the password Correa had used to access the Astros' systems was the name of a player "who was scrawny and who would not have been thought of to succeed in the major leagues, but through effort and determination he succeeded anyway." That password— which a person with knowledge of the case said was six letters with no numbers—is known to have belonged to Sig Mejdal. For his part, Mejdal felt he had screwed up, and that if he had been more diligent with security, the break-in might never have happened.

The plea deal answered some questions about breaches into the Astros' systems, but left plenty of others. It did not, for example, address the chain of custody of the Astros' trade-talk notes that Deadspin published to great embarrassment for the organization.

"That wasn't part of the crime charged in this case," Magidson said. "The crime charged in this case, remember, is pleading to five counts of unauthorized access. So it's his actions that are being focused on, of what he did."

The information Correa reviewed was determined to be worth $1.7 million. In court, Chu said the negotiations to arrive at that figure were lengthy, and influenced by the Astros themselves. The calculation focused on the 2013 draft, centering on the number of player reports Correa reviewed. The restitution Correa agreed to pay, or the actual monetary loss, was $279,038.65—still a staggering amount for a typical front-office employee.

Correa was adamant that he had broken into the Astros' systems to find what had been taken from the Cardinals. But all the different information he had viewed suggested the effort evolved into a maneuver to steal new information as well.

"I originally accessed, trespassed the Astros' resources based on suspicions that they had misappropriated proprietary work from myself and my colleagues," Correa told the judge.

"Which colleagues?" Hughes asked.

"My colleagues at the Cardinals," Correa said.

"So you broke in their house to find out if they were stealing your stuff?" Hughes asked. "That didn't strike you as peculiar?"

"It was stupid," Correa said.

Correa said in court, too, that he found Cardinals information in the Astros' systems.

"Did you find any Cardinals information in the computer?" Correa was asked. "I did, your honor," he said.

Astros general counsel Giles Kibbe responded quickly, saying, "The Astros refute Mr. Correa's statement that our database contained any information that was proprietary to the St. Louis Cardinals."

How deeply the FBI looked into whether the Astros indeed stole from the Cardinals is unknown. Through its Department of Investigations, MLB had the capability, sans subpoena power, to run an investigation into the Astros. The central office chose not to, at least in part because the Cardinals did not ask for the matter to be pursued. "I didn't request anyone to do a counter-investigation," Cardinals owner Bill DeWitt Jr. said. "We didn't think it was necessary and thought it best to resolve the matter as expeditiously as possible."

Correa said in a 2017 statement that Commissioner Rob Manfred was "unresponsive" to requests he made to meet with the commissioner to discuss his "concerns about intellectual property theft." Said Correa: "I am unimpressed with Major League Baseball's commitment to fair and just action in this matter. The Cardinals were not the organization that benefited from unauthorized access."

Manfred responded by saying that MLB decided to wait until the federal investigation concluded before interviewing witnesses. Manfred said he told Correa in July 2016 that he would be banned for life if he didn't cooperate. "Mr. Correa not only steadfastly refused to answer any questions, but also opposed the release of any documents by the government to the office of the commissioner," Manfred said.

With a short time remaining before he went to prison, Correa didn't feel a sit down with Manfred was high on his priority list. MLB permanently banned him from the sport in January 2017. In his statement, he elaborated on what he thought the Astros did wrong.

"On December 21, 2011, a Houston Astros employee accessed proprietary data on a St. Louis Cardinals server. Later, I would learn—through unlawful methods—that Cardinals' data were used extensively from 2012 through 2014," Correa said. "Houston Astros employees used the data to replicate and evaluate key algorithms and decision tools related to amateur and professional player evaluation. Many individuals throughout the Houston organization, including the General Manager and Assistant General Manager, were included in email discussions about these efforts."

In 2015, Luhnow had told *Sports Illustrated*, "I didn't take anything, any proprietary information."

Correa believed he had found evidence that the Astros had used what the Cardinals called PV, or present value, to help reverse-engineer and create what the Astros called RV, or run value. The Astros, he believed, had a report on how well those two measures correlated, and what could be done to improve RV to make it further aligned with PV.

"I know that Sig and him [Luhnow] took stuff," one Astros employee said. "Absolutely they took stuff, because I was a recipient."

Among Correa's suspicions was that the Astros had data tagged with ID numbers from Red Bird Dog, the Cardinals' database.

"As far as I know, yes," another Astros employee said.

Another was that the Astros had the biomechanics grades done by Tim Leveque, who works for the Cardinals.

"Yes," the employee said.

Did the Astros have the Cardinals' PV values from the days in St. Louis?

"No," the same employee said.

"As far as I know, no one ever breached the Cardinals database or performed any sort of criminal act," an Astros employee said. "But there was a lot of bad shit that would get people who currently have jobs in baseball fired. It would probably also vindicate Correa a little bit, even though I think it's clear as water he did everything he was accused of.

"His whole defense was like, 'Well, Sig did it first.' And then that was that part that no one was really able to ever prove. And what Sig did first was basically just take a bunch of stuff with him when he left. Like Leveque. Like research on replacement level that [Cardinals executive Mike] Girsch had done, whatever."

Back in 2014, around the time the Astros learned they had been hacked, Kibbe, Jim Crane's right-hand man, was said to have directed an assessment of what Correa had accessed when he broke into the Astros' systems. Part of the assessment included a review of Mejdal's emails and his database access points.

"It's not good for Sig. It's not good for Correa. It's not good for the Astros. It's not good for the Cardinals. Baseball would hate it," a person with knowledge of the findings said. "The truth of it is that what Correa did, and how many times he did it, all that is worse than what's known. And whether Sig took stuff from the Cardinals, and whether Jeff knew that Sig took stuff, is worse than is known."

○

Spring training 2016 was upbeat. Now five years into his job, Jeff Luhnow had gone back through his email and came across the plan he had presented to Jim Crane when he took over the team.

"I had it in a spot where nobody can find it," Luhnow said that spring with a slightly awkward laugh, seemingly a reference to the hacking scandal with the Cardinals. "'Cause I haven't shared it with anybody."

How did it look half a decade later?

"I wanted to answer that question: Are the principles the same?" Luhnow said. "How much will this plan have changed today versus five years ago, five seasons ago? And I was pleasantly surprised that the principles that were articulated were still applied today, although some of the practical implications are different."

Just one season of winning allowed the Astros to project a greater sense of harmony and oneness. Dallas Keuchel, the newly minted Cy

Young Award winner in the American League, admitted that the relationship between the clubhouse and the front office had been adversarial.

"I guess everybody starts somewhere," Keuchel said. "Luhnow started with the Cardinals, basically the scouting director, and then he gets this role, the GM, and he's got a little bit of experience probably from talking with Cardinals guys or previous GMs. But until you actually experience it yourself, you're kind of doing your job on the fly, just like a player coming into his own.

"So I think at first it was kind of more standoffish and trying to figure out his role, but now that he's kind of figured out his role, Mr. [Jim] Crane with his role as the owner, you see them in the clubhouse more often. You see them engaging with the players more often instead of the whole kind of gate between the players and the front office. In years past, there's no communication—or I guess, connection—between the two."

Luhnow's explanation for why he hadn't visited the clubhouse more in the past was that the players, in essence, were too disposable.

"Quite frankly, we have more of our minor league players in the clubhouse now than we did before—and more players that we know are going to be around for a while longer—so it's a little easier to walk down there when at least I hope these guys are going to be around for a while and are going to be a big part of what we do," Luhnow said. "Whereas, the first couple years, I knew there were a lot of players that were probably not going to be here in a few years. Maybe I didn't take quite the same time to invest . . . in those relationships. But I'm glad to hear them say that it's feeling more positive."

They were at least projecting an image of newfound harmony, albeit awkwardly. Now, the hunt for separators would continue.

"From my experience here, the front office is really hungry for finding competitive advantages, and they'll not stop until they find it," manager A.J. Hinch said, entering his sophomore season in Houston. "Whether it's, you know, a deeper understanding of the analytics, whether it's an understanding of the baseball side of things, whether it's the medical process, whatever the area—the draft. I've listened to this front office preach competitive advantage my entire time through the interview process, all the way to now.

"It is very difficult to alter Jeff from his plan that he believes in. . . . How intense he is in his willingness to help us win is pretty remarkable."

The roster, though, had a problem entering 2016. Luhnow simply hadn't done much to upgrade it. The loudest move of the winter was picking up a young, hard-throwing reliever from the Philadelphia Phillies, Ken Giles, in exchange for prospects, including Mark Appel. The team was still only gently dipping its toe into the free agency waters.

"We addressed what we felt were some [needed] areas as a contending team," Luhnow said. "And when I talk about contending, I really do mean contending for a championship, not just contending for a wild card.

"I think we did everything we can. And it's not about how much money we spent, and it's about the team that we have on the field. . . . I'm not sure there was a clear answer—that we needed to go sign someone out there and commit the future resources that we may rather commit in some other area two years down the road—to get maybe incrementally better in a division that we think we can win with the guys we have."

General managers are obliged to toss around optimism before every season, but Luhnow was nonetheless off the mark.

One of the Astros' prized draft picks did arrive in 2016. Alex Bregman—the player the Astros drafted with the compensation pick for Brady Aiken—debuted in late July.

The Astros rolled into the midseason All-Star break with a 48–41 record, in second place. After a 13–5 loss to the Orioles on August 18, they had fallen to just one game above .500, at 61–60. They had lost five in a row, and 16 of 23. Hinch held a blow-up, team-wide meeting, addressing overall play while singling out a few players who were filling in for regulars. The message: don't just be happy to be here. Hinch, one person present said, "let 'em have it." A.J. Reed, a high draft pick in a classic Astros mold—great statistics in college, but disliked by scouts for his conditioning—was hitting a paltry .193, and didn't go on to have much of a career.

The next day didn't look much better at first. After facing just five batters, Collin McHugh had allowed four home runs. The Astros' hitters, though, responded immediately. They won 15–8, and won 10 of their final 12 games to finish out August.

That surge wasn't enough. A poor September put the Astros well out of the running. At 84–78, they won two fewer games than they did the year before, but finished in third. Injuries explained some of the underperformance, but the front office had also been too high on the supporting cast moving through the farm system.

"We relied too much on our upper-level, minor league talent to be everyday players," an executive said. "Tony Kemp, and Tyler White and A.J. Reed, a lot of guys that got service time in 2016 but didn't really perform all that well."

One player accomplished something of personal importance: George Springer played in all 162 games. Hinch and Springer had grown particularly close, and it was important for both of them that Springer, with a history of injuries, reach a milestone even the best players rarely can, to appear in every game. The feat was a little more special considering how adversarial the Astros had been in handling Springer's promotion to the big leagues in 2014, and the "eye exam" contract proposal.

Although his team was not in the playoffs, Hinch was encouraged. The bar had been moved. In just his second year, his group of players understood that 84 wins was unacceptable. The mindset he wanted was in place, even if the roster follow-through was not.

"We had the same team in '16 as we did in '15, but they didn't add a starter. Like I feel like we could have won the World Series if they would have added a couple starters," said Pat Neshek. "I was really pissed. . . . All they had to do was add a couple starters, and they just left us hanging, man, and that really pissed off the clubhouse.

"That whole '16 was such a shitshow at the end. We had all the guys, man. We had the hitters. We had the bullpen. It was just like: 'Add a couple starters, man.' Hinch was good. I don't know how much pull Hinch had, but Hinch was awesome with his communication. He was the best. He was kind of stuck in a hard place where the front office would tell him what to do and stuff, but I've seen way worse. Hinch was the man for the new-age baseball stuff."

It might have been wishful thinking, though, for Neshek to suggest that a couple more starting pitchers would have done the trick. At some point in a GM's tenure, a team has to start winning consistently. Luhnow was entering year six.

"The tone heading into the 2017 season was we need to up our game, and become more legitimate in player procurement through free agency," an Astros executive said.

Although litigation was still ongoing, the Astros' television carriage debacle had finally settled down, increasing revenues. Jim Crane, in turn, had eased the belt on the budget over time, giving the Astros room to grow. The payroll jumped more than $24 million between 2015 and 2016, and was about to rise by more than $27 million for the 2017 season.

"That gave us room to get two or three decently good free agents plus some smaller pieces, so it's an acknowledgment to Jim I think that he really increased our budget, and said like, 'Get after it,'" an Astros executive said.

O

The 2016–17 offseason was Luhnow's second without assistant general manager David Stearns. Luhnow had not yet given Stearns's old title to Taubman, but this winter would be the first where Taubman effectively stepped into that role, as the primary liaison to player agents and other teams' front offices.

"Jeff was surprisingly OK with taking sort of a backseat," an Astros exec said. "I think he would agree that negotiation is not his strong suit. Brilliant guy, but just not a great negotiator."

In the vein of what he had built as a daily fantasy sports player in his previous life, Taubman constructed a tool to look at the optimal deployment of money. It weighed every roster construction possible given the team's capital constraints, as well as the projected value of free agents, while also accounting for the Astros' internal talent. So if the Astros had a very strong player at a given position, the tool typically wouldn't recommend an addition at the same spot.

The front office had never been particularly inclined to rely on the recommendations of the pro scouting staff. Luhnow and Taubman had been planning for at least a year to reimagine pro scouting— or to nearly eliminate it, depending on your vantage—and by 2016, the process was under way.

"It became immensely awkward, because it was basically like Jeff wanted to get rid of the pro scouting meetings," an Astros exec said. "I remember KG [Kevin Goldstein] and the pro scouts feeling burned that Jeff didn't really give them the time of day in hearing their opinions. . . . We were really relying on the TrackMan data."

The focus for the winter landed on the outfield and starting pitching. The data pointed to a free agent pitcher, Charlie Morton, who showed an increase in velocity early in 2016 before a leg injury derailed the rest of his season.

Taubman led the acquisition and was pumped, believing Morton had one of the best curveballs in baseball, but hadn't been throwing it enough. Taubman also ran point when the Astros traded for a catcher from the Yankees, Brian McCann. That deal included a kerfuffle, though, when Luhnow allegedly tried to change the deal at the last minute. The Yankees were to send the Astros cash in the deal to offset McCann's salary, but Luhnow wanted the Yankees instead to take Jon Singleton, the first baseman who signed a long-term extension before playing a day in the big leagues and subsequently struggled on and off the field. Yankees assistant general manager Michael Fishman felt Taubman was going back on the deal, which Taubman was—at Luhnow's direction. Singleton was not traded in the end.

McCann was a well-liked veteran, excellent at handling a pitching staff. He also had a desirable offensive profile, as he could hit well without striking out much. In the last decade, the sport had seen a rise in what's known as the three true outcomes: home runs, walks, and strikeouts. Offenses with too many of those players can at least appear feast or famine.

"We focused on good players, and good players tend to strike out less and tend to make contact more," an exec said. "And we were really prone towards the three true outcomes—walk, strikeout, home runs—with our 2015 and '16 construction.

"Our mandate, or what we were solving for, was to have the team projected to win the most games possible. And based on the way that we evaluated our projected players, pitchers that strike guys out and batters that put the ball in play tend to be better, and therefore we're attracted to them."

Just as the Astros got done with the McCann deal, they landed an outfielder who represented, by far, the largest total dollar commitment Luhnow had ever made for a player in free agency—the means of player acquisition he favored the least. Josh Reddick, a skinny outfielder (who was one of the rare professional athletes who had a proclivity for cigarette smoking), had just hit 20 home runs in the prior season. He was on board for four years and $52 million, hardly a blockbuster. Although Luhnow would someday pay more to players who had not yet reached free agency, he would never exceed that figure for a player on the open market.

With McCann and Reddick on board, the Astros still wanted more help on offense, and had narrowed their sights to two veteran outfielders: Carlos Beltrán and Matt Holliday. Both had once been top free agent prizes themselves, but their best days were gone. They would have to spend at least some time as the designated hitter, or DH for short, a role in which they would bat, but not play defense.

"Beltrán was a huge controversy, because he did not represent a marketable improvement over Marwin Gonzalez in left field," an Astros exec said. "In fact, he projected as a worse player, so there was this question of, where does Beltrán fit in? And if at only DH, there's other players that are just as good as a bat-only sort of player. And Beltrán was a hard guy to figure out because he had been sort of volatile in performance as he moved around from New York to Texas, and he had an OK projection, but it wasn't seemingly as reliable as some other players'."

The Astros' projection used a three-year exponential decay, taking the past three years of performance and providing an assessment for the future. Beltrán had done well overall in the 2016 season, but his numbers had been considerably better in the first half of the season.

"He was actually a player that didn't fit the mathematical answer," the executive said. "But there was this idea that we needed more Latin leadership for Carlos Correa and more veteran presence in the clubhouse."

Chemistry and leadership can't easily be quantified, so it was a positive that the Astros, nonetheless, were thinking about those traits. There were whispers in spring training 2016 that Carlos Correa's head was getting too big, that after his debut the year before, people thought he was more concerned with so-called Carlos Correa Inc., the business side of his rising stardom, than his play. And although Jose Altuve was a standout performer, he wasn't at that time particularly vocal in the clubhouse.

"There was like no veteran that was of Latin descent, and so it was sort of like Marwin Gonzalez was the leader of the Venezuelan players. All of our Dominican players were really young," an Astros exec said. "It was very important to A.J., because we had a lot of young Latin players, and it was one of these things he wanted: we need more leadership for the Latin players."

All things being equal, then, the scales likely would tip in favor of a Latin player for the veteran role. Beltrán also had some notable history in Houston. The Astros traded for him in the middle of 2004, giving way to one of the greatest postseason performances ever. Beltrán hit a whopping eight home runs in just twelve playoff games. The tryst was memorable but short; he left as a free agent ahead of the next season.

But Luhnow appeared more concerned with a different history. In 2010, when Luhnow was with the Cardinals, the team had signed Holliday to a contract that was, at the time, the richest in St. Louis history. Luhnow wasn't the GM in St. Louis, but an Astros colleague nonetheless detected favoritism.

The moment of choice had arrived, and Luhnow directed Taubman and Mike Fast to figure out the best answer. Luhnow, the same day, happened to have his wisdom teeth removed. While Luhnow was gone, Taubman and Fast concluded that they didn't really want either player, but if one was needed, they preferred Beltrán because he was versatile as a switch hitter—meaning, he could bat left-handed or right-handed—and because he brought the benefit of Latin leadership.

When Luhnow checked in, he had what one colleague called "one of his worst moments as a GM."

"He was a complete asshole," the colleague said. Luhnow yelled at Fast and Taubman, but not in a way that made any sense. He was laying into the pair of underlings in "this drunken stupor coming out of surgery," and it left Taubman and Fast feeling terrible. Luhnow wanted to know if their logic was sound, "but he wanted Holliday because he had an emotional attachment to him, and I think that he was pissed-off that's not the answer."

The conclusion went unchanged: the Astros would sign Beltrán to a one-year, $16 million deal, and neither player would do well in 2017.

"It wasn't like this very exciting acquisition for us. It came from this idea that we needed veteran leadership," an executive said.

But in all, the 2016–17 offseason was a win for Luhnow and his roster. It was a positive signal for the clubhouse, too, for Hinch and the players who had waited so long for the Astros to arrive at serious contention.

"Switching gears and getting McCann and Reddick and Beltrán, going from high strikeout, high [isolated] power, to more quality at-bats, tougher to strike out, more balls in play—Jeff showed versatility in his team-building," one member of the 2017 Astros said. "And I do think that should be said."

○

Hinch needed a new bench coach and turned to a rising star, an ex-player who already had interviewed for managerial jobs elsewhere, Alex Cora. Smart and instinctual, Cora was one of the sharper baseball minds on any team he played for and was on a path to someday become a manager himself.

Like Beltrán, Cora was from Puerto Rico, and at the time Cora agreed to come to Houston, Cora was actually the GM of Puerto Rico's national team. He had been a star at the University of Miami in the 1990s, but didn't find the same success in the major leagues that Beltrán did. Cora spent the later years of his playing career in a utility role, helping out where needed on the infield for various teams. His talent and clubhouse reputation helped him to play for fourteen seasons.

Cora's charisma and confidence had also made him a fit as an ESPN broadcaster. Between his media experience, his reputation as a player, and the work he was doing running Team Puerto Rico, he was in a spot where he could have pursued most any job he wanted in the sport, including a front-office gig. But he wanted to manage, and about the only thing he lacked was coaching experience. Not all teams required it, but it wouldn't hurt.

○

Luhnow and Taubman's push for new technology beyond TrackMan and Edgertronic cameras had a dual effect: new gains, and new conflicts.

In 2016, the team had hired a sport science analyst, Jose Fernandez, to work under Bill Firkus. Sport science is a crossover discipline, ranging from health and fitness and physiology to typical on-field performance. It's something of a bridge between technology and training, often involving wearable devices. The Astros were trying new things in the weight room and the trainer's room: the measurement of recovery, for example.

In player evaluation, a lot of the early edge the Astros held was in pitching, the data they interpreted through TrackMan. Hitting, then, presented itself as the obvious next frontier. The Astros had demoed different devices that could attach to a bat and measure a player's swing. Pete Putila, Mike Fast, and a few other Astros staffers took to the diamond at Minute Maid Park in the prior offseason, testing one company's offering, Blast Motion, themselves.

Houston first distributed Blast Motion to minor league players during spring training. Taubman and one of Luhnow's minor league hires from St. Louis, hitting coach Jeff Albert, would run to the back fields every day, get the sensors, and analyze the data. One of the best ways to read the data, they found, was to take high-speed video of the swings at the same time, so that they could line up the Blast Motion data with the video. In all, Blast Motion would be "the first time we had insights on hitting," an executive said.

Once again, the Astros were an early adopter, and struck a business deal with Blast Motion. The Astros agreed not to use any other hitting sensor, and in return, Blast Motion sold them the sensors at a big discount, and also held the rights to market the Astros as clients. (As he had with TrackMan, Jim Crane considered attempting to buy the company.)

In 2016, Putila had taken over as farm director, and "Pete was amazing at having a feel" for how players would see and use the new technology, a colleague said. But getting minor leaguers to use new technology is almost always easier than convincing major leaguers to do the same. Everything minor league players do is geared toward climbing, which means that saying no can be dangerous to their careers. Minor leaguers didn't have a union of their own to bargain for their interests, like setting boundaries over the use of tech.

When the front office tried to get their major league players to use the bat sensors going into 2017, resistance followed.

"Because the data could be used against them, in theory," an Astros executive said. "That was the main theme of it. We were asking them to agree to put on technology which would then give the front office insights into how sound their swing mechanics were, and they were thinking, Why would I give that extra information up, what's my incentive? And our response was, 'So we can help you be a better baseball player, the same thing we're trying to do on the pitching side with the TrackMan data.' But they were basically receiving advice from their agents not to, and part of it was because we were pretty cutthroat in arbitration."

How the Astros handled their contract negotiations with their young, arbitration-eligible players was coming back to bite them.

The arbitration process can play out in two ways. The team and the player can settle on a salary, or they can go to a hearing where a panel of three arbitrators hears arguments and chooses which salary is fairest: the one the player asked for, or the one the team asked for. The arbitrators won't split the baby, so, most often, players and teams settle on their own.

But there's strategy involved in the entire process, and if it gets to a hearing, it can get really ugly.

Taubman was leading the Astros' process, along with another executive, Samir Mayur, who had also come from the business world. It used to be the province of David Stearns, who had been a diplomatic type, in arbitration and otherwise. "His attitude is to get deals done," a colleague said. But when Taubman took the reins, he was very keen to demonstrate to Crane and Luhnow he could save them money, knowing that would please them.

At quarterly owners' meetings, Major League Baseball would have reports "about how the different clubs were performing in baseball operations in arbitration and also across all the expense categories," an Astros executive said. "So they would say, 'Here's who's spending the most on scouting and in player development.'" These were opportunities to make Crane proud, so that the owner "could see in front of his peer group that we were cheaper or better or winning more or whatever."

MLB's Labor Relations Department advises teams during the arbitration process, just as the players' union does for the players. The LRD was said to have recommended to Taubman that the Astros move to "a file and trial" system, or "file and go."

In arbitration, players and teams formally propose salary numbers in the early winter if they haven't already settled. Normally, once that exchange happens, the player and team can keep negotiating before the case reaches a hearing around February. But a "file and go" approach meant that once the numbers were exchanged, the team would cut off negotiations—essentially ensuring the case would go to a hearing.

Theoretically, such a stance could pressure players to agree to a deal. Taubman, trying to impress Luhnow to become an assistant general manager, took the league's recommendation to Luhnow, and the Astros moved to "file and go."

In 2016, for the first time in Luhnow's tenure, and for the first time for the franchise since 2011, the Astros went to a hearing. The team had internal debates as to how aggressively they and the LRD should argue that catcher Jason Castro didn't deserve the salary he wanted. There were two ways to make that case: gently, or by bludgeon.

"Basically, we killed Castro," an executive said. "We made the argument that he was on a precipitous decline and also that he was among the worst offensive players in all of baseball."

Said a witness to the hearing: "Castro was bad. They basically referred to him as barely a major league player."

"We won," the Astros executive said, "but it was awkward as fuck, and Castro was upset at us for the way that we did it, and he should have been. It was intense. And so that created this early reputation for the new arbitration team."

The reputation of that group would depend on who you ask, and the front office knew it: "Some would say asshole, some would say badass."

What does that have to do with new technology? The front-office members asking the players to indulge new innovations were some of the same ones involved in arbitration, and that made implementation harder.

The tough-love arbitration process gave the Astros some financial gain, but they had slowed themselves down in efforts to improve and educate players: "a weird duality," one executive called it. "Sharing with them a pretty PowerPoint of their TrackMan and their player development slides and all that, and on the other hand saying, 'You suck, you're on a precipitous decline.'"

Additionally, players and agents were wary about how the Astros would ultimately use the information collected from the bat sensors, or any other device. Top agent Scott Boras at one point advised his players in Houston not to agree to data collection.

Players and agents were concerned about other teams' use of such data, as well, and the use of wearable devices was collectively bargained by MLB and the union in 2016. But in general, players and agents looked at the Astros with as much skepticism as they did any single team.

"We had a bad reputation in terms of the extent we were willing to go to win our cases in arbitration, and I feel like that attitude, that stance, backfired on us," an executive said, "because when it came time to say, 'Hey, trust us, use this data,' they were like, 'We don't want to.'"

Carlos Correa appeared in some television commercials for Blast Motion. But he didn't much use it himself, an Astros employee claimed.

Over time, Taubman and the front office would try to correct course. But even if 2016 had brought improvement compared to the prior years, the Astros were still operating in silos. The players were not big fans of the front office.

"Some of that's normal. They have to be the bad guys, of course, and they're separate," a member of the team said. "But they just weren't very humane about things. Their people skills were bad. And they weren't around a lot; that never helps. None of them were particularly personable, in terms of like communicating with the group and all that. That's not to say [the players] didn't value the information they got, that side of things. I don't remember guys being like, 'Oh, these scouting reports suck.'"

O

Hinch's relationship with the front office had its own strains, and the disappointment of missing the playoffs the prior year played a role.

In 2016, there was an episode dubbed "Wandy-gate," after pitcher Wandy Rodriguez. Years earlier, Rodriguez had been a regular member of the Astros' starting rotation. After stints with other teams, the Astros brought him back to spring training to see if he could win a job.

The front office was intrigued, in part, by Rodriguez's ability as a left-handed thrower to neutralize left-handed hitters, a skill set teams sometimes covet late in games. Rodriguez had also been known to drop his arm slot when throwing a particular pitch, the slider, to a positive result. Instead of releasing the ball near or close to twelve o'clock, if one imagines the hands of a clock, he would let the ball go from a lower angle, and more toward the side: ten or eleven o'clock. The Astros wanted him to try to do that more regularly.

Conventional logic says that having a pitcher change his arm angle for just one pitch is a mistake, because a hitter could figure out what is coming based on the angle alone. But the Astros' thinking was that if Rodriguez appeared only to face a batter or two, then it wouldn't be as big a deal, particularly if the pitch was ultimately strong. So in spring training, the front office had encouraged pitching coach Brent Strom to work with Rodriguez.

"But A.J. flipped a shit about it because Brandon and Strom

didn't check with him first," an Astros executive said. An airing-of-the-grievances meeting followed, and those became common.

Hinch liked the premise of helping Rodriguez improve. The manager's concern was the pipeline of communication. Perhaps the most important part of a field manager's job is talking to and knowing the players.

Say Hinch had been in the outfield before a game, chatting with players while they were warming up, and Rodriguez mentioned something new he was doing. Hinch wouldn't have known anything about it, and he wanted to be in the know. He encouraged the front office, as one person familiar with Wandy-gate put it, "to not be so damn secretive."

Hinch could also be territorial about the teaching of catcher's skills, a front-office member said, recalling the manager pushing back when Mike Fast wanted to work with backup catcher Hank Conger in a prior year. Fast was a pioneer in understanding how a catcher framed pitches for the umpire, but catching was near and dear to Hinch, as he had played the position himself. "He felt marginalized, when it was like, 'We can tell Conger what he's doing wrong,'" a front-office member remembered.

Even if Hinch could be territorial, the environment Luhnow built was not one where front-office staffers, particularly at this period in time, had other people's comfort in mind. It was Hinch's job, and an outsize part of his job, to mitigate the front office's lack of touch. Hinch had a combined experience of both playing the game and working for other front offices that no one else in Luhnow's group did. "I see a goal, and I miss the point on how I garner the cooperation and buy-in," one younger Astros executive said. "And arguably, didn't get a lot of help learning on that front."

Luhnow and Hinch had a frustrating but still functional relationship, usually. But they saw the world very differently.

When Sig Mejdal was taken off his post atop R&D a year earlier, he told Luhnow that the Astros needed someone to handle change better. Luhnow agreed, and told Mejdal that the task was his. Mejdal felt the opportunity for the Astros at this stage would not be in squeezing out another inch and a half in the draft, where the rest of the league was catching up, but in taking advantage of findings in player development. Now, heading into 2017, after the Astros missed the playoffs, Mejdal was to turn his focus on another area where the brass felt there was room for improvement: Hinch's in-game decision-making.

On the one hand, Luhnow had always been rightly concerned about the in-game moves a manager makes, among other smaller details. Little advantages add up.

"How much of an impact do the cutoff and relays make?" Luhnow had once said. "How many games a year are really determined by cutoff and relays? Maybe one, maybe two. How much of a difference does lefty-righty matchups make? Maybe one, maybe two. Infield positioning, maybe one, maybe two. Catcher framing, maybe one, maybe two. You add all those things up, you certainly don't want to be giving away chunks of half-games advantages to other clubs. . . . Doing things the right way can make the difference between a ninety-win season and an eighty-win season."

But the timing of Mejdal turning his focus on Hinch was not insignificant, even if it wasn't apparent to Hinch.

"There's tension between Jeff and A.J. after we had a really shitty season in '16," an Astros executive said. "And Sig had done basic data science to [see], on average over a fifty-year history, how value-add or -minus are different decisions that managers make."

Ultimately, though, the manager is always going to have more context for in-game decisions, the ability to see what the data misses. One of the Astros' younger staffers, Tom Koch-Weser, would say that the best way to think about managers was relative to one another: "Because they're all stoic and handsome and all have big dicks or whatever, they're all going to be kind of cocky. A.J.'s the best of them," a colleague recalled.

But the full-steam-ahead front office still had complaints.

"For people pushing the tech, A.J. gave a healthy amount of pushback," one Astros employee said. "One was, let's use TrackMan in bullpen sessions so pitchers could practice with intent. . . . Astros did it first. A.J. didn't want it.

"Sig was the socializer and change-management lead to get A.J. to change his behavior. A.J. started to embrace the TrackMan stuff more and believe in it for roster decisions, and he allowed us slowly, with quite a bit of resistance, to start doing TrackMan goals and stuff like that for major leaguers."

Mejdal was to be in regular contact with Hinch during the 2017 season, discussing the manager's choices after the fact, be it pitching changes or when to run certain plays. Among the things the math showed was that Astros pitchers should almost never issue intentional walks. Meanwhile, the infield in—a defensive positioning meant to give infielders a better chance to prevent a runner from scoring—should be used much more often.

Mejdal wasn't the only one who would review Hinch's moves in 2017, however.

"That's when McKinsey came in," a member of the Astros said. "That's when the whole paranoia started."

○

By the end of 2016, the Astros, like some other forward-thinking teams, had realized they could use their gaggle of video cameras, high speed or otherwise, for advance scouting. Using video from prior games, they could closely watch a pitcher to see if he would tip his pitches, looking for signs of physical tells in their throwing motion that indicated what kind of pitch was likely coming. A pitcher might hold his glove higher or lower depending on whether he's throwing, say, a slider.

"I noticed that they upgraded the shit out of their cameras," said Pat Neshek, whose last season in Houston was 2016. "Their video room, they had all the cameras everywhere. They had all the analytics, and they had different programs for you to look up. I liked to use that stuff a lot. . . . They just had millions of camera angles. It was kind of unique, it was like, 'Hey, do you want to see from this side, or this side or this side, or two degrees over?'"

But more nefarious usage was proliferating. Electronic sign-stealing via the video room is known to have reached at least two teams by 2016: the Yankees, who had started no later than 2015, and the Red Sox, who had joined the party by the next year. At least part of the reason the Red Sox were said to have adopted the practice was that they signed someone who had been on the Yankees, veteran outfielder Chris Young.

"He came over in spring training in '16," a Red Sox player said of Young. "He goes, 'We always knew most of your guys' signs.'"

"Oftentimes it takes a player to show up and be like, 'You fucking morons, you're not doing this?'" said one American League executive.

The execution in Boston was largely the same as it had been in New York: use the video room to get sign information to the dugout, so that if a runner reached second base, he would have an easier time figuring out what was coming. This is called the baserunner method.

In 2016, the Astros were particularly suspicious that the Texas Rangers, their division rival, had been stealing signs electronically. The Astros did terribly against Texas, losing 15 of 19 games overall, and the Rangers hit 16 home runs against the Astros in ten games played at the Rangers' home park.

"When I was with the Astros, we were definitely leery about Texas for sure," Neshek said. "I don't know what they were doing, but we had to have a whole different sign group with the '16 Rangers. The '16 Rangers scared the shit out of Strommy. . . . I think Seattle, we thought they may have had them too with something, we don't know what they did.

"But it would have been so easy, I mean if you want to cheat, it would take two seconds to put a guy in right field with a walkie-talkie," Neshek continued. "It would take two seconds to do it. I always said that if I was a hitter, man, I'd fly my dad into every city and have him sit in center field and radio right into my earpiece. I mean, with the money that's being made? I think that's the biggest thing. These guys are tempted by that. It's not morally right, but when you get a taste of it, you know you want more, and I think that's what happened with the Astros."

What the Astros believed that the Rangers were doing—and belief isn't necessarily fact—was positioning someone among the crowd in center field who would stand and signal to hitters what was coming. If true, most people in the sport would consider this more egregious than the baserunner method. It was a suspicion of direct communication from someone off the field of play to a hitter, without a runner as intermediary.

○

The Astros needed a Spanish translator in 2016, and Luhnow brought in someone who had flashes of his own background: a business-minded kid out of Penn, Derek Vigoa, whom a colleague described as a Luhnow "pet." As a member of the traveling party, Vigoa had assisted the advance staff, Tom Koch-Weser, and the group of lower-level employees who aided the team's daily prep work.

When Luhnow had an opening at traveling secretary for 2017, Vigoa made his pitch, and got the job. His work on one particular project may have helped.

"In September 2016, then-intern Derek Vigoa gave an in-person presentation to you in which he discussed 'Codebreaker,' an Excel spreadsheet in which he logged pitchers' signs and used an algorithm to determine sign sequences for those pitchers," Commissioner Rob Manfred would write to Luhnow. "You acknowledged to my investigators that you recalled his PowerPoint slide about Codebreaker and you asked him some questions about how it operated."

The title "Codebreaker" and the word "algorithm" made the project sound more intense than it was. Codebreaker wasn't an example of advanced programming.

For one thing, figuring out the catcher's signs usually didn't require high-level effort. At this point, most pitchers and catchers around the league were not going to great lengths to disguise their signs beyond the standard practice of flashing several in succession. Were no runner on base, teams might not disguise their signs at all.

"Oh, it's not hard. The signs are so easy to break," a member of a rival team's R&D department said. "People have very distinct patterns, and so, by one or two batters, you can figure out what the pattern was. And particularly when no one's on base, then it's really simple. Then it's just mapping which signals to which pitch."

Relative to the *kind* of technical work that the Astros could pull off, then, Codebreaker was a rudimentary undertaking. Vigoa wasn't a member of the Astros' R&D department, where the analytical fire-power rested.

It is probably accurate to call Codebreaker a "predictor" of signs, but what Vigoa developed was more of a catalog, an aid to prediction. Codebreaker wasn't running off artificial intelligence, nor did it have incredible accuracy.

"It was a spreadsheet that Derek punched pitch types into and some probabilities to understand that when a catcher flashes a 1 [one finger], eighty-five percent of the time, it's a fastball," a member of the Astros said, offering a hypothetical. "Stuff like that.

"What they were doing was building a catalog of the sign, or the sign sequence, and the actual pitch that's thrown. And they could say 'OK, eighty percent of the time that a [catcher puts down three fingers], it's off-speed.' Therefore, if you see a 3, it's going to be an off-speed pitch. It was not wildly sophisticated. It couldn't have been. . . . I'm basing that on my understanding of Derek and Tom's quantitative skills."

Another member of the Astros described Codebreaker as an effort of brute force. "People think it's so sophisticated. There was no algorithm. Some of the sign sequences are simple, and some of them I think are harder, and you don't get [them]. . . . You've got to watch all the pitches and all the sign sequences and you got to write 'em down, or type 'em into Excel and then look for the patterns as a human."

At some point, the advance staff asked the R&D department for help with decoding. But R&D felt it would actually be more effort to write coding than it would be for the staff to just look at their Excel spreadsheet. The fact that Codebreaker was in Excel was, in itself, a sign of low fidelity. Doing one-offs in Excel wasn't going to help the Astros move forward in the big picture.

As a joke, one Astros executive in 2016 said that the team should take away everybody's copy of Excel.

"Because our software development practices were so bad that the front office was using Excel to patch around our lack of Tableau or whatever," was their feeling. Tableau is a data visualization and business intelligence company that was sold to Salesforce in 2019 for

$15.7 billion, and their service was not one the Astros had ponied up for. "We had like three overworked software developers, and a bunch of people building their own shit in Excel," the executive continued. "And I'm like, this is untenable."

So cryptography, Codebreaker was not. But the advance staff nonetheless knew it wanted a better look at the signs, because players like Alex Bregman wanted better knowledge of the signs, too.

The feed from the telecast did not always provide a great view of the catcher's fingers, but a dedicated camera, one fixed on the catcher, could more effectively provide that footage.

"We put in the camera, the center field camera, to see the catcher signs. I don't remember when it was, but it was before the 2017 season," an Astros employee said. "On the broadcast video, it often cuts in after the catcher signs had been given. And so we don't get the sign sequence, and so we've got gaps in our knowledge, and we want all the information."

Most important, Codebreaker's development was not wrongdoing at the time—not on its own. Rather, Codebreaker's legality, in baseball's meager rules, would depend on how and when it was used.

If signs were decoded as preparation for an upcoming game, it was fine, considered just another form of advance scouting. Vigoa and Koch-Weser could review the sign systems a team had used in the past, and then, in a future game, if the opposing team hadn't switched up their signs, the Astros would have an advantage.

Because Codebreaker had a purpose that could be considered legitimate, its existence didn't need to be top secret. It was not widely broadcast, but at least some members of the front office were aware of its development.

"I knew that Derek had a way to input the signs that the pitchers throw down and then the actual pitch that's thrown," an Astros executive said. "I wish I could tell you that I was like, 'This is immoral,' but my actual thought was, 'Is there any data efficacy to what you're doing?' And also what I understood that he was doing was trying to figure out the opposing team's sign-stealing system ahead of the game. Which is basically everything that advance [team] does, is looking at video and data for past games to predict how players will make practical choices in upcoming series. . . . We're going to learn it, and we're going to tell our players about it for the upcoming game."

What would be a problem, however, is if Codebreaker was used live, inside a given game. To that end, the Astros' advance staff had plans for a new deployment for the upcoming 2017 season.

The rules seemed to be an afterthought in Houston, if they were a thought at all. Innovation, improvement—"Data efficacy"—that was the mindset Luhnow had long fostered.

"Vigoa did not explicitly recall whether he explicitly told you that Codebreaker would be used during games, but he presumed you knew because that's where the value would be," Manfred wrote in his letter to Luhnow. "You told my investigators that you thought he was simply deciphering sign sequences from prior game footage that would be provided to players to look out for if they got to second base."

Vigoa wasn't the only one who told MLB he discussed Codebreaker with Luhnow.

Per Manfred's letter to Luhnow, Koch-Weser said he spoke to Luhnow about it in one to three meetings in the 2016–17 offseason. Koch-Weser, too, told investigators he had provided Luhnow "some detail of the intent to use Codebreaker during games in 2017, and that it was understood among you that Codebreaker would be used for in-game sign decoding and communication to players," Manfred wrote.

In response, Koch-Weser told MLB, Luhnow would smile and "giggle" at the title. The GM appeared "excited" about it. Luhnow denied to MLB that those conversations occurred.

# 11

# MCKINSEY AT THE BAT

COMMUNICATION WAS THIN, AND RELATIONSHIPS WERE STRAINED. TECH-
nology was ubiquitous, and the goal was singularly to win. It's hard to
say the Astros were the most likely team in baseball to start cheating.
But there couldn't have been a team more poorly prepared to *stop*
cheating.

In Houston, the future had always been the thing, until now. Jeff
Luhnow's 2017 roster was talented enough to be perhaps the best in
baseball, although the brain trust wasn't convinced the group was
quite that good, not yet. Over time, the vaunted farm system had produced a spate of stars: Jose Altuve and George Springer and Carlos
Correa and Dallas Keuchel and Lance McCullers Jr. and now, entering
his first full year, Alex Bregman. Luhnow had filled in the rest of the
spots with mostly capable veterans.

On May 15, the Astros were in Miami, playing the Marlins. The
Astros had gotten to their team hotel at five in the morning, and were
shut down in the early innings by Marlins starting pitcher Dan Straily.
Down 1–0 heading into the top of the sixth inning opposite reliever
Junichi Tazawa, Josh Reddick doubled for the Astros with one out.
Altuve flied out before Correa walked and Evan Gattis was hit by a
pitch, loading the bases with two out.

With the count 2–1 against Astros batter Yuli Gurriel, Correa was
said by a teammate to be leaning forward with his chest. The gesture

was said to be his signal to Gurriel—*a fastball is coming*. Gurriel ripped a line-drive home run to left field, giving the Astros a 4–1 lead.

"After three seconds like chest out, he knew what was coming," a member of the team said. "I wasn't impressed by the grand slam. I was impressed by that."

The Astros won the game, 7–2.

The team had already joined the ranks of teams that were decoding signs in the video room and getting the information out to runners during the game—the baserunner method.

As planned, Codebreaker, the spreadsheet that Derek Vigoa had created the year before, was a help. Some players and staff understood generally that the Astros' advance staff was trying to decode signs. But the specific means, the use of an Excel document, Codebreaker, wasn't common knowledge.

Alex Cora, the new bench coach, would often man the phone in the dugout. He would communicate with the advance staff, the video replay crew, including Koch-Weser, about what the sign sequence was. Sometimes the video room staff would let the dugout know by sending a text message, "which was received on the smart watch of a staff member on the bench, or in other cases on a cell phone stored nearby," MLB found.

"He was calling the nerds inside," a member of the team said of Cora. If a runner was on second base, the dugout would get that message out to the runner, who then could let the hitter know what was coming.

But early in the season, what was most notable about Codebreaker and the decoding efforts was their frequent ineffectiveness. Two Astros leaders, in particular, felt the team needed to do more. Cora and Carlos Beltrán, heavyweights in the clubhouse, wanted a better way to get the signs, a more direct way.

"What happened was Cora and Beltrán decided that this video room stuff Koch-Weser was doing was just not working, inefficient, too slow," a person with direct knowledge of MLB's investigation said.

Beltrán in 2017 was still a player, but he was effectively an additional coach, too—as one member of the team put it, the highest-paid coach they had ever seen. Members of the 2017 Astros used various terms to describe Beltrán: *El Jefe*, the Godfather, the king, the alpha male in the building. "He was revered," one member of the 2017 Astros said. "He was very much the checks and balances on everything that went on."

Beltrán was forty that season, capping off a twenty-year career, and no one else in the Astros clubhouse carried the same stature, not even catcher Brian McCann, who was thirty-three. Beltrán always had a particular flair for studying the opposition and using video to do so. In 2016, the year before joining the Astros, he explained to the *New York Post* that he had been studying pitch tipping—a legal practice—since 2002, a discipline passed on from other top veteran players at the time. Some pitchers have tells as to what pitches they are going to throw, positioning their body differently depending on the selection. The growth of technology in the sport had only helped Beltrán's studies, which were legal.

"It could be during the game, it could be video," Beltrán told the *Post*. "If I never [have faced] a guy, I go in the computer to research and kind of like get some videos and compare them with when they throw the fastball, when they throw the curveball, and when they throw the changeup."

Cora, the bench coach, had similar guile, a reputation for having a keen eye for picking up pitch tipping or the opposition's signs. Again, a permissible and encouraged behavior.

Beltrán also had been a member of the New York Yankees from 2014 to 2016—and he spent the second half of 2016 with the Texas Rangers. In New York, if not in Texas as well, Beltrán had lived the early stages of video room electronic sign-stealing, and he brought that knowledge to Houston.

"Hey, we gotta get a system going here," Beltrán said inside the Astros clubhouse.

It was about two months into the season, MLB found, when Cora arranged for a video monitor to be hung on a wall in the tunnel at Minute Maid Park—just steps from the Astros dugout, but shrouded from the field of play. But team members said the scheme began earlier than May. One thought it kicked off in the first week of the season, against the Royals at home from April 7 to April 9.

Tony Adams, an Astros fan, reviewed audio from any 2017 Astros game he could get his hands on and posted the findings online. He found evidence the Astros had started even with the first series of the season, which began on April 3.

As you walked in from the field and down a few steps through the dugout, the screen was on the right. The monitor was hooked up to a center field camera that fed live footage, with no delay, of the catcher's signs. Or, as one member of the team put it: "Intern-level guy gets bullied into putting up a camera."

Stationed across from the TV were some massage beds, and during games, chairs. Astros players and staff would sit there and scribble the signs on pieces of paper, using their eyes to decode what the signs the catcher was giving were in real time, sometimes with the help of Codebreaker.

Once the signs were decoded, the Astros in the tunnel told the hitter what was coming by making noise. They experimented with clapping, whistling, and yelling, before settling on—of all things—banging on a trash can, often with a baseball bat.

No bangs typically meant a fastball was coming: one or two bangs signaled a breaking ball or changeup.

The new cheating system only worked at the Astros' home stadium, Minute Maid Park. They couldn't get the logistics to work on the road, where they were relegated to simply using the baserunner scheme. But at home games, they had an advantage, or at the very least, the clear appearance of an advantage.

"We felt in our hearts that we were being more efficient and smarter than any team out there," Beltrán told the Yankees' YES Network in 2022. "That's how we felt."

The note takers were varied. From the advance staff, Koch-Weser contributed, as did Matt Hogan, a member of the team said.

With Vigoa now the traveling secretary, the Astros needed a new translator for Spanish-speaking players, and Alex Cintrón, a former major league infielder, got the gig. Cintrón was said to help out with decoding as well.

Naturally, the Astros' bench players, those on reserve at the start of the game, were more readily available.

"There were so many guys taking notes," one member of the 2017 Astros said.

Some of the chairs were even said to have name tags.

Most every day, the advance staff would take the TV down. Sometimes they would cover it with a piece of cloth or curtain.

Although he was a regular player, Bregman was alleged to sometimes hit the trash can, too. On occasion, he used a massage gun, if not against the trash can, then against the restroom door in the same area. The sound was even louder when the massage gun was used.

"He had so much fun with that," one member of the 2017 Astros said.

One Astros employee thought using the massage gun was the "most ridiculous thing" they'd ever heard, so much so that they didn't believe it at first.

During the first inning of one game, after a couple of batters had already gone to the plate, Beltrán grew frustrated the monitor hadn't been set up yet for the day. He approached the advance staff.

"Where's the TV?" Beltrán asked.

The staff said they were busy.

"No, get the TV and connect this," he said, growing frustrated. "I'll do it on my own, don't worry about it, let me do this."

Beltrán did it himself, and when the staffers saw him carrying the TV over, they apologized. After the game, he complained to teammates about the staff's lack of urgency.

"We need to sit down with these guys," Beltrán said. "We need to get it going earlier, fifteen, twenty minutes before the game, Jesus Christ."

Codebreaker had been an entrée, but the Astros had graduated. Baseball's rules weren't a help, because it was, at the time, legal to have a monitor in the tunnel and a camera set up in center field. But what was clearly not legal was how the Astros were using them.

"Front office is infiltrating clubhouses, and the technology being brought into the game, created the temptation, and then people lost their mind," a team member said. "The monitor was legal. The live feed was legal.

"The ethical line was stealing signs. Having it in the tunnel was legal. It just couldn't be seen from the field. Well fuck, man, every tunnel can't be seen from the field, as if that matters."

On the night of May 24, Koch-Weser sent an email to Luhnow, cc'ing Brandon Taubman and Matt Hogan. It was the first installation of a series Koch-Weser wrote that he wanted to do monthly, "Road Notes." Luhnow, like most GMs, didn't go to every road game, but Koch-Weser was a member of the traveling party. He offered observations about how the team was performing and preparing, like the poor play of Gurriel at first base.

"I think it's evident to anyone watching," Koch-Weser wrote, "that Yuli is a vulnerability for us defensively on the infield. He drops balls, is continually adventurous trying to find the base with his right foot on throws over, and gets caught in no man's land frequently on GBs [ground balls] to the right side."

There were five underlined topics in all, none of them particularly long or arduous to read. The fourth was "The System."

"I don't want to electronically correspond too much about 'the system' but Cora/Cintrón/Beltrán have been driving a culture initiated by Bregman/Vigoa last year, and I think it's working. I have no proof that it has worked, but we get real good dope on pitchers tipping and being lazy. That information, if it's not already, will eventually yield major results in our favor once players get used to the implementation."

The next day, Luhnow replied, "These are great, thanks," before replying again about three hours later.

"Tom, how much of this stuff do you think AJ is aware of?" Luhnow wrote. "For the things he is not aware of, what do you recommend as the best way to educate him and eventually the entire staff? I think it all starts with him, of course."

Much of this email exchange, up to this point, had been previously reported. What has not been reported is what followed.

Koch-Weser responded quickly, and once again mentioned "the system."

"He is certainly aware of the low-ball issue, defensive alignment, and our initiative with 'the system.' I talked with him about those last week," Koch-Weser wrote in an email that totaled five sentences. "I haven't (but should) approach him about the Yuli thing. The baserunning and RISP [runner in scoring position] swing decision issues we just discovered. I can approach him about those but don't want to unload on him with negatives all at once."

Luhnow got back to him the same day.

"I do think it's important that you guys communicate what you are seeing and what your opinion is, but it's equally important that you do it in a respectful way and not to be critical of anything in front of the players, or quite frankly other staff members. Hopefully you feel comfortable approaching AJ once in a while and going through some of these items especially when you have facts to back up what you are saying.

"If staff members approach you then it's fair game to tell them what you think, but generally speaking we should let AJ be the one delivering the message to his staff about where they need to improve."

On May 25, the Astros began an eleven-game win streak that put them a whopping fourteen games up in the American League West.

Their cheating scheme was an evolution and fluctuation. They didn't use the trash-can system on every pitch of every home game, but it was steadily available.

"It wasn't being worked on behind the scenes, and all of a sudden, we debuted it on July 1," one member of the team said. "It was all sort of pieced together, and it gained steam, and we looked up, and it was a big snowball."

But not everyone was on board, at least, not in hindsight—particularly pitchers.

"Looking back, I don't know what we could have done as pitchers," Collin McHugh told reporters in 2020. "It wasn't really our territory. Maybe we could've gotten together and somehow tried to stop it. Yeah, it was tough watching that. You feel for guys out there who are working their tails off, whether they're on your team or against you."

Said another member of the Astros, Charlie Morton, to reporters in 2020: "Personally, I regret not doing more to stop it."

Morton privately at the time said he absolutely hated it, that he felt it was cheap, a member of the team said.

One player on the 2017 Astros described the feeling as like being an accessory to a robbery, like sitting in the backseat of a getaway car.

The doors are locked, the driver is speeding away, and you're unable to escape.

Of course, how much some players really disliked it at the time can be hard to decipher after the fact.

"I think it's always going to be super convenient now to disapprove more at some percentage than you really did," one member of the 2017 Astros said. "I'm just being honest. It's always easy to say, 'No, I fucking hated it.'"

In 2017, Hinch would spend less time directly in the clubhouse with players than he did at any other point in his Astros career, before or after. Whether it was out of deference to the veterans or outright fear, that would prove a mistake.

○

In the middle of 2017, Jeff Luhnow took on a project that was his most fractious yet.

A year and a half after Brandon Taubman made a presentation to the Astros' front office pushing for a change in pro scouting, he made another to Luhnow, this one focused on a vision across scouting, including amateur. The theory was that the Astros needed to employ scouts who could do at least some of the basic data analyses that the front office was doing regularly: "technical scouting," it was dubbed.

Alex Jacobs, one of the Astros' young pro scouts, had spent most of his time on back fields in Florida, where he lived. He drove to games that were sparsely attended at the spring training complexes dotted throughout the state, trying to identify diamonds in the rough who were often many years away from contributing in the majors, but worth targeting while they were still relatively anonymous.

In May 2017, Jacobs went to Houston. When he arrived, he had increased access to Ground Control, the Astros' database. He and another young scout, Will Sharp, were to test-run technical scouting.

"When we got there we learned how to evaluate the way the Astros wanted to evaluate in the future. It was an experiment to see the difference between traditional scouting and scouting through numbers," Jacobs said. "Two-day like crash course in all the technology to evaluate players. We were given twelve players each to literally break down anything you possibly could through numbers, using technology, anything you could. Public sources, private sources."

Kevin Goldstein, Jacobs's boss, told Luhnow he didn't want Taubman leading the TrackMan training, although Goldstein relented. Goldstein and Taubman had never jelled, in part because of the direction Taubman was pushing pro scouting. Taubman was ticked off by Goldstein lobbying for Fast to lead the sessions, in part because he had friendships with Jacobs and Sharp.

By this time, pro scouting had already been mostly tuned out by Luhnow and Taubman anyway.

"Jeff was relying like eighty percent on [Taubman] and Fast to evaluate pitchers and to give him full evaluations and twenty percent on Kevin and the pro scouting team," an executive estimated. "So Kevin felt like he had lost his voice, the pro scouts had basically lost their voice."

Taubman and Sharp continued to do the new analysis once they left Houston, the experiment rolling into July.

"Two to three a day. It was a lot," Jacobs said. "Just analyze every possible aspect and tell you what happened and why it happened rather than doing a subjective scouting report."

Back in late 2015, Luhnow and Taubman knew where they were going with pro scouting. But Luhnow, who had been more hesitant to rip the Band-Aid than Taubman, wanted to take one more step before moving forward. He wanted the approval of McKinsey & Company.

Every June, when baseball's amateur draft rolls around, teams fly in their amateur scouting staffs, who rarely visit major league stadiums. They spend all their days visiting college and high school games across the country. Then, when June arrives, with a year's worth of work behind them, they converge for final preparations and discussions, and for the big day itself.

In this way, the Astros were no different than any other team in 2017: they brought their scouts to town ahead of the draft. But what their scouts were greeted with in breakout meetings was a scene unprecedented in baseball.

"These people are from McKinsey," the scouts were told.

In the middle of a momentous season, Luhnow had hired his old management consultant firm to do a study on the Astros. Not on the price of hot dogs or tickets or foam fingers, or any other of the rote business functions McKinsey usually evaluates. Consultants descended on Minute Maid to study the most insular and core functions of the team—baseball operations—and only baseball operations. No other MLB team is known to have hired a consultant firm for a similar engagement before or since. (The famously dysfunctional New York Knicks, the basketball team, had hired McKinsey in 2013.)

Scouting was one area the consultants were studying, and at least one amateur scout had never heard of McKinsey before walking into a room with their consultants.

"I didn't know what they did," the scout said. "I thought they just wanted to see just how we do things for their benefit. I didn't know."

"Every scout in the room is fucking nervous as shit about this," an Astros executive said. "The 2017 draft was, I think, designed to give every scout there an ulcer."

The front office had been commanded not to talk to the scouts about opinions on players during the meetings, to "keep our mouths shut, to not say a thing, to just listen to the scouts." Once the daytime meetings ended and the scouts went off to dinner, the core group got together: Mike Elias, Taubman, Mike Fast, Colin Wyers, Pete Putila, and some junior staffers. The McKinsey people had left for the day.

"We would give our opinions on players, and Elias would rearrange the entire draft board," the executive said. "And then the scouts would come in the next morning, and they'd be like, 'What the fuck just happened? This is not where we left any of this last night. What is going on?'

"So the scouts, like, you have all these besuited people who don't work for the Astros in the draft room, taking notes, asking them questions. You have these late-night meetings that they're not invited to where the whole draft board's getting reshaped. I think they were all paranoid."

Luhnow didn't broadcast to the organization what he was doing, keeping information about McKinsey's work on a need-to-know basis. Ultimately, the firm's presence was not a secret, since the consultants were certainly visible around the stadium, holding interviews with different Astros personnel. But Luhnow didn't outline his thinking, the breadth of the planned engagements, to anyone but his core circle. Publicly, he also never directly acknowledged McKinsey's presence, but he did speak about it in oblique terms when I approached him in 2019.

"We have sought and paid for help in numerous areas across baseball operations, including adoption and rollout of emerging technologies; accessing, developing, and retaining the best baseball operations talent; and helping devise strategy and operational approaches in a quickly evolving environment.

"We don't disclose our partners in these areas unless it's mutually desired and convenient. We also do not discuss the specifics of any work."

Like most decisions Luhnow made, McKinsey's arrival made some sense on paper. For one thing, Luhnow was able to strike a low-cost deal with McKinsey through a barter. Had the Astros hired McKinsey at the usual price the firm charges, the cost likely would have been well into the six figures.

"It didn't cost us anything," an Astros executive said. "We had to cover travel and expense." That cost, the executive said, was in the range of $50,000 to $100,000 per year in the time McKinsey worked with the Astros.

Luhnow might have genuinely wanted some level of validation from an outside observer that firing pro scouts would be a smart move. But he also wanted cover for his plans.

"Jeff's strategy was: I have a connection with McKinsey. Let them come in and take some heat off me so that they're easier to market internally," a member of the inner circle said. "I don't think that's good change management, but that's basically his strategy. I'm not speculating: it's one hundred percent. McKinsey people are pretty smart, but they're naive. At times we'd be like, 'They don't know what they're talking about here.' Jeff is like, 'Don't worry about it.' It wasn't an earnest, truly independent valuation of our operations."

In pro scouting, then, Luhnow wasn't really seeking an answer he didn't already have. Elsewhere, though, he was lost, or at least, unsure.

"The McKinsey report," an executive said, "is what basically ended up leading to the destruction of the Astros front office."

○

In the middle of what was shaping up to be an incredible season, Luhnow directed McKinsey to study the most crucial area of the Astros' success, and the lifeblood of his own career: research and development, the department that most readily influenced innovation and analytics.

The R&D team was not given much of a heads-up, though.

"Jeff told all of us he was bringing in McKinsey to evaluate scouting," an Astros employee said, "and then I found out they were actually coming in to evaluate R&D."

Among those Luhnow kept in the dark was the head of that department himself, Mike Fast, who felt he had been naive. Fast believed when he was put in charge of R&D in late 2015 that he would be in control of that department, because he would be held responsible for it. He believed, too, that his title was tantamount to Luhnow endorsing his vision, which differed in some ways, notable ways, from the executive he replaced, Luhnow's close friend Sig Mejdal.

"Jeff didn't know who to listen to in terms of how we keep innovating at the Houston Astros," an executive said.

To an extent, Mejdal wanted to focus resources in other areas. There are dozens of areas and projects where a limited budget can be applied. But the heart of the issue struck at the Astros' Tao: With all these new technologies, bat sensors and TrackMan and information from the Edgertronic cameras, what data do you trust? What do you incorporate into Mejdal's baby, the draft model? Taubman, and to an extent Putila, were typically aligned with Fast.

In a way, McKinsey's arrival was an outgrowth of the way Luhnow had always structured the front office. He had deployed Taubman as something of a roving consultant, assigning him different projects to check on the validity of the work of others. "The Astros were run on conflict," an executive said. "That was Jeff's management style all over the organization," said another.

The experience in the prior year's draft, when the Astros debated whether to take Forrest Whitley and Fast and Taubman wanted to believe in data that wasn't yet incorporated into the model, was the matter writ large. The George Springer promotion debate, the lessons of letting J. D. Martinez go—all of it funneled into McKinsey's arrival.

"That's exactly what the conflict was: Do you trust that data?" an Astros executive said. "How do we know it's good? There was no sort of burden of proof there. There's just an assumption that was good data to make draft decisions on, and that made Jeff very uncomfortable, and that was at the core of his trepidation with Fast. And Fast was underappreciated for all this great shit he was doing, but Jeff was right with sensing there was a risk with moving away from our draft model, but wrong for the way that he dealt with Fast and bringing McKinsey in, letting Sig challenge Fast but not in a way that was productive, in a way that was detrimental to their relationship."

"I don't know what was going through Jeff's head at that point," another front-office member said. "I think that must have been part of it, yeah: I've got this war between Sig and Mike and I trust both of them to some extent, but I don't know how to pick between them, or I need a third party to help me."

Although Mejdal was now spending more of his time on player development and discussions with Hinch about in-game moves, he was still involved in the direction of the draft model. For all of Luhnow's desires to remain objective, over time he had shown favoritism in different ways to those who had been with him in his Cardinals days— evidence to colleagues that Luhnow was not truly robotic. Yet that favoritism was a different sort of flaw.

"Sig was no longer actively involved in maintaining the draft model, but he still had say," an executive said. "[Luhnow] still trusted Sig. This is his right-hand man who he's leaned on, was in his wedding. He was sidelining Sig from active management of that, but it wasn't like he no longer believed anything Sig was saying. Sig's voice still was important to him."

The draft model, ultimately, is designed to produce a player order to guide selection, which was run by Elias.

"The model has these inputs. It spits out a draft order. That's supposed to be how you draft," an executive recalled. "Elias still has freedom to move guys for a lot of reasons: signability, health, and his feel for the draft. But 2017 was the year where we really started like looking at player swing mechanics off of video, or, we have TrackMan data from pretty much every D1 school. So you had this pitcher who's a college stat guy, a college junior who gets good results. But you go, OK, here's this TrackMan data, he doesn't have good enough spin on his breaking balls. Even though he gets people out in college, we don't think he's a major league pitcher. Because he doesn't have the spin on his breaking balls. We don't think we can teach him.

"Pete [Putila] was in the 2017 draft and he's sitting there like, 'We can teach a player this that and that, so this flaw's OK. But no, we can't teach a player this, that, and that, don't take him.' So 2017, we're successful, but we're sitting there in the draft room throwing out this draft model that—I'm choosing my words very carefully . . . that has its conception all the way back to Sig's time in St. Louis—where he had to fight for every inch of this. So Sig is very defensive of the draft model. And it has a successful track record up to this point. But at the same time, you see other clubs picking players that two years ago they wouldn't have picked, and were there for St. Louis to take that, you know, you weren't all of a sudden going to get anymore. Because more teams were looking at college stats.

"So what's the next competitive advantage? It's Edgertronic. It's TrackMan. It's Rapsodo [which also produces tech to evaluate performance]. And it's like, well, none of this is in the draft model. So there's this tension between the people who are Sig, and are incredibly emotionally invested in the draft model, and if we're going to be doing all these other things, it needs to be in the model. So Sig is screaming at Jeff, you know, 'These fucking cowboys are fucking doing all this shit, and it's not in the draft model.'"

With McKinsey anointed the adjudicator, Fast was put on the defensive from the get-go. The questions McKinsey asked read like a list of grievances received directly from Mejdal. In a sense, that had played out before: Fast or Wyers might talk to Mejdal about an issue, only to have Luhnow parrot the same questions Mejdal had already asked at a later point.

"To Sig's view, this was backsliding," an executive said. "Replacing his objective process with scouts again, and to the view to some of the rest, we're exploiting a market inefficiency that won't be there forever. And that's sort of at the core of the whole McKinsey thing, was, are the Astros trying to execute the plan that they thought they were, which was to finish the project they started in St. Louis, but without so much internal fighting? Or are we trying to build the thing that comes after Moneyball?"

The choices, then, were significant, but many Astros employees who sat down with McKinsey were worried the consultants didn't have enough grounding in baseball.

"Like many breathing, sentient humans, I was highly skeptical because they're consultants," one employee said. "Baseball is unlike any other business in the world, period. And for them to walk in and understand how we do things, I think, is a fool's errand."

Or, put more harshly by a colleague: "They're a bunch of idiots. They're not a bunch of idiots in what they were used to doing, but they weren't used to doing what they were coming in to do."

For the R&D study in particular, consultants from a McKinsey offshoot called QuantumBlack, which has its roots in Formula One racing, contributed prominently. "The QuantumBlack people are really data scientists," an executive remembered. "They were the people that really came in under the umbrella of McKinsey and worked with [R&D] directly. QuantumBlack only worked with us in '17. They're this elusive, even more expensive specialty service in McKinsey."

Two of the consultants had flown in from London. McKinsey took space on the second floor of Minute Maid Park in 2017, before moving around more often the next year. The Astros' baseball operations office was on the fifth floor.

"Didn't really have official space because there wasn't like any big room open available for them," a member of the inner circle said. "It pissed people off because they took over the fifth-floor conference room. They never had cube space or office space. It was never permanent, always squatting basis. Which like frustrated some people. . . . It didn't create a good energy in the office space that these consultants were always here. That was bad."

The consultants also needed time with Astros personnel to learn how different departments worked. Not only that, McKinsey needed time from Astros executives when they brought their own clients to Minute Maid Park.

"I would just write things in emails to McKinsey people, and they would just copy and paste them into the reports," one Astros executive said. "I think that's what management consulting does a lot of anyways: is find discontented people in the organization who know where all the skeletons are hidden and just anonymize that feedback and report it up the reporting chain without intermediation. That's the sense I've gotten from reading about McKinsey since then, and talking to other people who have been management consultants."

Fast, a colleague said, would dread meeting with McKinsey. In a meeting with the consultants and multiple team executives to discuss the future of Astros modeling, Luhnow and Fast got into an argument.

"It really was sort of unfortunate," a colleague said. "Mike didn't show well; he literally stomped his feet and it was because Jeff was being an asshole to him. He was demanding Mike fix this complicated problem about how to get TrackMan and Blast Motion into our projections, and also make our draft model better. But doing both of those things at the same time is impossible, and even McKinsey was saying that, and Jeff was in a mood, and something got lost in translation, and it was very unfortunate."

○

Mejdal took on an unusual role for a front-office member with no playing background: He was to be a uniformed coach for one of the Astros' minor league teams in upstate New York, on the premise that being on the ground could help him better understand the needs of player development and players, and help minor league staff and players better understand the mindset of the front office. He was now the Astros' change management guru, after all.

There was a more cynical read, as well. At least some in the inner circle wanted Mejdal out of the office. "I loved all the articles that were talking about how great and forward-thinking it was, when they just literally didn't want him to have time to check his email," an Astros executive said. "I'm not even kidding. Like, they just wanted to give him something to distract him from getting involved with various parts of the operation."

While living the minor league road life, Mejdal was still focused on communicating with Hinch about in-game moves.

"Interfacing with A.J. on the road a lot," an executive said. "Even when he was away at the affiliate, he was still sending emails to A.J. and back and forth. . . . I think A.J. felt that Sig was his watchdog in '17."

To at least some around the team, Hinch would vent about Mejdal. Mejdal might write a long email about why Hinch used a sacrifice bunt. "A.J.'s like, 'Sig's not even watching the game, he's in bumble-fuck, and Jeff probably tells him he was bothered.' . . . It was a weird dynamic."

Few managers could have effectively mitigated the new-age gunslingers in Houston's front office, and Hinch did enjoy at least some of the work with Mejdal, in part because he missed the daily back-and-forth about game decisions he had when David Stearns was around. But Hinch did feel strained, too, because as one person close to him put it, "They wanted to measure everything, and unfortunately, not everything can be measured."

What was more annoying for Hinch was that McKinsey wasn't just there to talk to the front office and scouts. During a demanding 162-game major league season, McKinsey interviewed the manager, plus some players and coaches as well. One executive recalled George Springer and Carlos Beltrán going for chats.

Beyond R&D and scouting, McKinsey was also directly reviewing in-game decision-making and the processes Hinch had with his staff, including the advance team.

"They were deeply entrenched," a member of the field staff said. "McKinsey was just hard to deal with in season."

"One of the initiatives for McKinsey was to be a change consultant so that like A.J. and Jeff could get along better," a member of the inner circle said. "Design a communication protocol for a good platform for airing of the grievances. And Sig was in that role of 'Hey, A.J., you drag-bunted with Nori Aoki last night—data doesn't support it.'"

Luhnow was the so-called sponsor and chairman of what's known as the steering committee, the group that guides McKinsey with a given engagement and organization. Some presentations were prepared for the stakeholders, typically the top management officials involved in a relevant area. Other reports, the most blunt and detailed, went to the steering committee, which was limited in audience. Taubman was part of the steering committee, Mike Elias sometimes as well.

What McKinsey found in its review of major league decision-making and advance scouting was that Hinch needed more people around him to support data. "Current staff has not fully embraced analytics and tech," McKinsey noted in an August 3 presentation that did not include Hinch. "Front office + coaching staff should build new feedback model together."

McKinsey also did a mapping of Hinch's decision-making, a chart that showed where, by their analysis, he had succeeded in-game as a manger, and where he failed. Hinch might not have had his best showing in the McKinsey process, because in the words of one Astros employee, he "never gave it any respect." He was professional, but looked at the consultants' presence as a necessary evil.

Although the steering committee received feedback on the manager, Hinch never got a direct follow-up from McKinsey. He never saw the mappings, and ultimately, the manager didn't know how closely McKinsey was studying him. McKinsey, above all, appeared to be serving Luhnow's interests.

○

Dallas Keuchel, who had lived through the losing in Houston and gone on to become a Cy Young winner, spoke for the clubhouse when the July 31 trade deadline passed and Luhnow hadn't made a major upgrade. The Astros at the time weren't in trouble, with a 16-game lead, but the idea would have been to improve the team for the playoffs.

"I mean, I'm not going to lie, disappointment is a little bit of an understatement," Keuchel told reporters. "I feel like a bunch of teams really bolstered their rosters for the long haul and for a huge playoff push, and us just kind of staying pat was really disappointing to myself."

The Astros had certainly tried to make deals. Luhnow was particularly keen on a young relief pitcher on the Toronto Blue Jays, Roberto Osuna. But the Blue Jays and Astros couldn't find a fit.

The offense was rolling. Through the first half of the season, Jose Altuve was hitting .347 and Carlos Correa .325. George Springer had 27 home runs. Keuchel himself had been phenomenal, with a 1.67 ERA through mid-July's All-Star break. But a pitching boost would have made sense.

As August arrived, the Astros' front office and field staff began thinking ahead, to advance scouting. They had the luxury to do so: even with two months to go in the regular season, the Astros, with a record of 69–37 on August 1, were a virtual lock for the postseason, holding a 15-game lead over the second-place team in their division, the Seattle Mariners.

Teams traditionally had prepared for the postseason by sending scouts on the road to closely watch their potential opponents. But the last time the Astros made the playoffs, in 2015, they had just one scout out on the road, which was notably less than other teams.

"Advance scouting is different than scouting for player acquisition," Luhnow said in 2015. "And there are certain things you learn by being in the stadium and having a trained scout observe that you cannot pick up via TV, because you're able to see the signs between the manager and third-base coach, you're able to see people's leads that they take that you might not see on TV. You're able to see a lot of how they react in real-time that you might not be able to see on TV.

"At the same time, on TV, you're able to slow things down, see replays, see angles that you might not have visual angles of in person, so they really are complimentary. For us, we need 'em both in order to make the best decisions."

Now, two years later, the Astros were even more bent on pivoting to video. Pro scouting director Kevin Goldstein had started to notify the scouts of potential advance plans, which would include both in-person work and video. But part of his request to scouts also made some scouts uncomfortable.

"One thing in specific we are looking for is picking up signs coming out of the dugout," Goldstein wrote in one of the messages he sent to scouts. "What we are looking for is how much we can see, how we would log things, if we need cameras/binoculars, etc. So go to game, see what you can (or can't) do and report back your findings."

Taping signs out of the dugout, not from the catcher, was not unheard-of in the scouting world, but it was also uncouth to some.

"Nobody wanted to do that, and take a chance of getting caught and ruining their reputation, not only as a scout but then even further damage what the Astros had going," one person directly involved in the conversations said.

To an extent, the ask sounded worse than it was. For one, the signs that Goldstein was asking scouts to tape were not the pitchers' signs the Astros were already stealing during games. "Can't see catcher signals from the stands," Goldstein said in an interview. "It was geared towards signals coming from base coaches and coaches in the dugout. In-game strategy signals, if you want to call them that: bunt, hit and run, positioning."

The scouts also weren't going to be relaying anything in real time. The footage was to be reviewed after the fact.

More to the point: the scouts had no clue about the concurrent trash-can scheme the Astros were undertaking. All of them worked remotely. Goldstein, who did not live in Houston, also said he was unaware. "It wasn't connected at all, because I didn't know the shit was going on," he said. "It was involved with a plan . . . to do some advancing on playoff teams, which is not something we had done in the past. Our advance was kind of in-house, video-based. And so, it was a plan to move in all around that. This was about scouts, in person, in the stands, at non-Astros games."

The sport's rules at the time also offered inadequate guidance. Taping coaches' signs from the stands with a handheld camera was not specifically addressed, or prohibited, as the practice would become a few years later.

"It was something I wanted to get right and help. It didn't seem wrong at the time," Goldstein said. "Catch the signals, and try to decode them later and say, 'Hey, A.J., this is the signal for this.' . . . Later found out it's a gray area at best, and that plenty of people inside the game go, 'Man, you did nothing, this is nothing. Don't even think twice about it.'"

The Astros' pro scouting staff had a mix of backgrounds, some younger, some older. The veterans seemed the most dubious of Goldstein's request. It was untrue, however, that none of the scouts were interested in the task, as one scout had suggested. Alex Jacobs wanted to go try it out, but the logistics didn't work.

"I was disappointed I couldn't go to a game. I thought it'd be pretty cool," Jacobs said. "Because I'm competitive. . . . I would have loved to sit down the line and try to steal signs and look into the dugouts. I remember getting the email vividly."

In Arizona, the Astros had a scout in a similar role to Jacobs's. Mild-mannered and bright, Aaron Tassano joined the Astros after working as a scout in Korea, an unusual background for a US-based scout. He, like Jacobs, normally worked the back fields at team spring training complexes, and the schedule left Tassano with an opportunity: the Chicago Cubs, who had won the World Series the year before and were bound for the 2017 postseason, were playing the Arizona Diamondbacks in Phoenix on August 11–13.

"I went out and bought a pair of binoculars, which I returned, but I sat up in the third deck above the D-backs dugout and was trying to literally steal signs," Tassano said. "But it didn't cross my mind that really what I needed was a high-speed video camera."

To Tassano, this was an assignment, first and foremost, and he was excited to have a chance to contribute to the playoff preparation, considering how few assignments the Astros handed out to the pro scouts for playoff prep normally.

"There weren't rules against it," Tassano said. "I embraced it. I mean because again, that's what the Astros were all about, is disruption. And if there wasn't a rule explicitly against that . . . We were just salivating."

The effort, which lasted just one game, was fruitless. Tassano couldn't see the signs being given in the dugout well from such a distance. He emailed Goldstein to tell him as much, but there was no response.

It probably wouldn't have mattered. The idea died, and so too did the department. Less than a week later, on August 18, Luhnow ripped the Band-Aid. At least eight scouts, some in pro scouting and some in amateur scouting, were fired.

Luhnow had gotten the thumbs-up from McKinsey he sought. Not only did Luhnow and Taubman think the Astros would be more effective in their new form of scouting; they would also be saving considerable money compared to the cost of sending scouts on the road. One executive said the budget would eventually become 30 percent of the seven-figure sum it once was.

"Any decisions made regarding personnel and staffing matters have been and will continue to be internally driven and not based on any third-party work," Luhnow said a couple of years later.

Nonetheless, through the overall process, McKinsey did make specific recommendations about at least some Astros personnel to the steering committee, an executive said, adding that it "was sort of bullshit, because they didn't know people well enough."

Goldstein was not told the scouts would be fired until the day it happened, nor was he presented with any formal findings from or by McKinsey. He was simply informed of the team's new direction. He cried as he called up his scouts.

Goldstein's own role would now be vastly different. Taubman was to assume control of pro scouting, while Goldstein would become a special assistant, giving player evaluation advice to Luhnow. "That was a real sour moment for KG," a colleague said. Goldstein, though, was hurt most at the time for the scouts who were let go. At least he still had a job, and one whose new look he had input designing.

Tassano, who was not fired yet, found out about his colleagues inadvertently: he went to check the normal Slack channel, and it was locked.

"And I went to Ground Control, that was kind of my next move, and so I clicked on the schedule, and half the names were gone," Tassano said. "That whole thing, I guess it hit me like a ton of bricks. I mean, it was out of nowhere. And it changed everything from that moment."

Though he was temporarily sticking around, Tassano would be moving to the amateur scouting staff. Other pro scouts were in search of greener pastures of their own volition, including Jacobs before the season was over.

The Astros were again turning a swath of the baseball community against themselves. For so many scouts to be fired when the franchise was finally a contender after so many painful years "just went too far," an Astros executive said. "It certainly hurt the reputation in the scouting community. But at the same time, for better or for worse, many other teams followed suit."

Goldstein, the following spring, would be cursed out by a scout with the Colorado Rockies. But the scouts he employed by and large loved him. If Goldstein had one flaw in his time in Houston, it was an unflinching loyalty to Luhnow.

When the scouts were axed, even Hinch was annoyed. The field manager had started talking to some of them about the advance process for the postseason, and a week later, poof, they were gone.

○

On August 25, the Astros announced a reorganized front office. Taubman was still not an assistant general manager, despite taking on so many of the responsibilities normally associated with the job. Instead he was now senior director of baseball operations, research, and innovation. The duties were significant: R&D would report to him, with Mike Fast maintaining his role as the day-to-day department director. That was in addition to Taubman's new oversight of pro scouting, Goldstein's old territory.

Mike Elias was no longer solely the amateur scouting director, but international scouting as well, putting all amateur acquisitions under his umbrella.

Had Taubman had his way, the Astros would have moved closer to a singular scouting department. He disliked that the Astros had different processes, different reports across the international, amateur, and pro scouting groups. But Luhnow was being somewhat deferential to one of his top lieutenants, Elias.

"When McKinsey came in, one thing Jeff was sensitive to was not ripping away amateur scouting from Elias," an Astros executive said. "He didn't want Elias to be relegated to a strict scouting role."

Taubman's ideal model would have had him running all the technical scouting, the in-house work, while Elias would manage the scouts out in the field. Instead Luhnow had a message; "Mike, you're going to continue to run amateur and international, but I'm expecting that you're going to embrace the ideas," a colleague remembered.

Matt Hogan, of the advance staff, received a title bump as well.

A day after the announced reshuffling, on August 26, the team was in Anaheim, California, for a quick trip, just a three-game series against the Los Angeles Angels. Koch-Weser sent another edition of his road notes, this time to Luhnow, Taubman, Hogan, and Fast.

"Gents, I wanted to put together some notes before the waiver deadline and rosters expanding. We've gotten our first helping of humble pie over the last month. We've been unable to bludgeon teams with runs like we did most of the first half, and some of our flaws now appear as bigger obstacles to winning," Koch-Weser wrote. "Our pitching seems to be on the rebound, but offensively we've stalled since the break—especially this month—where our team OPS is down about 200 points."

The baserunning had been poor, and Springer's "most alarming," Koch-Weser wrote. Koch-Weser also broke down some of Springer's offensive struggles, with screenshots of Springer at the plate recently compared to the past. "George was informed of this before the 8/23 game and was noticeably trying to get his hips cocked earlier. . . . Seems like he's heading in the right direction even if the results haven't shown up yet."

Under the headline "Other Offensive Areas," Koch-Weser reviewed the Astros' sign-stealing scheme once again. A.J. Hinch, Koch-Weser wrote, was starting to grow concerned because the system was affecting the Astros' baserunning.

"The system: our dark arts, sign-stealing department has been less productive in the second half as the league has become aware of our reputation and now most clubs change their signs a dozen times per game. I've mentioned to you guys that the last place teams like TOR and OAK seem not to care as much. We've been able to take advantage of them. WAS surprisingly was pretty sloppy for a first place, playoff-seasoned club.

"Marwin I'd say does the best job with getting this info as he (usually) shuts it down on offSp and just goes after the FB," making references to Astros player Marwin Gonzalez's ability to handle off-speed pitches and fastballs. "We've seen huge declines from him in chase and swing rates. Beltrán, who is the godfather of the whole program, ironically just swings at everything after taking a strike and probably does the worst with the info. AJ is starting to not like the program altogether as he feels it hinders our secondary leads. We will keep gathering the information and working opponents nevertheless and the coaches can use the info at their own discretion."

Luhnow responded a couple of weeks later.

"Tom, this type of write up is very helpful," the GM wrote back. "Seems like our baserunning is still pathetic. What the hell happened to our pitching this series? I mean that was historically bad. . . ."

# 12

## THE HURRICANE

WHILE THE ASTROS WERE IN ANAHEIM, WHERE TOM KOCH-WESER HAD submitted his latest road notes, Houston and the surrounding areas were in grave danger.

Hurricane Harvey made landfall in Texas on August 25 as a category 4 storm, and for five days, torrential rainfall and flash flooding destroyed homes and took at least ninety-four lives, according to an April 2018 report from Texas Health and Human Services. More than 39,000 square miles and 32 percent of the state were impacted. Adjusted for inflation, Harvey stood in 2018 as second only to Katrina as the most costly hurricane in US history, with a projected cost exceeding $7.2 billion.

During the storm, the US Army Corps of Engineers released water from two overfilled reservoirs in West Houston, with the intent of avoiding a collapse of the reservoirs' dam. But it put thousands of homes at risk in the process. Officials never before had to release water while rain was still coming down.

For the Astros, baseball became secondary to their concern for a city and region in need. The players and staff were worried about their own families, too, with many of them residing in Houston. As a team, the Astros would find an elevated sense of purpose: winning baseball games won't fix a destroyed home, but the team hoped to provide a small distraction.

The heightened anxieties of the time were also a backdrop to growing fissures inside the club.

Once the Astros' visit to Anaheim ended on August 27, the schedule called for the Astros to return to Houston to take on their in-state rivals, the Texas Rangers, August 29–31. But holding the series in Houston was not an option. August 28 was an off day for the Astros, so they flew to Dallas, near the Rangers' home park.

"We can't get home," an Astros employee recalled. "Everybody's wives and family, my wife and family, are huddled underneath the stairs, and so is everybody else's in the organization. So we fly to Dallas; they put us in Dallas kind of in a holding pattern."

The Astros saw a solution for the series against the Rangers. In late September, the Astros were scheduled for a three-game set in Arlington, at the Rangers' park. The Astros wanted to simply swap the series: play in Arlington now and relocate the September series to Houston.

The Rangers didn't like the idea, in part because it meant in September they would have to play twelve straight games on the road. The Rangers were also worried about their season ticket holders who had planned to attend the September series.

The Rangers made a different offer: the August series could be hosted in Arlington, and the Astros would be technically considered the home team. The Rangers would give all the profits from the August series to the Astros.

The Astros remained peeved that the Rangers wouldn't just flip-flop the series. Team president Reid Ryan called out the Rangers, as did Lance McCullers Jr., who wrote on Twitter: "Classy as always, should be absolutely ashamed. Greed never takes off days, apparently. Stay strong #Htown! We hope to be home soon."

Rangers president of baseball operations Jon Daniels didn't agree with the portrayal, but the internet backlash in Houston and elsewhere was swift. The final determination was that the series would move to a true neutral site in St. Petersburg, Florida, the home of the Tampa Bay Rays.

Many with the Astros still weren't happy, but others were at least accepting of the outcome. On August 28, the off day, Astros bench coach Alex Cora sent a tweet: "Playing the Rangers in Tampa for the right reasons. Let's focus on what really matters."

One of the team broadcasters, Geoff Blum, was peeved at Cora's message, particularly once a Rangers beat reporter retweeted it and added on that Cora would be a manager soon, because "He gets it."

Everyone was an emotional wreck, including Blum and Cora. Relative to coaches, broadcasters might not appear important. But Blum wasn't some kid out of broadcasting school. He played fourteen years in the major leagues, the same number of years Cora played. Of his fourteen, Blum spent five with the Astros, making him an established presence in Houston. He was not a Hall of Famer, but his decade in the big leagues is a notable accomplishment, and he had a strong friendship with Hinch to boot.

As the team was traveling to Florida, Blum went up to Hinch and showed him Cora's tweet.

"Are you seeing this stuff?" Blum asked.

Cora was sitting right behind Hinch, and Blum wasn't exactly discreet. Hinch, though, wouldn't indulge the drama.

"F it, man, we're going to do this. Go sit down," Hinch told Blum.

For the moment, Hinch had defused the situation.

On the final day of the relocated series, August 31, Hinch's time in the dugout was short. He was ejected by an umpire after arguing a play in the first inning, and when a manager is thrown out, his successor is the bench coach. Cora, who had aspirations to sit in the big chair himself, had assumed Hinch's job for the day.

Hall of Famer Craig Biggio had met the Astros in Florida, mainly because he was looking for a way to get back to Houston with the team. Biggio wasn't involved with the team on a day-to-day basis, but he still had a role with the club, as dignitaries often do, and he happened to be on hand for this game. Cora, though, grew fearful Biggio was watching over his shoulder.

"He's standing in the tunnel behind Alex Cora the whole game, so Alex Cora is already flipping out," a person on the road trip recalled. "'Why is Biggio watching me?' He's already paranoid."

Meanwhile, pitching coach Brent Strom was telling Cora what to do as far as pitching: when to warm up relievers and so forth. "Get these guys up, get this guy up, giving him all kinds of recommendation out of the bullpen, saying, 'A.J. told me to do this, A.J. told me to do this.'"

Cora removed the day's starting pitcher, Collin McHugh, in the fifth inning, even though the Astros were ahead 2–1. McHugh, typically mild-mannered, wasn't happy and let Cora know it.

"McHugh comes back, of all people, and starts airing out Alex Cora for taking him out early," a person with knowledge of the events said. "He kept it in the clubhouse, but he let him have it."

The Astros won 5–1, and Cora went into Hinch's office and started screaming.

"Why do you have Biggio watching me? You don't think I can do this on my own?"

Hinch was taken aback. He wasn't aware that Biggio had positioned himself in the tunnel.

"Why are you telling Brent Strom who I should bring in out of the bullpen?" Cora continued.

Hinch tried to calm Cora down: in fact, Hinch told his coach, he hadn't told Strom anything. Hinch brought in Strom, who admitted to Cora he was freelancing.

"Strommy was like, 'Yeah, you're right, I kind of lied to you,'" one Astros person recalled. "And so, Alex is just livid."

What was bizarre is that if Hinch, after being ejected, had been attempting to manage Cora from inside, that wouldn't be unheard-of. An ejected manager isn't supposed to still be part of the game, but it's not a rule that's always followed.

Of all days on a baseball calendar, though, August 31 was one where Hinch had something else to worry about in the sport, even beyond the hurricane. When he was ejected, he jumped on his phone, texting and calling. This was the last day teams could make a trade and still have the newly acquired player be eligible for the playoffs. A premier pitcher, Justin Verlander of the Detroit Tigers, was a target.

At the standard July deadline, the Astros' lack of a splash had left the clubhouse disappointed to the point that Dallas Keuchel said as much publicly. But there was still time to inject new energy into the clubhouse. Hinch, more than most field managers, was well connected to other front offices, because he had worked high-level jobs as an executive with two other teams, in Arizona and San Diego.

For now, the fight with Cora was over, and the Astros were heading back home to Houston. "But we're all kind of on edge, 'cause that's the first time we've been back to Houston," a member of the team recalled, "and immediately we see devastation, debris on everybody's front lawns."

At the airport in Houston, the Astros boarded two team buses, including one that primarily carried staff such as Hinch, Cora, and Blum. Normally Cora's seat was right behind Hinch, but someone else had plopped themselves down: Biggio. Cora relocated.

On the drive to downtown Houston, Cora started playing music loudly on a speaker. Blum was trying to get a hold of his wife, and some of the broadcast crew were also trying to reach out to families and figure out which roads were open.

"The logistics of disaster," one person on the bus recalled.

One of the TV crew members noted that they couldn't hear their phone call. Blum, annoyed by the music, quietly went up to Cora's seat.

"Any other day, crank it," Blum told Cora. "But if you can just turn it down a little bit, and let us kind of figure out how we're going to get home, see the families are OK—"

"Oh, you want me to turn it down?" Cora shot back. "You want me to turn it down? I'll turn it down. How about I just turn it off?"

Blum said thanks and went back to his seat. About five minutes later, Cora walked past Blum, before all of a sudden he was hovering right over the broadcaster.

"I bet if Puerto Rico was going through this you'd be playing the music," Cora said.

Blum snapped.

"You got to be kidding me! How dare you say that? There's no way I'd be doing that. You can't bring that up right now," Blum said.

Cora called Blum a c***.

"What are you talking about?" Blum said.

"I saw you talking to the manager," Cora said, referring to Blum's relationship with Hinch.

The bench coach laid into Blum, who was trying to convince Cora this wasn't the time or place, almost pleading.

"Let's not do this here. Alex, you don't want to do this," Blum said. "Let's just talk when we get off the bus."

For about five minutes, the yelling continued, and people on the bus assumed a fistfight was inevitable. Blum is a sizable guy, at six foot three, 220 pounds, according to his playing days listing. Cora isn't tiny, but is smaller at six feet tall, about 200 pounds.

"People are like, seriously, here it comes," a member of the team said.

Finally, Cora stopped. He briefly went to talk to Hinch, came back, and told Blum, "You, me—after the bus."

Team travel back to Houston was supposed to be dry, although it's not uncommon in the sport for those rules to be bent. Nonetheless, Cora was clearly drunk, and people in the traveling party had seen him drinking. "On the bus you could see it," one person said.

When the bus got to Minute Maid Park, Hinch and Cora went down a ramp off to the right, where the TV trucks are. Blum followed, and told Cora he was sorry. Cora immediately snapped and started screaming again on the loading dock—not just at Blum, but at Hinch this time, too.

"He's your buddy, you want him to be your bench coach, you don't trust me," Cora said, accusing Hinch of showing favoritism to Blum. "It's been like this all year long. This is just business."

Cora called Hinch "a fucking c***," and his second rant, this one directed mainly at his boss, lasted about ten minutes, in front of most of the team to see as players and staff filed off the buses.

"He sounded very aggressive, like, if you tried to break it up, you're going to get hit in the face, you're going to get punched in the face," a witness said.

Said another: "Holy crap, I'm going to watch our manager deck our bench coach."

"I was not on the trip where things blew up, but I talked with a lot of people that were," an Astros front office member said. "And it seemed like Cora was sort of being a drunk asshole and then A.J. had some pent-up rage and just let it rip."

At the loading dock, Craig Bjornson, the Astros' bullpen coach, was trying to shuffle players out of the way, although the fight was hard for nearly anyone who had traveled with the team to miss. Carlos Beltrán came over and tried to calm Cora down, and Alex Cintrón, as well.

In the past, Cora and at least a couple of others on the team had noticed Blum and Hinch's relationship.

"We used to tell Cintrón, 'Look at Blum, he's going to go up A.J.'s ass,'" one member of the Astros said.

But for as much as Blum and Cora were miffed at each other, the root of the explosion appeared to lie in Cora's relationship with Hinch. Hinch, colleagues said, felt the trouble started the first month of the season, even back in spring training. "A.J. said that that wasn't the first time they actually had that kind of interaction," one said. Cora was said to be insecure about his role with the team—which might explain caring so much about Biggio's presence, or about Strom's directives allegedly on Hinch's behalf, or about Blum having Hinch's ear.

In Cora's short time in Houston, he had shown he could be erratic or simply immature. "He totally disenchanted the coaching staff," one member of the Astros said. "He blew up one day in the coach's office with A.J., and said, 'You expect me to do all this stuff for two hundred and fifty grand?' And you know, all the other coaches are making, like, seventy-five grand."

Another version of the story had Cora making $275,000. Either way, it wasn't big money for ex-ballplayers like Cora, who made upwards of $15 million over his career as a player, before taxes. But, in the coaching world, a salary approaching $300,000 was significant, particularly in Houston, where purse strings were tight.

"Two seventy-five, I mean, that's like what, forty thousand, fifty thousand dollars a month?" another person with the team said, referencing the pay schedule during the roughly six-month-long regular season. "Come on, man."

Fights can happen in long seasons on baseball teams, between players and staff and others. But this one stood out to some who had seen plenty before. "It was crazy, man," one longtime player said.

Cora had more on his mind than baseball. He was worried about his family, and he was worried about Puerto Rico, where Hurricane Irma's arrival was imminent. (The more powerful and destructive Hurricane Maria, which would not reach Puerto Rico until September 20, had yet to form.)

"Between Harvey and [Irma], it was a combination of a lot of emotions on a personal level," Cora said later that year. "We're flying everywhere, man, and then the team, we weren't playing good. I learned that we can be—honestly, honestly, on a personal standpoint, I learned that boys are boys, and it's a family and you're going to have your good days and your bad days."

He was also, ultimately, trying to downplay what happened. No matter how good a team is, having a bench coach berate not just a broadcaster, but the manager of the team, in front of so many others wasn't something that could repeat itself. The rift between manager and bench coach had to be patched immediately, or what choice would Hinch have had but to fire Cora in the middle of an otherwise amazing season? "He should have been fired a long time ago," Hinch vented to others.

The front office and Jim Crane were aware of what happened, and an executive confirmed that if the rift had continued, a dismissal likely would have been afoot.

"That's right," an executive said. "It got smoothed over pretty quick. It was a bad, embarrassing moment for the organization and for A.J. and Cora. It sort of showed some of our dysfunction."

(The Astros successfully kept the story hidden from the public for a few months, until after the season.)

Hinch's own insecurities may have played a role as well. One Astros staffer felt that in general, Hinch and Cora were in many ways similar: smart, talented, charismatic, and carrying big egos. Cora had become a go-to for pockets of the clubhouse, which shouldn't have been a bad thing. Alex Bregman, for example, had become very close with Cora.

"Cora was doing such a good fucking job that a lot of players were coming to him for advice, feedback, coaching," a colleague said. "Cora challenged A.J. a lot and disagreed with his decisions and was vocal about it, but in a respectful way. A.J. was pissed-off at Cora a lot.

Because you know what he would do, A.J. would be like: 'I was debating this decision at this moment and Cora said this, and thank God I ignored him, because things worked out the way they did.' And so it was a little awkward, and of course A.J. wouldn't bring up any instances where Cora gave a recommendation that maybe would have led to a better result for the Astros."

"Cora really likes to drink," said someone who traveled with the Astros. "Any road trip I was on with him, or plane flight I was on with him, he was drinking a lot. Him and Craig Bjornson, CB, were basically wasted on every single flight. So much so that Cora would turn into the equivalent of like, the scary homeless person that's talking to themself doing like drunken tai chi in place, and you're like: 'Oh my God, what's wrong with that guy?' Like, Cora would get that level drunk on basically every single trip."

O

The bizarre night took another turn as players and staff left the ballpark and went to their homes. The Astros had landed the big fish, Justin Verlander, in a trade.

Verlander may be best known to non–baseball fans as the husband of model Kate Upton. But he's also a big right-hander with a powerful fastball who will likely wind up in the Hall of Fame. At the age of thirty-four, Verlander wasn't as dominant as he once had been. But the Astros believed they could get more out of him, and Verlander still had something to fight for: he had never won a championship.

Publicly, the glory for the trade to this point has largely rested with the biggest names involved: Luhnow, and his counterpart in Detroit, Al Avila, as well as owner Jim Crane, because Verlander was a highly paid player and it was ultimately Crane's money.

"The way that story was told is basically that Jeff did this deal at the deadline while he was on vacation from a phone that had spotty service and Jim is on the phone with Verlander," an Astros employee said.

But it was a partial picture.

"Jim was the real muscle behind it—at the end, with Jeff," said another colleague. "But, you know it's hard. Jeff really did pull the trigger at the end. All of that stuff is true in its own right. It's hard to capture where the actual influence was. To think it was just two GMs who got together grinding out a deal, that's not accurate."

On the final day, Luhnow was not front and center. He was "largely unavailable on vacation" for the whole night, "hard to get in touch with." Luhnow's right-hand man, Taubman, and the manager, Hinch, had actually spearheaded the endgame—along with the owner, Crane. This was the first time Taubman was leading a trade process, along with a counterpart on the Tigers, Sam Menzin. The two front-office members had been exchanging names on prospects for about a week, and on the Astros' side, Taubman was gathering evaluations, talking to the scouting staff. Technical scouting, reviewing TrackMan and beyond, had helped the Astros home in on Verlander as someone who had room to improve.

Hinch's connections around the league were always a sore spot for Luhnow, presumed to be born out of jealousy. Between the two, Hinch was always much better liked in the industry, with friends across the sport. Hinch knew Luhnow's sensitivities and didn't want to be mistaken as playing GM. But those connections were also quite valuable when push came to shove, and one of Hinch's closest friends in the sport happened to be a higher-up in the Tigers' front office, Scott Bream.

"That deal was dead, and A.J. basically reinvigorated that deal by back-channeling conversations to his friend Scott," an Astros executive said. Hinch's ejection on August 31, then, had produced a silver lining: it gave him time to chat.

One of the main holdups to the trade was whether the Astros would include a fourth player. Hinch was actually the first to suggest Astros prospect Daz Cameron's name to the Tigers. Technically, Hinch couldn't authorize anything, but Cameron did wind up in the deal, and Houston didn't have to include a fourth player.

"It drove Jeff crazy that A.J. would back-channel on all this stuff," the executive said. "This is a prime example where it helped our organization a lot that A.J. had connections with front-office people, and knows what a reasonable trade is."

Luhnow was involved at the point that the Astros had to deal with

Verlander's no-trade clause. And ultimately, the GM's willingness to use prospects to acquire a win-now player was important, if not a full-on departure from the conservative approach the front office had otherwise adhered to. Sig Mejdal always favored the odds, and the future value that the Astros were giving up to acquire Verlander was significant.

"Once Jeff started having to make decisions of, 'Should we sign this free agent? Should we trade for Verlander?' Sig started pushing back on him a lot on those sort of things," a different executive said. "Sig was never able to switch gears. He wanted to hoard every single, not even prospect-prospect, but like, org piece that we had. He didn't like spending free-agent money; he didn't like trading for established players. I think he really thought that building through the farm and staying with those players was the way to build a ball club."

The Verlander deal took until the very last minute, and maybe then some. The league told the Astros the deal was submitted about two seconds before the deadline. But the approved email came through about a minute and a half after the deadline.

"The written rule is the time stamp of the approved email," a front-office member said. "That time stamp was late. The league would say we made an internal decision: it was approved."

The Astros didn't play on September 1, holding a day of service in the wake of the hurricane instead. The next day, the Astros played at Minute Maid Park for the first time since Harvey hit. The team had a new patch: the Astros' *H* logo, and the word "strong," for Houston Strong. Hinch gave a speech before the game, thanking first responders and reaching out to the community.

# 13

# LINES IN THE SAND

WHEN VERLANDER JOINED HIS NEW TEAM, THE ASTROS HAD MOMENTARY panic about their sign-stealing system, a small moment of truth. "Nobody was proud of it," one person with the Astros said.

Earlier that same season, one of Verlander's worst outings had come against the Astros in Houston, in May. Now, wearing an Astros uniform, he didn't outwardly react negatively when he learned what happened. If anything, he newly had an excuse as to why he gave up three home runs that day.

"You fuckers," Verlander said, laughing when he found out. Verlander noted, too, that when the Tigers left Minute Maid Park in May, they had a feeling the Astros knew what was coming. The Astros weren't the only team Verlander remembered leaving him with that feeling. True or not, he was adamant to his new team that the Cleveland Indians (now the Cleveland Guardians) had done something similar.

In September, for the first time as commissioner, Rob Manfred had to publicly confront his growing electronic sign-stealing problem—not in Houston, though. The two members of the sport's most famous rivalry, the Red Sox and the Yankees, had leveled crossfire accusations at one another in August, and the commissioner was now going to make a public show of his findings.

Both teams accused the other of using the baserunner method.

The Yankees had recorded video of Red Sox athletic trainer Jon Jochim looking at a wearable device on his wrist in the dugout. He then relayed the information he received on the device—the sign sequence—to players.

The Red Sox filed a countercomplaint, suggesting the Yankees were using a camera from their television network improperly.

The ordeal became as known as the Apple Watch scandal (even though Boston's trainer was wearing a device from a different maker). In response, Manfred made choices that had profound effects.

Manfred did not find the Yankees had used their TV station to cheat. But he did find that both teams had, in fact, been using their video rooms to decode signs in recent years. And instead of just bringing the information out on foot, the teams were speeding up the process: the Yankees by communicating to the dugout through a phone, the Red Sox via that wearable device.

"Players complained: they didn't want to have to run up the stairs, run down. They're just like, 'Our trainers wear watches, can receive texts, save us that time,'" one member of the Red Sox said. "It was out of pure laziness. Just stupidity and laziness, and also annoying [that Yankees manager Joe] Girardi blew the whistle—we fucking learned it from them. They were using a YES Network camera to zoom in on signs. So it was like so stupid that they blew the whistle, because they're doing the same fucking shit."

Manfred now had a choice to make. He had a rule on his books that was broad, but nonetheless clearly prohibited using electronic equipment to steal signs. It would have been a reasonable interpretation, if not the obvious one, to find that decoding signs in the video room was illegal. What was the replay rig, if not electronic?

Instead, Manfred found that the only crime committed was the subsequent means of relaying the information: the use of the phone, in the case of the Yankees, or the watch, in the case of the Red Sox. Both teams were fined, the Yankees $100,000, the Red Sox a larger amount.

"The Yankees and the Red Sox at the time were saying, true or not, 'Oh, every club has people walking from the video room to the dugout, so you're nailing us for a more efficient means of communication,'" a person with direct knowledge of the league's investigations said. "The answer was, 'Yeah, the way you were transmitting it was clearly illegal, right?' . . . This is September of '17. Going before that, [MLB] identified walking from the video room as the gray area."

But it was very much Manfred's choice to define it as a gray area, and that choice came with certain gains for the league office.

The playoffs were approaching, and Manfred would not have wanted to dramatically punish a pair of postseason-bound clubs, distracting from the league's most profitable time of year. The Red Sox and Yankees have also always been, let's say, important franchises in the sport. Punishing players would have meant taking up a fight with the players' union, too.

The sense of convenience didn't stop there. Manfred was avoiding setting a precedent. Were other teams to be subsequently caught using their video rooms to steal signs prior to September 2017, Manfred wouldn't have to retroactively punish them.

In addition, because Manfred determined that the video room behavior was not grounds for punishment, he didn't have to detail publicly what was going on in those rooms. He could be outwardly vague.

Manfred put out a statement on September 15. It gave a general sense of what the Red Sox had been doing. But the explanation of the Yankees' behavior was word soup. Most people reading it would have no clue what the Yanks were up to.

"In the course of our investigation, however," went the statement, "we learned that during an earlier championship season (prior to 2017) the Yankees had violated a rule governing the use of the dugout phone. No Club complained about the conduct in question at the time and, without prompting from another Club or my Office, the Yankees halted the conduct in question. Moreover, the substance of the communications that took place on the dugout phone was not a violation of any Rule or Regulation in and of itself. Rather, the violation occurred because the dugout phone technically cannot be used for such a communication."

In a separate letter Manfred wrote at the time directly to Yankees general manager Brian Cashman, he was much more direct and succinct about what the Yankees had done.

"The Yankees' use of the dugout phone to relay information about an opposing Club's signs during the 2015 season, and part of the 2016 season, constitutes a material violation of the Replay Review Regulations," Manfred wrote. "By using the phone in the video review room to instantaneously transmit information regarding signs to the dugout in violation of the Regulations, the Yankees were able to provide real-time information to their players regarding an opposing Club's sign sequence—the same objective of the Red Sox's scheme that was the subject of the Yankees' complaint."

The world didn't have access to that letter until five years later, by which time what the Yankees had done had been reported on by Ken Rosenthal and me. But the letter's 2022 court-ordered release still revealed a stark contrast between Manfred's public and private phrasing, between what he wanted to portray to the world in 2017 and what he didn't.

Manfred never meant for the letter to Cashman to become public at all, but it became part of the record in a lawsuit brought by daily fantasy players who were accusing MLB and some teams of defrauding them. In a court filing, Yankees president Randy Levine, a politically connected and powerful figure in the sport, accused MLB of mistakenly allowing the letter to be submitted in court in the first place.

Both the Yankees and MLB fought the release of the letter, which became known simply as "The Yankees Letter." They lost in an appeals process that took nearly two years.

September 2017 proved a major juncture in the sport's history. Manfred's goal was to keep the damage minimal, and put an end to the cheating. At the same time he put out his public statement and he sent Cashman that letter, the commissioner sent all thirty teams a memo "putting all Clubs on notice that future violations would be taken extremely seriously by my office." Manfred also outlined who would be held accountable in the future: the general manager and field manager.

But the commissioner had made two large mistakes.

First, by aiming future punishment at the manager and GM, Manfred was beginning to build a certain precedent: management, and not the players themselves, would most likely be punished if this ever happened again. He didn't consider how the world might react were a team someday caught and players not held responsible.

Of course, Manfred didn't think he would have to punish this behavior again at all, at least not prominently. In just his third season presiding over the sport, the commissioner believed that merely fining the Red Sox and the Yankees—while simultaneously letting them off the hook for how they used the video room—and issuing a threat of more severe punishments in the future would be sufficient deterrence.

The day before he announced the Red Sox' and Yankees' fines, I asked Manfred in a press conference at Fenway Park about his goals for the impending discipline.

"When I think about punishment, I think you need to think about deterrence," Manfred said. "I think you need to think about how the violation has affected the play on the field, and I think you need to think about how it's affected the perception of the game publicly. All of those things are something that you have to weigh in terms of trying to get to appropriate discipline."

In the middle of September, this was the commissioner's second failure: he believed he had drawn a line in the sand.

O

At times in 2017, small groups of Astros discussed their misgivings with the sign-stealing system. Brian McCann at one point approached Carlos Beltrán and asked him to stop, two members of the 2017 team said.

"He disregarded it and steamrolled everybody," one of the team members said. "Where do you go if you're a young, impressionable player with the Astros and this guy says, 'We're doing this'? What do you do?"

Locker room rules have always prized secrecy and protectiveness, as well as seniority. The pecking order was, rightly or wrongly, viewed as a hindrance.

"I was in my first year, man," Astros pitcher Joe Musgrove, a rookie in 2017, said in an interview on MLB Network years later. "Along with [Alex] Bregman and a lot of those guys, and in your first year in the big leagues you're around guys like Beltrán and McCann, some big names. And I'm not going to be the pitcher to walk up and tell 'em to knock it off."

Ultimately, MLB found that most if not all of the regular Astros players knew what was going on. But there was some frustration over the system, too.

"We weren't even good at it," one member of the team said.

The Astros weren't dominating at home as compared to the road. There were still days they would cheat and lose, and days they would cheat and win—likely not for any reason owed to their cheating.

But they kept at it, on the belief they were gaining a leg up. "What we did in 2017, yeah, it was an advantage. Yeah, it was wrong," Carlos Correa eventually said publicly—and no one was putting a stop to it. Pitching coach Brent Strom was said to have noted to others on the team that the scheme appeared to be working.

"Strommy or A.J., they can't be like—'Hey, dude, hey, stop doing that,'" one member of the team said. "I mean, they're winning. Why would they tell them, 'Let's stop that, let's play fair'?"

Someone would have to stick their neck out to bring it to a halt, but whistleblowers are uncommon anywhere. Max Bazerman of Harvard Business School has spent a lot of time studying the unintentional unethical behavior of otherwise good people.

"Within baseball, the notion of accepting cheating as OK has sort of a very significant tradition, and I think that to tell a team to stop it requires an awful lot of courage," he said. "If we think of the act of saying something as a player on the team, this is the equivalent of whistleblowers in corporate contexts, and whistleblowers are pretty rare, and they are typically punished. And I think if you think of a player stepping forward to say, 'My team's cheating,' I think that the likelihood that their career would have lasted is pretty small.

"Can you identify a situation where any athlete has ever stepped forward to be the whistleblower to say my team is cheating? I can't come up with an example of that."

Twice during the 2017 season, Hinch damaged the television monitor the Astros were using in the tunnel to steal signs. The first occasion coincided with a time when Hinch at least briefly reduced playing time for Beltrán. Afterward, Cora and Beltrán didn't directly come to Hinch and fight to keep the trash-can system going, but there was nonetheless some pushback.

The second time Hinch damaged the monitor was in August, some time prior to the blowup with Cora on the bus and the Verlander trade.

Wild as it sounds—the manager attacking the means of cheating—these were not dramatic, demonstrative flashpoints in front of the whole team. There were none of those from the manager, which would become Hinch's biggest regret: that he never stood up in front of everyone and permanently put an end to it.

Both times, a monitor wound up back on the wall again. Hinch told MLB that he never brought the matter directly to Luhnow.

The manager was operating out of fear. He didn't have a World Series win under his belt yet. He had already lost a clubhouse once, in Arizona, which led to his firing. Now, in Houston, he didn't want to disappoint high-profile players. He was reticent to stand up to the Hall of Fame legacy of Beltrán. He didn't want to actually fight Cora, or any of the players, or find the players who looked up to Cora or Beltrán turned against him. And the team was playing well.

Jeff Luhnow was one of the recipients of Manfred's September 15 memo, the one that the commissioner's office had intended to be a firm warning after the Apple Watch scandal. But after the email landed, Luhnow "admittedly took no steps to investigate whether the Astros were violating the regulations," nor did Luhnow forward the memo to anyone, Manfred later found.

"You claimed that you fulfilled your obligation by asking manager A. J. Hinch and then Senior Director of Baseball Operations Brandon Taubman to make sure to not have electronics in the dugout, after which Taubman assured you that the Astros 'were not using electronics downstairs,'" Manfred wrote to Luhnow. "Even if true, this response was woefully inadequate, but Taubman and Hinch told my investigators that they had no recollection of that conversation, and Taubman said that he did not give you such assurance and was not in position to do so without further investigation."

Luhnow has always denied knowledge of any of the Astros' cheating, the trash-can set-up or the concurrent baserunner system. MLB's public report stated that the "investigation revealed no evidence to suggest that Luhnow was aware of the banging scheme. The investigation also revealed that Luhnow neither devised nor actively directed the efforts of the replay review room staff to decode signs in 2017 or 2018. Although Luhnow denies having any awareness that his replay review room staff was decoding and transmitting signs, there is both documentary and testimonial evidence that indicates Luhnow had some knowledge of those efforts, but he did not give it much attention."

Yet, when speaking to MLB, Tom Koch-Weser said that Luhnow "almost certainly" observed him or Matt Hogan communicating signs using the replay phone during the end of away games in 2017.

"While unable to identify an instance of it occurring, and noting that your visits were brief, Hogan and another video room staffer Antonio Padilla believe that you may have seen Hogan or Koch-Weser decipher and communicate sign information," Manfred wrote to Luhnow. "Padilla and Hogan both noted that there was no effort to hide it from you, and Hogan said he did not have any 'trepidation' about doing it in front of you—in fact, he thought 'it would have been something to show we were working and get validation of our work.'"

Koch-Weser told MLB that Luhnow often stopped by the video room during games and made comments such as "You guys Codebreaking?"

At group dinners, Koch-Weser said Luhnow would make passing references to Codebreaker and had a "sense of glee" about its use. To league investigators, Hogan couldn't recall a specific conversation with Luhnow about Codebreaker, but was "almost positive" Luhnow talked about it in his presence.

Luhnow denied those accounts. He told MLB that team dinners were infrequent and often had a large number of people, and that he watched the end of games from the road video room on only a handful of occasions—none in 2017 and four times in 2018. Luhnow denied ever seeing evidence of sign-stealing or improper phone use, either.

O

On September 21, just six days after the commissioner's league-wide warning, the Astros hosted the Chicago White Sox at Minute Maid Park, where Houston trailed 3–1 in the eighth inning. A veteran pitcher, Danny Farquhar, was on the mound for Chicago.

The White Sox were a bad team, and Minute Maid Park wasn't exactly full, with 24,283 tickets sold, and even fewer fans left in the seats late in the game, making it easier for anyone on the field to hear loud noises.

The first batter Farquhar faced was Evan Gattis. After six pitches, Farquhar stepped off the mound, and his catcher walked out of his crouch to meet with him. Farquhar had heard something, some sound just before he threw anything other than a fastball.

"There was a banging from the dugout, almost like a bat hitting the bat rack every time a changeup signal got put down," Farquhar said. "I was throwing some really good changeups, and they were getting fouled off. After the third bang, I stepped off."

Farquhar and his catcher changed the signs to a more complex set, the kind teams normally used when a runner was on base, even though the Astros had no one on.

"The banging stopped," Farquhar said. "My assumption was they were picking it up from the video and relaying the signs to the dugout. . . . That was my theory on the whole thing. It made me very upset. I was so angry, so mad, that the media didn't come to me after."

Panic ensued in the Astros dugout. They were worried they had been caught. Alex Cora turned around and told at least one player, rookie Derek Fisher, to take the TV down. Fisher didn't play that day. MLB found that "a group of Astros players removed the monitor from the wall in the tunnel and hid it in an office."

The Astros were still cheating, even after Manfred drew his supposed line in the sand, and the playoffs were just a couple of weeks away.

Tony Adams, who listened to every Astros game from 2017 that he could, found the banging curtailed after the Farquhar game.

Throughout the season, according to Adams's findings, the hitters who heard the most "bangs" at the plate were: Marwin Gonzalez (147), George Springer (140), Carlos Beltrán (138), Alex Bregman (133), Yuli Gurriel (120), Carlos Correa (97), Jake Marisnick (83), and Evan Gattis (71). The list dropped off from there: Brian McCann was next, at 45.

"There were guys who didn't like it," said Mike Fiers, who led all Astros pitchers in innings pitched during the regular season. "There are guys who don't like to know [what's coming] and guys who do."

The peak of the banging was recorded by Adams as August 4, against Toronto. The pitcher for the Blue Jays that day, Mike Bolsinger, never pitched in the majors again. He faced eight batters and retired one. He eventually sued the Astros, and lost.

Throughout 2017, the Astros relied on the belief they were not alone—that other teams were doing *something*, never mind whether it was comparable.

"I don't know if we really had any hard proof, but I'm sure there was [some evidence of other teams' conduct]," pitcher Mike Fiers said. "Going into the playoffs, we had veterans like Brian McCann—we went straight to multiple signs [with our pitchers]. We weren't going to mess around. We were sure there were teams out there that were trying certain things to get an edge and win ball games. I wouldn't say there was hard evidence. But it's hard to catch teams at home. There are so many things you can use to win at home."

O

As the playoffs approached, Jose Altuve, who rarely used the banging scheme himself, expressed excitement to others on the team.

"We're going to beat those guys at their ballpark and then when we come back here, we're going to have the boom-boom-boom," he said, doing an impression of banging noises, a teammate recalled.

The Astros rolled onward, defeating the Boston Red Sox to advance to the American League Championship Series.

Not everyone with the Astros, to this day, is convinced the cheating continued into the postseason. About a third of players later told MLB they could not remember or did not know if it was used in postseason, but some could have been covering, and plenty of people with the team said they were sure it was used, both to MLB and to this reporter. One common thread that came up was noise: banging on a trash can wouldn't be consistently effective in a postseason setting where the crowds are very loud.

"I think it was used. How often, how much, whether they can hear it, I mean, those are questions that you just can't answer," one person with direct knowledge of the investigation said. "Maybe some players can, maybe they can't. Maybe they don't even remember, honestly."

It's an exaggeration to say that every moment is so loud that it could never be heard. One moment people with the team pointed to was a home run in the final game of the second round of the postseason, against the Yankees, a winner-take-all Game 7 at Minute Maid Park.

In the fourth inning, there was no score, so the crowd was buzzing, but not at a fever pitch. Evan Gattis hit a breaking ball out to left field for a 1–0 Astros lead. A member of the team had a clear memory of hearing the garbage can prior to that home run. The Astros won the game 4–0, behind stellar pitching from Charlie Morton and Lance McCullers Jr., who between them struck out 11 Yankees hitters.

The Astros had made it past two of the game's powerhouse franchises, Boston and New York, and one more stood in their way.

For Houston, the Los Angeles Dodgers were something of a foil. Although Los Angeles had a much larger payroll than Houston, its top baseball executive, Andrew Friedman, had been a target of Jim Crane's before he hired Luhnow. The Dodgers were among the most progressive teams in the sport, after Friedman, formerly of Bear Stearns, had established himself as one of the premier executives in his years running the small-market Tampa Bay Rays.

The Dodgers had reverence for the Astros in a few areas: how well the latter's pitchers' spin rates improved, for one, became a topic the Dodgers would themselves pursue. The Dodgers, too, had heard about all the Edgertronic cameras. "It was always my impression that, you know whether or not it was true, they were farther ahead on the motion capture stuff," one Dodgers employee said.

Teams had two main buckets in which to be innovative: the actual analytics—which encompasses all the math and the technological capabilities—and their implementation. The Dodgers had more people with highly technical advanced degrees in their R&D department than the Astros, and more people in the department overall. But some with the Dodgers still considered the Astros to be leaders in the second bucket, rollout.

The Astros, though, didn't come by that advantage without a cost. Friedman's Dodgers had no qualms about living in the gray area. Friedman, too, liked to push the envelope. But Friedman managed to initiate change without alienating as many in the process as Luhnow. (That doesn't mean no one was unhappy, however.) Dodgers employees spoke of a desire to find a balance in speed of implementation. "Which like, if you wanted to be completely rational, you could argue that games are being lost because of that," said one. "But the other side of it is, people aren't as upset about that change process because it's at a more manageable pace."

On the sign-stealing front, the Astros and Dodgers were suspicious of one another. One member of the Dodgers said during the 2017 season, they indeed did use a baserunner scheme, determining sign sequences with the help of their video room, an analog to what the Red Sox and Yankees had done in recent years, and to what the Astros were doing on the road. Another member of the Dodgers said that everyone was doing that until MLB cracked down on it in 2018. But there is no known evidence that the Dodgers were doing something as flagrant as the Astros' trash-can system.

Inside the Dodgers offices, different theories abounded as to what Houston was up to: were the Astros' base coaches helping? Were signals coming from the bullpen, where someone was wearing an earpiece? (There's no known evidence on those fronts.) Some people inside the team started to try to run the numbers, to see if they could find anything.

When the World Series switched to Houston for Games 3, 4, and 5, top Dodgers brass met with the starting pitchers for those games: Yu Darvish, Alex Wood, and Clayton Kershaw. The Dodgers brain trust didn't want to freak out their pitchers, but they delivered a message: we have suspicions that the Astros are up to something, so let's use multiple signs even when no one is on base.

Kershaw and Darvish both declined to heed that advice. The only pitcher who agreed to deviate was the least-renowned pitcher of the bunch, Wood. It just so happened that Wood fared the best: he didn't allow the Astros a hit until the sixth inning of Game 4, which wound up a 6–2 Dodgers win, evening the series at two games apiece.

On the next night, Game 5 of the World Series produced one of the most epic back-and-forth contests the sport has ever seen on its biggest stage, and the Dodgers felt in hindsight that the sign-stealing scheme had particularly helped the Astros that night, as well as in Game 3.

Even in real time, Game 5 had a surreal feel to it. Every time one team would take the lead, the other would storm back immediately—almost like they all knew what was coming. The Dodgers scored three runs in the ninth to tie at 12, and in the tenth inning, the Astros walked off winners, 13–12.

The series moved back to Los Angeles with the Astros ahead three games to two.

During the ALCS, the Astros had believed that the Yankees had positioned someone to relay signs in center field. For the games in Los Angeles, the Astros believed the Dodgers had a camera set up in center field with an iPad connected to it.

The camera was alleged to be zoomed in on the pitcher's glove, and the iPad on the camera is said to have had a preset button with the different pitches thrown by the pitcher of the moment: a fastball, a curveball, and so forth. A person manning the camera would hit the button, and the results would go to an iPad in the dugout, indicating what pitch was coming, and someone would verbally signal what was coming to a Dodgers hitter.

This was just an allegation, however, but the Astros believed they had caught the Dodgers doing at least *something*.

An Astros coach was said to have seen someone setting up a center field camera at Dodger Stadium prior to one of the final two games and yelled at the person. The guy working the camera simply left. Some members of the Astros went up to the center field camera well and asked other crew members who the person was, and TV crew people in the vicinity said they did not know. The operator was said to be wearing a Dodgers hat, and to have laughed when the coach approached.

○

The Dodgers won Game 6 of the World Series, sending the Fall Classic to a winner-take-all Game 7 at Dodger Stadium. On the road—which is not where they're known to have done their best cheating—the Astros prevailed, 5–1. The players, jubilant, celebrated on the field and in the locker room. MLB Network, the league-run television station, set up a stage on the field and interviewed Astros catcher Brian McCann.

Analysts asked McCann about all the mound visits he had with Astros pitchers, about the possibility of the Dodgers knowing the Astros' signs. McCann looked pained, with a face that said, "Come on."

"There's a lot more going on than . . ." he started to say. The conversation moved on.

Carlos Correa, in the postgame celebration, proposed to his girlfriend. The Astros were the toast of the town, the darlings of baseball, and the accolades kept coming. Early in the offseason, Jose Altuve was announced as the American League's Most Valuable Player, over second-place finisher Aaron Judge of the Yankees. Carlos Beltrán retired from playing, and Alex Cora was hired by the Boston Red Sox to be their manager.

The following spring, the Astros visited the White House. A president's invitation is customary for sports champions, although teams and individuals sometimes stayed away during Donald Trump's tenure. Kevin Goldstein is the only known member of the Astros front office who did not attend on political grounds. Luhnow was a Trump supporter, multiple colleagues said. "Jeff's a rich white guy, of course he's a Republican," said one colleague.

One prominent name, Correa, did not go to the White House, instead spending the day in Florida where, in the wake of Hurricane Maria, he arranged aid for his native Puerto Rico.

Up north, Trump threw around canned praise as Astros leadership basked.

"Jeff really came in six years ago and, you know, restructured the whole organization," Jim Crane said at the podium. "And it's his plan—his twenty-one-page plan that he delivered to me six years ago that got us there for the first time."

The president ushered up Luhnow for the last remarks from the Astros. He thought back to an old headline in the *Houston Chronicle*.

"We had a vision in 2011," Luhnow began. "It was a little different than what the media and the fans were expecting. 'Radical ways,' they called it. But at the end of the day, our goal was to win a championship as soon as possible, and to build an organization that could compete for multiple championships. We did it."

# 14

# HERE WAS AN INEFFICIENCY

FROM THE OUTSET, THE ASTROS WERE EASY FOR MEDIA AND FANS TO RO-manticize because they were different. They were shiny and smart and new-age. They seemed fearless, too, the pioneers marching across baseball's new frontier. Six years into Jim Crane's tenure, he and Jeff Luhnow had scaled the mountain. Even before they won, any public doubt that arrived on their step was rebranded as adversity to over-come, and sometimes, rightly so. Now, though, the Luddites had lost, and what else had their critics been? The goal had been singular: a championship, and it was theirs.

Most teams are focused on winning. But in Houston, most any-thing else, eventually or immediately, faded out of view in pursuit of that goal. Luhnow and Crane's tolerance for pushing the envelope cer-tainly wasn't about to diminish now, nor would their sight lines reach beyond the only horizon they'd built for themselves: victories.

Put another way: "We all got cocky," an executive said.

A title in hand, Luhnow was also receding.

"Jeff got really disengaged," an executive said. The GM had a re-duced presence at Minute Maid Park, taking on occasional corporate speaking engagements. In the middle of 2018, he also secured a title bump and a raise: he was now the president of baseball operations, as well. On days Luhnow would come in late, one of the lower-level baseball operations members would often turn on the lights in Luhnow's office, so it had seemed he had already been there.

"After we won the World Series, he changed a lot," an executive said. "And started to come into the office at eleven a.m. on average most days. Especially days where we had night games. And often didn't come in until like BP, and he would go straight from the players' lot to batting practice because there was an entry way there. . . . That started to happen more and more in '18 and '19."

Manager A.J. Hinch wanted a contract extension heading into 2018, but Luhnow preferred a one-year deal. Shortly after the World Series, Luhnow told the well-connected Hinch that he didn't need "a GM in a manager's chair."

Just after the Astros clinched their championship, Hinch had advised one of his best friends in the organization, scout Chris Young (no relation to the player of the same name), to leave. Luhnow had forbid Young from joining the team in Los Angeles for the final two games of the World Series, fearing in part that Young—the only advance scout the Astros sent on the road to watch opponents in person—might conflict with what the regular advance team, Tom Koch-Weser's group, was advising. But Young's close relationship with Hinch appeared consequential as well.

"I know you've got A.J.'s ear," Luhnow once told Young. "If there's things that he's unhappy about or complaining about, man, I'd love you to reach out and call me and share them with me. We can make this thing work. We know he tells you things."

It took until August for Hinch to receive a four-year, $12 million deal running through 2022. The contract was only finalized because Crane stepped in. And for 2018, Luhnow made sure Hinch's coaching staff had more of the GM's own imprint, with a pair of coaches he brought into Houston's minor league system from St. Louis, Jeff Albert and Doug White, joining the major league group.

In many of the choices Luhnow made as the Astros became competitive, speculation was rampant internally that Luhnow was angling for credit. That part of his motive to have so much turnover was to become the last man standing, the glory predominantly his.

"Just remember: Jeff will turn over this whole place so that he's the only one who's been here, at some point," one high-ranking Astros employee told another.

The central fight still hung in the balance: Were the Astros still building on the vision that Luhnow and Sig Mejdal had built in St. Louis? Or was it time for the vision Mike Fast was pushing for?

Luhnow again arranged for McKinsey to proctor in 2018, this time with an engagement reviewing player development. But the 2017 recommendations were still being sorted through.

"One of the big reasons to bring McKinsey in was to tell Jeff if Sig or Fast were right," a member of the inner circle said. "And they sort of got the worst of both worlds out of that process, where McKinsey was honest enough with Jeff that Sig felt really undermined by the whole McKinsey report, but they sort of hedged enough that Mike didn't feel supported by it."

In a cost-saving measure, the Astros hadn't arranged for McKinsey to formally guide implementation.

"We bought the cheap version of McKinsey consult, so they came in, they parachuted in, they spewed out a ton of PDF files, and they left," one employee said. "And so, there was not a lot of guidance."

McKinsey's R&D recommendations were taken by the department to be mostly reasonable—and mostly in line with what Fast and Taubman were interested in pursuing. The problem was support. Luhnow, colleagues felt, cherry-picked what he wanted to iterate on.

For the draft model, McKinsey's recommendation was that the Astros had to develop software better. Because that's what the draft model essentially was: software.

McKinsey "had a very keen ear for what Jeff was going to be happy about hearing and not," an employee said. "Jeff hears this presentation, hears that he needs to fix X, Y, and Z in the draft model process to get what he wants, and goes, 'OK, fine.' But you know, there's parts of it that he didn't hear, and then Sig gets in his ear later.

"Sig I think felt very threatened by that, because he understood he thought how the draft model was put together then, and he wouldn't have near the same level of ability to understand or contribute to it if moved to this different world of software development."

One McKinsey consultant expressed shock to an Astros employee about the difference between what McKinsey had recommended and what the Astros actually put into action.

"McKinsey came in and told Jeff a lot of things that he probably needed to hear, but Jeff did not turn around and clean house afterwards," an employee said. "Like he would have if they were people that he had inherited [back in 2011]. He kept Sig around.

"Jeff was too slow to reward certain people, and to recognize them. I think part of that was personality, but I think part of that was paranoia."

One recommendation was a cliché: the Astros need to go to the cloud. "Yeah, everybody needs to go to the cloud," one front-office member said. "This is the sort of thing that businesspeople do where they just tell you the obvious. Because they have MBAs, you listen to them. It's on the magic quadrant now, so you do it."

McKinsey agreed that the department needed about five more people. But Luhnow thought that was too many. Instead, R&D could try to hire a software architect. One person, as a starting point.

Jim Crane had an idea. His primary business, Crane Worldwide Logistics, had some success in software development, enough so that Crane spun off the group into a company that became known as Modiant. Crane saw an opportunity for corporate synergy: Why not have Modiant handle the Astros' shift to the cloud?

"They're doing a very similar thing. They're trying to figure out how to take all these big-data sources and use 'em to make decisions and build a software infrastructure around that, and that would dovetail nicely with what you're doing," one Astros employee recalled of the message.

Crane was always game to leverage one of his businesses for the benefit of another. When he started to explore owning restaurants in Houston, he asked Taubman to review financials. But the latest crossover threw a wrench into a front office already fraying.

For one, the Astros were said to have paid a seven-figure sum to Modiant, which would have been enough for the Astros to go hire a handful of people of their own. Astros executives felt that Modiant preferred high-cost solutions, which had obvious benefits for Modiant. Astros employees also noted that the monies going to Modiant were going to a different Jim Crane–run business, effectively using the Astros to help fund that software start-up's operating capital.

In the end, Modiant was just another headache for Taubman and Fast. The financing aside, Modiant was missing deadlines. The R&D group was unsurprised because Modiant was barely off the ground.

"It was a fucking disaster," one Astros employee said. Yet Luhnow didn't seem to mind it. "Jeff supported Modiant because it didn't appear as an R&D expense. It appeared as an Astros expense. He celebrated his efficiency, and this was a way we could grow head count without having a head count appear on the budget. All else equal, he preferred it."

Modiant took up office space on the second floor at Minute Maid Park. The space where the Astros convened for the 2017 amateur draft was now Modiant's, which contributed to the 2018 draft being conducted from Florida. And even with a presence inside the building, the Astros tried to, and effectively did, keep Modiant mostly hidden from the public, save for a quick mention in the team's 2019 media guide.

They were always trying to keep initiatives quiet. Take the time that Taubman was testing the sweet spot of baseball bats, the place on the barrel where a hitter always wants to make contact with the ball. He was overseeing a study of the trampoline effect.

"Is this against the rules? No. Is this bad in any way? No," an employee remembered. "Literally they're just doing bat quality control. We couldn't put any information about it on our project management tracking software; the people working on it couldn't tell people what they were doing. They just would show up, you know, go downstairs in this secret room where they were testing the bats."

One McKinsey recommendation in R&D had been a monthly stakeholder meeting. As R&D was growing, Luhnow wanted more transparency from the department. The meetings devolved into Luhnow berating Fast in front of the core members of the front office over "anything and everything," one witness said. Another described the meetings as couples counseling.

In March 2018, Fast approached Taubman to say the status quo couldn't continue. His contract was up at the end of October, and he was nearing a breaking point: when the deal was up, he might be better off leaving.

Taubman told Fast to call Luhnow, who was on the road. They talked for an hour, an encouraging chat. But when Luhnow returned to Houston, he called Fast into his office to say that Mejdal wouldn't be going anywhere. He's my right-hand man, Luhnow said, and you'd better toe the line.

"One way in which it always worked, is that there were people who had worked together at the Cardinals and people who hadn't been at the Cardinals, and there was always this sense that if you weren't one of the people who had been at the Cardinals, you had to work harder and be better to get noticed," one Astros employee said. "Sig, Elias, to a certain extent. Oz [Ocampo]. Like it's funny, where the Astros had this reputation of being very cutthroat when it came to firing people, and it was often the case that this was true. I'm not trying to say that this was a fabrication. But at the same time, if you look at people like Oz and Sig who were sort of eased out of jobs, it's like there was an exception of being cutthroat if you used to work for the St. Louis Cardinals."

The Astros were again an excellent team in 2018. In the spring, Luhnow gave out the largest contract he ever did to an Astros player, extending Jose Altuve, the reigning American League MVP, on a deal worth $151 million. Altuve had not reached free agency, but had switched back to the agent he had parted ways with years earlier when he signed his first long-term contract, Scott Boras.

As with Hinch's extension, Crane got involved to make Altuve's happen, although it wasn't as acrimonious. In the early going, Crane and Luhnow had both been adamant that the Astros would spend at the right time, and by ensuring Altuve would stick around, they were making good. Crane and Luhnow still never wanted to use free agency as anything but a supplement, but the extension for a homegrown star, even at a team-friendly price, was encouraging.

"It comes down to a question of how much of your payroll do you want to tie up in one or two players, and when you have a lot of good young players coming through that you're going to have to pay through arbitration and potentially locking them up in free agency, you have to keep that in mind," Luhnow said about a month before Altuve's extension.

In the offseason, Luhnow had traded for a former first overall pick, Gerrit Cole, a power pitcher with major potential whom the Astros believed they could optimize if they got him into their clutches. They were correct. The right-hander struck out 177 batters in the first half of the season alone, when 200 strikeouts in an entire season is considered a high mark.

When the July trade deadline arrived, one deal that would have knocked everyone's socks off fell through. The Astros had agreed to acquire star outfielder Bryce Harper from the Washington Nationals, but Nationals ownership nixed it.

In a search for bullpen help, Luhnow was drawn to a pitcher he had tried to acquire the year before: Roberto Osuna of the Toronto Blue Jays. But the deliberation was vastly different this time.

In early May, Osuna had been arrested in Canada and charged with assaulting the mother of his three-year-old son. In late June, Commissioner Rob Manfred suspended Osuna for seventy-five games under MLB's collectively bargained domestic violence policy. It was then the second-longest suspension that had ever been issued under the policy—one that, remarkably, had not been instituted in the sport until 2015.

Canadian privacy laws have kept the details of Osuna's arrest out of public view. But, when Manfred announced the suspension, he did so noting the decision was made after a review of "all of the available evidence," and the length of the suspension Manfred settled on was a suggestion that the incident was particularly severe. Osuna did not appeal the suspension.

Suspensions, however, end, and Osuna's would wrap up August 4, just days after the July 31 trade deadline.

A little more than a month into his tenure as Astros president, Luhnow had heard that the Blue Jays were looking to move Osuna. He would be available to play for any team that was willing to take him in the stretch run of the season. Luhnow knew that nothing in the rules at the time barred a player who had been suspended under the domestic violence policy from playing in the postseason that same year. If acquired, Osuna could pitch in October.

Luhnow would come to view Osuna through one prism above all: playing ability. The twenty-three-year-old's talent throwing a baseball had not diminished. He struck out many batters and walked few. He also was early in his career, and therefore an inexpensive, controllable asset.

Beyond that, Luhnow looked at Osuna as a distressed asset. He could be snagged at a discount. Most teams wouldn't pursue a player who had just been charged with attacking a woman, limiting Osuna's market.

"Here was an inefficiency. And did domestic violence matter? Yes. I think Jeff really thought so," one Astros executive said. "But winning mattered more."

Before taking the idea to a larger group, Luhnow had Taubman do some due diligence. Quickly, Taubman was struck by two things: the length of Osuna's suspension and a sense that Osuna was not actually as attractive a player as other options available.

Taubman didn't want to go after him and started trying to steer Luhnow to other relievers available, Ryan Pressly among them. Luhnow dropped the topic for about a week before hearing that the parent company of the Blue Jays, Rogers Communications, was said to be forcing the Blue Jays to either trade or release Osuna.

"So Jeff was like, 'We can get this guy cheap, we need to get him,'" one colleague said.

The commissioner's office was said to be clear in its communication with Taubman: this is a guy to stay away from. When Luhnow got that message, he decided to bring it to the larger group.

The Astros front office would have roundtable discussions at the trade deadline, blocking off a conference room for the final week or so before July 31. The core group advising Luhnow at the deadline was Taubman, Mike Fast, Kevin Goldstein, Matt Hogan, and Will Sharp, a group that discussed Osuna multiple times and saw Goldstein and Fast as the two most opposed.

"The first time he brought it up, I remember most people were silent, because they were almost afraid to talk," one witness said. When Luhnow left the room, the opposition was clear. More meetings took place.

"Jeff consistently got back from the group that we did not want this guy, and yet, Jeff would ask for more and more due diligence on it from various people," one colleague said. "Eventually Jeff got tired from getting feedback from the rest of the team, so he cut everybody out of the conversation."

A few days shy of the deadline, the Astros did pull off a deal for a reliever: Pressly. Now they had a shiny new bullpen piece, and Taubman felt Pressly's arrival should have been enough.

Luhnow kept talking to Blue Jays general manager Ross Atkins on his own. Normally Luhnow had Taubman sit in on phone calls with opposing GMs, but not these—not for a time. Eventually Luhnow told Taubman he wanted to get a deal for Osuna done.

Taubman wasn't up in arms on moral grounds alone, but an overall sense that the move was irrational, as well. One final war room discussion approached.

Luhnow asked the group to grade the different iterations of an Osuna trade, how they would vote on one version of the deal versus another. Goldstein rated everything the lowest score.

"I voted zero on any Osuna trade proposal, be it like a real baseball deal for players, or for a bag of balls, I was just a dead zero on it. And spoke up loudly about it," Goldstein said in 2021. "At one point, Jeff said to me, 'You know, I'm not asking you for your moral opinion. I'm asking you for your baseball opinion.' And I said, 'This is my baseball opinion. I think he's bad for the team and bad for the clubhouse. I think it sets a bad vibe overall and that actually, this is a baseball decision.' Not completely, but there's certainly a baseball aspect to it."

Luhnow's reply to Goldstein stood out to another onlooker as particularly condescending, as though he really were saying, "I don't want your hipster liberal opinion."

When Goldstein explained his point—that, if Luhnow must view through a baseball lens, Goldstein felt it was bad for the team—

Luhnow's response came off as "Well, whatever, fuck that," the witness said.

Fast, meanwhile, could not believe Osuna was even up for discussion. He appeared to be beside himself. But he was worn-out from the R&D update meetings and everything else unfolding in the front office, shell-shocked. He didn't say much.

"Basically clammed up," one friend said. "Sort of at his wits' end."

Talking to colleagues outside of the trade-deadline war room, Fast was livid: What the fuck are we doing here? What the hell are we thinking?

"It was pretty clear that no one really supported this," an executive recalled. "Everyone was a no or a soft no."

The trade was announced on July 30. "Jeff had agreed to a trade where Jeff ousted his whole decision-making group there because he didn't like what they had to say," one member of the inner circle said.

Goldstein made clear he thought it was the wrong move.

"He's a domestic abuser," Goldstein said in 2021. "I don't think someone like that should still be in baseball. It's not hard."

Why didn't Luhnow see it the same way?

"It's not like Roberto Osuna is the first," Goldstein said. "And winning is a bottom line, and it's something that not just Jeff, but a lot of people in this industry only care about, anything else be damned. And you know, the things people look aside for if a player is really talented is—Osuna's not the only one. There's several others, and a lot of them are still playing."

Other players in the sport have indeed been suspended for domestic violence, and the sport's rules allow for players to eventually return, which some people find abhorrent. Which actions should merit second chances in baseball and what form and length of rehabilitation are appropriate is not an irrelevant discussion—but it is one that could be leveraged. Publicly, Luhnow would lean heavily on a belief that Osuna deserved a second chance.

"I think that one of the reasons I personally supported this deal was, we have an environment here that will allow Roberto to succeed, and I'm not just talking about our clubhouse," Luhnow said shortly after the trade, via the *Houston Chronicle*. "I also think the city of Houston, the fact that I was born and raised in Mexico—I understand the Mexican culture, [Osuna] and I can speak in Spanish anytime—and Houston is a predominantly Mexican, Hispanic town in terms of the demographics. I think that also provides opportunities for Roberto down the road. There's going to be some positives that come out of this situation."

Even if he was sincere, Luhnow was still, in service of a baseball team, attempting to squeeze value out of the impact of a horrible act. From the fallout of an allegation of violence, Luhnow had seen opportunity.

In the war room, Luhnow was far and away the top dog. The front office he had built was young; his lieutenants' only experience working for a team had been under his guide. There was no veteran of twenty or thirty years who had been around the block.

"We didn't have a lot of experienced people at the Astros," an executive said. "I think there's a number of reasons for that, some of them good, some of them bad."

A.J. Hinch directly addressed the Astros clubhouse after the trade, and within a few days, Crane and Luhnow spoke to the team as well. But regardless of whether the concerns of Osuna's new teammates were, in fact, adequately addressed, the Astros' efforts to prepare the rest of the company were lacking.

Astros workers spoke of emotional devastation immediately following the trade, both for themselves and for others inside the organization. For the message Osuna's arrival sent to the team's own employees—and specifically women—about domestic violence. Employees saw no significant resources allocated to dealing with internal concerns, no meaningful action addressing the impact on others inside Minute Maid Park who had to newly reckon with the core values of their workplace. But some posters about domestic violence were put up.

Luhnow, after speaking to the media, took one of his trips to Mexico, leaving Taubman as the lead representative of baseball operations. Taubman was upset that Luhnow had left him alone. Taubman addressed staff at an internal town hall meeting, and also spoke one-on-one with a few women who worked in baseball operations. But Taubman wasn't trained for such conversations, and a more comprehensive system of support was not in place. Human resources did make some overtures, offering employees an opportunity to talk, but it felt hollow to people on the ground.

The Astros' president, Reid Ryan, as well as Matt Brand, senior vice president of corporate partnerships, were said to be looking for Luhnow while he was away and were "amazed that he was nowhere to be found, and they were pissed they were not consulted in the decision," a colleague said.

Typically, business-side executives were not welcome in Luhnow's baseball decisions, particularly not Ryan. But with such a massive decision, "you can make an argument that Reid should have been involved," a baseball-side employee said.

Where was the owner? Although hands-off, Crane was also made aware of every significant baseball move.

"Jim gave him permission to make this deal, and that was upsetting as well," an executive said. "Jim bears some responsibility for that."

Before or even after the trade, Crane and Luhnow could have carved out more time to plan to make sure women and the overall staff at Minute Maid Park received enough support. What burned the owner and the GM, many times, were not so much the things they valued, as what they did not.

In September, Canadian authorities dropped charges against Osuna. The woman Osuna allegedly attacked had returned to Mexico following the assault, and a Canadian prosecutor said the complainant had made it clear to authorities that she would not return to Toronto to testify against Osuna, reported Colin Perkel of the Canadian Press. Osuna agreed to stay away from the woman for a year and to undergo counseling.

But for the first time since the Astros won the World Series, the public and the industry were paying extra attention to how Luhnow and Crane were operating. Reverberations were felt internally, too.

"It was just divided," one Astros employee said. "It was divided upstairs, it was divided in the fan base. Divisive. It created another checkmark in the industry. Like, 'Of course the Astros did it.' That type of shit."

Taubman felt his boss had ignored him. Fast, meanwhile, had his final confirmation: he did not want to work for Luhnow anymore.

In many ways, Fast knew as much prior to the trade. Yet, before Luhnow swung that deal, Fast occasionally wondered if he was overreacting. He would remember the cool things that the Astros had accomplished and the ways in which he enjoyed the innovation.

It wasn't worth it any longer. In mid-September, three weeks before the Astros would enter the postseason as the reigning champions, Fast was offered a new contract. He would not accept, and left the only major league organization he'd known.

"The Osuna trade was the nail in the coffin," a colleague said. "But there was a lot of bad blood leading up to that point."

# 15

# A LION AND A DEER

THE COMMISSIONER'S OFFICE HAD TRIED TO BEEF UP ITS ELECTRONIC sign-stealing rules for 2018. A year earlier, the rules were seven paragraphs long. Now MLB had grown them to three pages, and had explicitly outlawed, in bold letters, using video rooms to steal signs—be it via the baserunner method or otherwise.

But it's one thing to make a rule, another to enforce it. During the 2018 regular season, MLB didn't have any personnel permanently assigned to watch over team video rooms. A security agent was supposed to occasionally stop in, but that wasn't going to stop a team bent on cheating.

To this point, the public's understanding of sign-stealing was limited to the Apple Watch scandal. What the Astros had done the year before was still a secret. But many teams, particularly the top contenders, had grown highly suspicious of one another. In some cases, those suspicions grew into paranoia. But there was a kernel of truth, too, even if few in the sport knew as much definitively.

The Astros had moved their video room closer to the dugout during the 2017 playoffs, and a similar relocation was permanent for 2018. MLB blessed such a move for the Astros and other teams, a decision that showed Rob Manfred and MLB still didn't grasp the extent of the problem.

Tom Koch-Weser had told Luhnow that moving the video room

"would not be an issue because" it was "moving closer to the dug-out, and the Astros' video room staff could relay sign information in-person," according to the account Koch-Weser gave to MLB. Luhnow denied that account.

The Astros' garbage-can system, the direct relay of signs from the tunnel to hitters, did not continue into 2018, league investigators would eventually find. But the Astros were still using the baserunner system in 2018.

They weren't alone. A loaded Red Sox team, fresh off their 2017 fine from the Apple Watch scandal and with new manager Alex Cora at the helm, were right back at it in 2018, decoding signs in the video room.

The Sox effectively had two video rooms at home games: one right near the dugout, the formal video room, and one in an upstairs area, an auxiliary station. Around their new team, Cora and Craig Bjornson—the former Astros bullpen coach who took the same role in Boston—would occasionally talk about the Astros' sign-stealing from 2017, even brag, sometimes in a late-night setting. "Especially when they started drinking," a member of the Red Sox said.

"We stole that fucking World Series," Cora would say, and his comments would shock some people.

"We knew the Astros did [steal signs]," another member of the Red Sox said, "because Alex Cora told us. He said that when they played the Dodgers, 'We already knew what everybody was throwing before we even got on base. We didn't have to get on base.' And everybody was like, 'What the hell does that mean?'"

Some teams knew what others had been up to in the past, and some didn't. But the finger-pointing was growing extreme. The Red Sox were convinced that the Yankees, who had been no strangers to the baserunner method in years past, were cheating in 2018 after a game in May when the Yankees came back to beat the Sox' best relief pitcher, Craig Kimbrel.

Some people in the sport started looking into the most conspiratorial suspicions, all theoretically possible: What's in this guy's back pocket? What about that wrist guard? Could they have a wearable device tucked somewhere on their body to receive a signal of what pitch was coming? Allegations were flying inside various clubhouses, particularly among contenders.

The Astros had a mind to fend for themselves through an informal counterespionage operation. Throughout the 2018 season, they took steps to ensure other teams weren't cheating against them. Luhnow was "more into counterintelligence than he'll ever care to admit," a colleague said.

Tom Koch-Weser would use the camera angles he could access to scan center field at road ballparks, to see where the opposition might have a camera placed. Front-office members traveling with the team would sometimes peek around in person. Taubman, for example, might try to see if there were any flashing lights that looked coordinated.

When the Astros headed to Yankee Stadium in late May, they arrived with a belief that they knew what the Yankees were up to.

Cora's replacement as bench coach in Houston, Joe Espada, had been a Yankees coach from 2015 to 2017. Espada, one Astros employee said, had alerted multiple Astros officials, including Luhnow, "that when he was with the Yankees the year prior, they had a sign-stealing operation in center field." Espada is said to have pointed out, too, where the alleged setup was, in a camera well in center field. A person manning the camera allegedly would be texting the signs to the clubhouse.

Another member of the team said they were not aware of the tip about the Yankees originating with Espada, nor did they think the tip was presented firmly. By that person's account, the Astros merely had intel that suggested the Yankees had scouting cameras that had at least the potential to be used improperly.

Luhnow and Taubman were both on the trip to New York. Taubman, who grew up on Long Island, was sitting with his family when Luhnow summoned him and told Taubman he should go check out center field. Taubman went and found a young Yankees employee working an expensive high-speed camera, far more costly than the Edgertronics the Astros used.

Taubman believed the camera was fixed on the catcher's mitt. He reported back to Luhnow, who said he was going to call MLB.

Taubman, too, made calls, trying to get in touch with a pair of Yankees executives.

Taubman started to ask questions of the employee working the camera and was ignored. He then went into the camera well and stood next to the employee, who was still operating it.

"Hey, man, I do what I'm told," the employee said.

Taubman was recording the incident, video that he is said to have provided to MLB.

Yankees management was livid over Taubman's intrusion. Taubman wasn't alone in the encounter: he had another Astros employee with him in center field, by the name of Kyle McLaughlin. A player-autograph hunter on the side, McLaughlin first joined the Astros as an intern after caddying at Jim Crane's golf course in Florida.

The Astros' head of security was in tow, too.

"It was a whole tag team," a Yankees official later said. "[McLaughlin] was on his belly taking pictures, and then Brandon went into a secured area, was very aggressive, they just didn't give a shit. They blew right by security, they were very rude to people, it was unbelievable, making allegations."

Taubman didn't have much trouble going from zero to irate, but he also felt, in the moment, that he was just following Luhnow's orders, and that the Yankees were painting him unfairly.

After the game, the commissioner himself was on a conference call with the two teams. Luhnow and Taubman sat on the call from Hinch's office. MLB determined the Yankees had received permission from MLB to use and install the camera for review after games, not in-game.

Starting in 2018, the commissioner's office demanded every team catalog and submit the "scouting" cameras they had established around their stadiums. The Dodgers, for example, had two cameras in center field going to the catcher, an official with knowledge of the list said that year. "Clubs have between twenty and forty of their so-called scouting cameras," the person said. "You can't use it during the game to steal signs, but you can use it after the game for whatever purpose you want." The Astros were said to have closer to forty scouting cameras in their park.

But of course, having permission to use a camera for one purpose does not mean it couldn't be used for another. Nonetheless, MLB was convinced the Yankees had done no wrong. Over time, the Astros brain trust came to feel MLB was protecting the Yankees.

The Yankees claimed the camera was not fixed on the catcher's signs, but on the pitcher's release point, and that the catcher just happened to be in the line of sight. Taubman believed his video showed otherwise.

The incident didn't go public right away, though.

Although MLB was occasionally monitoring the video rooms during the 2018 regular season, it was easy enough for teams to use the video room to gain signs when the security agent was not around. All that was needed was someone to serve as a lookout.

In one of two meetings he had with Jeff Luhnow late in the year, Tom Koch-Weser claimed he told the GM he did not trust Oz Ocampo in his job as watchman.

Ocampo, removed by Luhnow as the Astros director of international scouting, was now a special assistant and the team interpreter. But he was also charged with keeping an eye out for the security agent during games. Koch-Weser told investigators that "Ocampo's failure to look out for the video room monitor almost resulted in them being caught deciphering signs in the video room."

Koch-Weser also told MLB that Luhnow "did not question why a 'lookout' would be needed or otherwise respond," and that it was clear Luhnow "knew the Astros had attempted to employ the Baserunner System during the 2018 season."

Ocampo and colleague Antonio Padilla both confirmed to MLB that Ocampo had served as a lookout in 2018. Luhnow told investigators he recalled "discussing Ocampo not being 'that helpful' . . . and remembered that Koch-Weser 'did not think [Ocampo] was a great worker.'" But, as Luhnow did with any allegation that would imply he knew the Astros were cheating, he told MLB he was "not aware of this specific complaint or of the 'lookout' expectation of Ocampo."

At the end of 2018, Koch-Weser was up for a contract discussion. Before an October meeting with Luhnow, he outlined in the messaging service Slack his arguments for an extension. He included the term "dark arts" and wrote: "Lastly, I know the secrets that made us a championship team, some of which he['}d definitely feel a lot safer if they were kept in-house."

Later, Manfred would write to Luhnow: "Koch-Weser told my investigators that he covered all of the points in his outline while meeting with you, and that he used either the term 'dark arts' or 'codebreaking' in touting his sign-stealing efforts for the Astros. You acknowledged that the two of you discussed other items in this outline, but denied Koch-Weser referenced the 'dark arts,' Codebreaker, or made a 'threat' regarding keeping the secrets."

O

The 2018 postseason included the Astros, Red Sox, Yankees, and Dodgers once again. If any team had mind to continue to try to cheat, it would have been difficult to pull off with frequent success, unless they were doing something particularly well concealed. For the first time in the sport's history, MLB was instituting full-time in-person monitoring of the video rooms, swarming the playoff games with warm bodies to discourage cheating.

Teams in the postseason, too, were all well versed in changing their signs in self-defense.

"You got a bunch of people who are really good at cheating and everybody knows that each other's doing it," said one person with the 2018 Red Sox. "It's really hard for anybody to get away with it at that point. . . . If you get a lion and a deer, then the lion can really take advantage of the deer. So there's a lot of deers out there that weren't paying attention throughout the season. In the playoffs, now you're going against a lion."

A member of the 2017 Astros, pitcher Mike Fiers, had played at least a small role in MLB's decision to beef up security. Fiers had been a member of the Detroit Tigers for the first half of the 2018 season, before being traded to the Oakland Athletics. He warned both his teams what the Astros were up to, and word got back to the Astros that Fiers was raising red flags.

"I told the teams I was on, I didn't know how far the rules went with MLB, but I knew they [the Astros] were up to date if not beyond. I had to let my team know so that we were prepared when we went to go play them at Minute Maid," Fiers said in 2019. "They [Astros personnel] all got pissed at me. The word got out. But it's just kind of bullshit because that's not baseball. That's not playing the game the right way. That's pretty much my side of it.

"As a pitcher, you have no control over stuff like that, other than going there with multiple signs and starting from pitch one. If MLB wants to have quicker games, good game flow, you can't do that when teams are doing that at home."

Before the postseason, Oakland A's general manager David Forst spoke with an official in the commissioner's office, Peter Woodfork, about what the A's had been told the Astros were up to. Forst and Woodfork had known each other since their shared playing days at Harvard, and the league office did not consider the report to be a formal complaint, a person with knowledge of the league's thinking said.

The manager of the A's, Bob Melvin, coincidentally was the manager who was fired in Arizona and replaced by Hinch a decade earlier. Melvin phoned Hinch after a 2018 regular-season game, after one of the two times the Astros pounced all over Oakland pitcher Brett Anderson, poking around on what the Astros were up to. Hinch denied wrongdoing.

The commissioner's office has long worked to keep the focus of the postseason on the field, so the league did not announce all of its increased security presence in a formal press release—not until it had to. Not until the Astros were smack dab in the middle of a controversy during the middle of the postseason.

Cleveland, the Astros' first-round opponent, caught Kyle McLaughlin around their dugout area, taking pictures.

The Astros had long thought the Indians were up to something, in part because one of their most prominent voices believed as much and were trying to figure out what. When Justin Verlander arrived in Houston in 2017 and learned of the garbage-can scheme, he had mentioned his suspicion of Cleveland.

Of all the members of the Astros' clubhouse, Verlander was perhaps the most keen on conspiracy theories. Now, a year later, he told the front office before a game what he suspected: In center field in

Cleveland, several trees are dotted around the park. "He was claiming the groundskeeper had a string that was attached to a tree in center field," an Astros employee said. The groundskeeper, allegedly, was pulling on the string or a rope to move the tree. That movement, supposedly, would indicate what pitch was coming.

For the postseason, Luhnow and his two assistant general managers, Taubman and Mike Elias, were all on hand, and the group went out to do recon, an Astros executive said. The front office seemed to come to the conclusion that the string setup had something to do with fireworks that would occasionally be set off at the stadium. Cleveland, at one point, became aware that at least Elias had been snooping around.

During the Cleveland series, pitching coach Brent Strom and some of the advance staff were concerned about televisions that were in a seating area behind home plate, but visible from the field of play. The Astros had noticed the TVs when they played in Cleveland during the regular season. Come the postseason, the Astros complained to MLB, but it didn't go anywhere.

The Astros advanced to the next round, where they met Alex Cora's Red Sox. Cleveland tipped off the Sox about McLaughlin's snooping, and sure enough, Boston caught McLaughlin again. This time the whole affair went public, including the incident from Yankee Stadium in May.

In the middle of the postseason, the commissioner's office briefly investigated the Astros and concluded that McLaughlin had done what the Astros said he had: counterespionage, rather than proactively stealing signs himself. MLB didn't punish the team.

The irony of the Astros taking up counterespionage efforts was not lost inside Minute Maid Park. Wasn't that what Chris Correa, the Cardinals executive who went to prison, had said he was doing?

"Jeff said we were playing defense, not offense," a member of the Astros said. "That's just a weak, Chris Correa approach."

MLB had leads about the Astros beyond McLaughlin that it could have explored, but ever protective of its postseason, the commissioner's office had no mind to look any deeper. During the ALCS, a top official at the commissioner's office came to Boston and told Luhnow, in a suite at Fenway Park, that MLB had heard of allegations the Astros had a system involving the banging of trash cans. Luhnow denied it to that official. It was "ridiculous," he said.

During the same postseason, one colleague claimed that Luhnow directly acknowledged that he knew the Astros had carried out a sign-stealing operation involving the trash can, a person with knowledge of that conversation said.

"It's real," Luhnow allegedly told that colleague.

Publicly, Luhnow has maintained he did not know at all until more than a year later.

○

Their usually explosive offense quiet, the Astros lost in the ALCS to Cora's Red Sox. MLB during the series had tried to see if Cora would spill any information on the Astros, but he stayed quiet. Cora and the Red Sox went on to win the 2018 World Series, defeating the Dodgers and making Cora a champion for a second straight year.

When MLB did lengthier investigations into the Astros and Red Sox a couple of years later, investigators determined that both teams' baserunner sign-stealing schemes ended prior to the 2018 playoffs. That, in other words, their postseason runs were clean.

"At some point during the 2018 season, the Astros stopped using the replay review room to decode signs because the players no longer believed it was effective," Manfred wrote. "The investigation did not reveal any attempt by the Astros to utilize electronic equipment to decode and transmit signs in the 2018 Postseason."

Would the schemes really just stop—and if so, fully stop?

"I basically think that it wasn't working anymore," an Astros employee said, echoing others. "That MLB put in safeguards on the video system—maybe on the basis of complaints about the sign-stealing from other teams about the Astros—that made the sign-stealing difficult to achieve moving forward. So no one stopped out of the goodness of their heart. They stopped because they couldn't do it successfully anymore."

Early in 2018, the Astros front office fielded a bunch of complaints from the dugout. The R&D team had built a tool that predicted the probability of a pitch being called a ball or a strike based on the count and the batter's height. Players had access to that tool in-game, and it was legal. The front office thought it was helping the players make better swing decisions: "'Yeah, that was probably a strike, you should have swung at it,' or 'That was probably going to be called a ball, you should have laid off.' That was our intention behind relaying that information to the players."

But the access to in-game video tools was starting to become a problem in a different way, and the team was at least mildly incentivized to cut back. Players were occasionally getting too wrapped up in the video. Marwin Gonzalez "in particular would complain to the umps that they had called pitches incorrectly because the TrackMan data said otherwise. And so we had to remove that from the in-game feedback," one Astros employee said. It's not a good thing for players to be constantly barking at umpires. "I thought about that story a lot when the sign-stealing stuff came out, just the level of stuff the players had access to during games."

Not everyone with the Dodgers believed the Red Sox stopped come the 2018 postseason. The Red Sox, likewise, believed the Dodgers were up to no good.

"The Dodgers have always been the thing that bothers me the most," a member of the Red Sox said. "Because they're the biggest cheaters in the whole fucking industry. . . . They were doing it against us in the '18 World Series. They got caught by Major League Baseball and Major League Baseball did nothing."

The story goes that Dodgers hitter Joc Pederson ran into the visiting video area at Fenway Park where teammate Chase Utley was, as well as one of MLB's officials.

"Hey, did you get his signs yet?" Pederson is said to have asked.

"And they're just like, 'Fuck—fucking idiot,'" a Red Sox source said of the league official's response. "Apparently, nothing is done by MLB except they say, 'Stop doing that shit, don't do that shit.' Then they go over to the Red Sox clubhouse to [video operator J. T. Watkins], and they're like proactively scolding him, making sure he doesn't do that.

"And he turns to the guy and says, 'Oh, you caught Chase Utley doing shit?'"

Watkins didn't get a response back.

"He caught them off guard because he called them out," the Red Sox source said. "I know those motherfuckers were doing shit."

One rival general manager recommended looking at the Astros' performance with a runner in scoring position—when a runner was on second or third base. The 2017 Astros led the majors during the regular season with a .294 average with runners in scoring position, and were second with a .282 average in that scenario when there were two outs.

In that vein: Through 2022, no team had ever produced a better batting average with runners in scoring position and two outs in the World Series than the 2018 Red Sox, at .471. No team had ever had a higher on-base percentage in that scenario, either, than their .609. Only one team had recorded a higher slugging percentage than their .882.

Say the Astros decoded signs in the video room during games through all of 2018, not just part of it, or beyond. Even in that case, the most offensive, known form of electronic sign-stealing they undertook would still have been behind them: the camera and garbage-can scheme.

# 16

# PRESSURE MACHINE

BY THE END OF 2018, MIKE FAST WASN'T THE ONLY TOP MEMBER OF THE Astros' front office out the door.

The other Mike, Mike Elias, one of Luhnow's first hires in Houston and a St. Louis defector, was an important figure, but he also wasn't in the thick of everything. He was in his own silo in amateur scouting, often out on the road. He also was more moderate than Fast or Brandon Taubman. He wasn't the tip of the spear driving progress.

In his own way, Elias was ready to get out. The front-office conflicts and drama-filled meetings were getting to him. He and Taubman were not mortal enemies, but Taubman was committed to his technical scouting plan. After implementing it in pro scouting, amateur and international scouting were the next steps. Those were Elias's departments, and the two already clashed on budgets.

Elias was often in lockstep with Luhnow. Both were Donald Trump supporters, and they would rag on Taubman for backing Bernie Sanders. Luhnow and Elias, too, went on a diet that almost exclusively involved meat. Elias might call Taubman a pussy for eating vegetables, one employee recalled. "Jeff would love it, so Mike would always do it."

Elias was keen to keep costs down, just as Luhnow was. The Astros had begun offering club option years in contracts not only to players, but to their own employees, including scouts. When he left the Astros in 2017, Alex Jacobs had an offer from Elias to stay for one year, plus an additional club option for another year, with a $10,000 buyout.

"If you're giving me more money, sure, but this makes no sense to take these club options that they can exercise at a discount. What they do it for is because it keeps you in there, it keeps you with them," Jacobs said. "That's not how you treat people. You give them what they deserve; you don't try to freaking cut corners. You don't make your pitching coach cry."

(Brent Strom, the Astros' pitching coach, was said to have had a difficult negotiation at one point, separate of Elias, that left him in tears.)

"We had a sense that we would unwind the scouting team over the course of time, but it was Elias that did all of those contracts," one Astros employee said. Elias, they said, "was responsible for keeping salaries as suppressed as possible across the departments he ran."

While Fast's exit was primarily motivated by conflict with Luhnow and morality, Elias had an offer he couldn't refuse: the Baltimore Orioles wanted to make him a general manager. In November 2018, he went off to run his own team, just as David Stearns once had. But Elias would take another of Luhnow's right-hand men with him: Sig Mejdal.

The one-two punch of Luhnow and Mejdal, the nerdy outsiders who came together thirteen years earlier in St. Louis, was no more. Luhnow's good-bye to one of his best friends was unceremonious.

Publicly, the move was painted as Mejdal's choice.

"It was me asking for some time to explore other opportunities," Mejdal told MLB.com at the time. "Jeff is an amazing manager and always been supportive of me and was again in this case."

The Astros were no longer a start-up. Mejdal hadn't lived in Houston full-time for a number of years, and he ultimately wasn't as happy as he could be, or had been. In his eyes, the team was winning 100 games, but he didn't have 100 units of joy. He was an agent of change, and again wanted to be part of a nascent process, which he could be in Baltimore.

Mejdal knew, too, that his technical skills were dwindling relative to the up-and-coming analysts. In Houston, it had been three years since he had run decision sciences. Discussing in-game moves with A.J. Hinch felt new for a time, but undergoing another rebuild in Baltimore, where the Orioles were many years behind the Astros in innovation, would better ignite the fire.

Yet Mejdal's decision to leave was at best, mutual, and at worst, primarily Luhnow's. "Sig was not offered a contract renewal," an Astros executive said, echoing others. "He did not choose to leave."

"I want to point this out about Sig: where like half of the people he had in his R&D department left baseball," a colleague said, exaggerating. "Which is weird."

Notably, Mejdal, who was always unflinchingly loyal to Luhnow, had also been Houston's most highly publicized front-office figure besides the GM himself.

"He never moved towards embracing bigger data," an Astros employee said. "Because he just didn't have the technical chops to analyze bigger data. . . . And that's sort of the whole big thing about the Astros, is that the public narrative about them was shaped by Sig for so long, because Sig was the guy that Jeff let talk to the press. But Jeff didn't do that because Sig was the person that was leading the charge. Jeff did that because he wasn't."

Luhnow, the theory went, would not want someone like Taubman or Fast to garner a ton of press, because it would make them a flight risk.

Most colleagues liked Mejdal, but one cracked a joke. It had been shocking, years earlier, when Chris Correa had hacked into the Astros' systems and Mejdal's digital accounts. The reaction was natural: Oh my God, how could this happen? And yet, by the time Mejdal left, "I don't think I'd break a federal law to get back at Sig, but, you know, I understand."

A year and a half after McKinsey & Company arrived in 2017 and tried to sort out the future of the Astros' draft model and research and development team, the two principals at the heart of the dispute—Fast and Mejdal—were both gone.

"The wheels started to come off," an employee said. "I had thought that Mike [Fast's] leaving was a wake-up call for them, they said Mike's leaving was a wake-up call for them, and then like, it was very fast how things reverted."

Add in Elias's departure and one executive would be more important than ever to the future of the Astros: Brandon Taubman.

Although he had a newborn baby at home, Taubman was spending all of his time at the ballpark instead. Taubman's ego was among those that had been inflated by the 2017 World Series. But he also felt insecure. He was growing more aggressive in pushing the initiatives he felt were best for the Astros, and more careless in how he approached people.

"You can tell he wanted to be promoted. You can tell Jeff was keeping him in his place for whatever reason," said Jacobs. "I think all he wanted was the assistant general manager's title, and this was right after David left. And I had to tell him, 'Dude, you're what, thirty years old, thirty-one, like it's going to happen. It's inevitable. Just be patient.'"

○

Colin Wyers, Fast's right-hand man, would stick around until later in 2019, but he, too, would leave, in part because he was at his wits' end with the Modiant experiment.

In April 2019, Wyers was among a group sitting with Jeff Luhnow in the GM's box during a game, discussing the departed. Luhnow asked Wyers about his pal Fast, and Wyers asked about Luhnow's good friends Mejdal and Elias. It was awkward, because it appeared Luhnow was barely talking to Mejdal, "but Jeff didn't want to come out and say that," a witness said.

Meanwhile, Taubman was on his laptop, pounding away on a study. Luhnow had a rule that executives in the suite were not supposed to have their laptop out during games—foul balls were known to fly into the suite at dangerous speeds—and Luhnow told Taubman to put it away, to watch the game. Taubman blew him off.

"I gotta do stuff to keep this team pushing forward," Taubman said. That sentiment left a sense of puzzlement in the room: What could Taubman possibly do on that laptop that very night that would meaningfully push the Astros forward?

Taubman was becoming even more obsessive about work, about innovation, about winning, and pushing others to act similarly. Late in 2018, Luhnow finally granted Taubman the title he had clearly risen to: assistant general manager. But so much of the Astros' day-to-day operations had fallen to Taubman by then, particularly after Luhnow had been bumped up to president of baseball operations, that Taubman arguably was already operating in an even greater role.

"Brandon was, I think, literally functioning as the general manager of the Houston Astros," a colleague said. "As soon as Jeff got his president contract [in 2018], he seemed to recede from things a lot. But at the same time he was very, very stingy on giving Brandon promotions to match his title to the level of his responsibility he was given. And I'm not saying that any of that justifies the way Brandon behaved toward people. But it's my opinion that that contributed to how Brandon behaved. That he was basically, constantly feeling underappreciated and having to earn things, that he had [done] all the work for them, but [received] none of the prestige. When the Orioles interviewed Elias and not him for the GM job, I think that was a real blow to Brandon's ego.

"Brandon has been the person actually doing an AGM's job and Elias has just been running the draft and blowing everything else off, and he's the one who goes to Baltimore."

Luhnow was adept at creating a sense of internal competition in Houston, and a sense, too, that nothing was ever good enough.

"There was no sense of Jeff noticing," another employee said. "The examples of Kevin [Goldstein] and Oz [Ocampo] being pushed out and relegated to lower positions. Sig Mejdal, who you can argue is responsible for all of Jeff's success in St. Louis and early success with the Astros, same thing. His role is marginalized and pushed out the door, and Jeff overturned eighty percent of player development. It was this, I guess, worry whether you'd be employed by the team next year, and what you had to do to survive. . . . He knew how to squeeze the most out of people."

In reality, neither Taubman nor the Astros were actually behind.

All the video the Astros were collecting with Edgertronic cameras—seven of them per stadium in the majors and minors—was folding into projects that were cause for excitement at Minute Maid Park. Taubman was leading the charge, continuing to move in the direction he and Fast had set.

The Astros were no longer just taping players with their Edgertronic cameras and reviewing footage after the fact. They were systematically capturing video in standardized ways and from fixed points. That allowed the team to start doing biomechanics analysis, through a branch of artificial intelligence known as computer vision: training computers to interpret images.

A picture is made of thousands of pixels, and each pixel ranges in color. Each color can be assigned a numerical value: pitch black is 100, pure white is 1, and every other shade in between is a different number.

"So imagine now you have a picture, you have a thousand pixels and for each of those thousand pixels, you have a number describing the shade," an Astros employee explained. "Now what you can do is say, OK, I'm going to take a second picture of the same thing just one second later in time. And I can do the exact same thing, assign a numerical value to each of the values in that picture. And what computer vision is doing is calculating or interpreting the change in pixelation from frame to frame. So now if I have a thousand frames per second, or a thousand pictures, and I know what the change in numerical values are that correspond to each pixel in each frame, I can begin to understand movement in space.

"The movement I'm quantifying is in two dimensions. It's a flat photo. But if I have lots of these cameras, positioned from different angles focused on the same point in space, and I can observe what the changes are from two dimensions from multiple points in space, then I can extrapolate to a 3-D rendering."

The idea was to build a model to interpret the video the Astros were capturing. Taubman and his group wanted to then tie the video back to the pitch-by-pitch data. What could be learned from the result of the pitch when it's linked to its movement?

"These technologies don't always talk to each other, so you have to build systems so that they talk to each other," an employee said. "So now you're talking about linking the video to the events data:

strikeout, pop-up, whatever, and you're also talking about mapping it back to TrackMan, the pitch-level data. And so that was part of the technology challenge. . . . How do we collate all these data sources such that we could do legitimate research and figure out what the hell's going on, and what attributes of a player's motion or whatever actually lead to performance?"

The Astros had started down this road in 2017. That year, they had seventy Edgertronic cameras in the organization, at a cost of more than $350,000. But it wasn't until 2018 and 2019 that their computer-vision capabilities started to become robust. It's a very powerful tool, to be able to track and quantify so many different actions or movements on a baseball field.

"If you could track basically anything that's happening on the field, you could do lots of different things with that data," one executive said.

One Astros employee said the extent of what the Astros could attempt to study with that video capability would inherently be controversial. They declined to elaborate, but the team was loading up on a huge amount of information about players. Questions of whom such data belongs to—what rights do players have to it?—and how that information can be weaponized by a team, in arbitration or otherwise, linger across the sport.

The Astros were also wading into machine learning in their modeling efforts. Machine learning is basically the automation, or partial automation, of statistical modeling. "Machine learning being more large-scale black-box techniques," an R&D specialist with another team explained. "When you use some of these machine learning approaches, you can sort of quickly get to reasonably good answers."

While it was theoretically possible, there's no evidence the Astros employed machine learning to help them steal signs. "People have assumed, people have written that we used it to find pitch tipping, which isn't true," a member of the Astros said. "We talked about that, we never really figured out how to do that."

The Astros continued to experiment with wearable technology: a wearable vest that tracked players' kinematic movements, called K-Vest;

and 4D Motion, a motion-capture system. But those projects weren't quickly successful, certainly not in the majors.

"Basically all those wearables were part of our minor league player development tool kit," an employee said. "Maybe once [major league outfielder] Jake Marisnick put on a K-Vest. But we never had adoption at the major league level, and more importantly than adoption is our ability to have concrete research insights from the data. And we had none."

Players were again leery of data collection efforts.

In the minor leagues, Taubman and Pete Putila arranged for every Astros player to have a team-issued cell phone with Slack installed, so that goals the front office developed for players could be discussed more easily. In the past, roving coaches would oversee those goals. But Taubman felt the organization could use tech to make the process better. Big companies often set targets for employees, but might not institute meaningful tracking. The duo wanted to give players an easy way to follow along.

○

Even as all this innovation continued, the workplace in Houston continued to sour in ways hidden by the team's success.

"Eve Rosenbaum left," an Astros executive said. "And it's not like she went to the Orioles because she just really liked working with Elias. I think that's why it was the Orioles, among other teams. But she left not knowing where she was going."

Rosenbaum was a young Harvard grad who carried the title of manager of international scouting from 2018 to 2019. Elias, as assistant GM, technically oversaw the department in 2018, but the team had no titular director of international scouting in 2019.

"They passed her over for a director's position," a colleague continued. "She's been running international scouting for what, two years at this point? And you won't give her a director's job?

"And meanwhile, the Astros are really stingy with promotions, unless they aren't. And that's I think part of the problem, where you see people getting promoted and you see other people not getting promoted; it's not always congruent with who are the people that are having the biggest impact. It yanks them around."

The Astros' cost-consciousness represented "Jim Crane and Jeff's weaknesses combining to make a super weakness," another employee said. "Just like, clamping down on costs like crazy, and how that harmed morale, it harmed whatever people's desire to stay there, so forth. . . . They grind everybody down."

But many people in Houston simply didn't know anything else until eventually they left. Those who had never worked for another team just assumed that the Astros were like the rest of baseball. That assumption was not entirely wrong, but Houston was as far toward one end of the spectrum as any franchise.

"It was after I became a free agent that I realized that I was underpaid," one executive said.

Although he didn't fully grasp it in the moment, Taubman's stress was building. He felt he was on his way to becoming a general manager—Jim Crane had directly indicated to him that he would someday get there—and the Astros were winning one hundred games a year. And yet Taubman had never been more anxiety-ridden in his life.

Taubman was as strong a candidate as anyone to become swallowed up in the Astros' and Luhnow's cutthroat environment. When Luhnow hired him six years earlier, Luhnow had purposely sought someone with either finance or a management consulting background. The job was supposed to be filled by someone who had a particular mentality. The more Taubman exhibited that mentality, the more he was, eventually, rewarded. Luhnow, after all, had turned Taubman loose as something of a de facto consultant, constantly reviewing different areas of the operation.

"This is my armchair psychology: Jeff was kind of that guy when he first came in: behaving like a consultant," a member of the inner circle said. "And he probably knew that there was value there. Brandon was so explosive in the way he went about it. It wasn't the positive diplomatic [approach]."

Some of Taubman's aggressiveness was inherent to his own personality, baked in before arriving in Houston. His willingness to bulldoze others to get to a desired result grew as he made the climb to an Ivy League school and into the world of finance.

But in Houston, Taubman became "completely obsessed with work and felt like if we weren't doing the best and the most all the time that the Astros were going to crumble to the ground," an employee said. "So it's just constantly putting people's feet to the fire to get more done. And that was the culture. That was the culture. Jeff will never, ever admit it. But that was it. It was do or die, all the time."

Unsurprisingly, Taubman turned people off even as he implemented smart strategies.

Collin McHugh, the diamond in the rough the Astros had found in 2014, twice went to arbitration hearings with the Astros, in 2017 and 2018, to determine his salary for the upcoming season. Twice, McHugh won. In the second hearing, the Astros waited until the end of their rebuttal period to essentially "introduce some medical records in an effort to say that Collin was damaged goods." One of the people arguing on behalf of McHugh went nuts, and called it a sandbagging.

Taubman didn't deliver the argument himself, but he had a part in the strategy. At the end of hearings, the two sides typically shake hands. When the same player-side representative reached Taubman, he told Taubman point-blank: "You're a fucking asshole."

# 17

# INCRIMINATING EVIDENCE

BRANDON TAUBMAN INCREASINGLY WANTED EVERYTHING DONE HIS WAY. With Mike Elias out of the picture, Taubman was more involved in the 2019 amateur draft, and charged an intern with developing an application to get feedback from the scouts in the draft room. The effort appeared redundant to others in the organization, because the Astros already had a way of integrating scouts' preferences into their process. But Taubman had an intern write it anyway, a colleague said, "because that was the only person he could directly control the output of. It didn't work. It worked on one guy's computer, but if you tried to have like ten scouts logging into it at once, it would fall over."

At midnight, Taubman would still be working on the project, telling people it was so important, and it had to get done.

Sometimes the frustrations would boil over. Another time leading up to a draft, Taubman had asked an analyst to do a study on a theory of his, about a way to improve hitting. One morning on Slack, he blew up at the R&D team: "If you won't support this, I'm gonna tell the coaches this, and I'm going to tell them it doesn't come up with the support of the R&D department."

"Just the most unprofessional thing in the world," a colleague remembered. "Here he was trying to get the code working so he could prove himself right. Part of that I think was just Brandon being Brandon, his personality. Part of it I think is that Brandon had a real anxiety that we weren't innovating anymore at the Astros in 2019. That Mike [Fast] was gone, we were going to fall behind."

No one in Houston questioned Taubman's acumen. He was "extremely talented and extremely hardworking and all of that, and it isn't that this is a guy without positive qualities," another colleague said. "Jeff was slow to give him the title. Jeff was aware of the issues."

But why would they concern Luhnow, who was grooming Taubman in his own likeness? Both master and apprentice were keen strategists, and both often lacked the touch to win over hearts and minds.

Luhnow "couldn't be aware of the degree he was sending ugly text messages and stuff like that," a colleague said of Taubman. "I'm not surprised by it, he had a lot of free rein running around. I think junior people had no real avenue for getting Jeff's ear about that, and I do think that Jeff was, first of all, sympathetic to a guy doing a ton of great work, and sympathetic to a guy being a bit of a change agent."

But one incident in particular, Astros employees believe, should have caught Luhnow's attention, and if not Luhnow's, then Crane's or human resources'.

In the offseason heading into 2019, not long after he'd been promoted to assistant GM in September 2018, while inside the baseball operations office at Minute Maid Park, Taubman verbally tore into another employee, leaving them in tears. Human resource officials with the Astros were said to have been aware of the incident.

The encounter was something Astros employees would talk about among themselves. Taubman is not known to have been disciplined, and it is unclear what follow-up human resources had, if any.

Taubman had become Luhnow and Crane's top weapon. He brought results. And the organization's inaction was an example of what mattered in Crane and Luhnow's business, and what did not.

"I don't think blind spot's the right term," one executive said of Luhnow's approach to Taubman. "I think willing to turn a blind eye is more accurate. Because he was contributing a lot in a lot of ways, he was willing to turn a blind eye."

○

The Astros expected to run the table in 2019, to be among the very best teams in baseball from start to finish, and they followed through. They finished with 107 wins with a group that, by most accounts, was probably the most talented team in franchise history.

Luhnow had signed a top outfielder, Michael Brantley, as a free agent. Combined with the incumbents, the Astros offense set a major league record with a .495 slugging percentage. The right side of the infield, second baseman Jose Altuve and first baseman Yuli Gurriel, hit 31 home runs apiece, and Alex Bregman hit 41. George Springer could only muster 39.

Their pitching allowed fewer runs than all but one team. Gerrit Cole led the majors in strikeouts, at 326, the most by any pitcher in the sport since 2002. Justin Verlander also topped 300 strikeouts, a feat that's rare for any one pitcher, never mind two on the same team. The Astros were a juggernaut, and the team's play was putting Luhnow and Hinch on the cusp of a dynasty. Another World Series victory would make for two in three years.

When they arrived in the postseason, the sign-stealing finger-pointing started right back up again. MLB had again updated its rules for 2019. Continuing the setup from the prior year's postseason, MLB for the regular season parked someone in video rooms to stand guard, which made cheating harder and more scarce. But it still wasn't an airtight system. The Red Sox felt they had the workers monitoring the video rooms "in our back pocket," one person with the team said.

The baserunner system, at least, was still occasionally possible. Talking about electronic sign-stealing, one Astros executive said to me during the 2019 postseason that, "It still happens." The comment seemed to be intended as an assessment of other teams.

Coaches on different teams would yell at each other from across the field during games when they thought the other team was stealing signs, as they had the year before. But by 2019, teams were also pro-actively trying to scare the other team into thinking something was happening, even if or when it wasn't. Movement and whispering in the dugout was, at least, a means of getting under an opponent's skin.

"Use the paranoia to your advantage," a member of the Red Sox said. "You guys think we're stealing signs? You know what, we're going to fake that we have everything and your catcher is going to go nuts and you're going to throw three wild pitches and we're going to score a freakin' run. That's it. Use it to your advantage. Oh, you think that we have something? You think that whistling was bad? Now we will whistle. Fuck yeah, we will."

As they had two years earlier, the Astros and Yankees met in the American League Championship Series, with a trip to the World Series on the line. "Gerrit Cole whistled his fucking ass off" during that series, and he wasn't alone. It got under the skin of Yankees coach Phil Nevin. "Fuck you to Nevin. Fuck you to [Yankees manager] Aaron Boone," one member of the Astros said of the sentiment. It was the same reason that the team had been whistling when they faced Mike Fiers in the regular season in 2019—because they had heard he was, to his teammates, accusing the Astros of cheating.

Of course, in reality, the Astros had been cheating in the past, and occasionally via whistle. Nonetheless, in a press conference at Yankee Stadium during the 2019 ALCS, A.J. Hinch made light of the idea the Astros could be doing something wrong.

"When I get contacted about some questions about whistling, it made me laugh because it's ridiculous," Hinch said. "And had I known that it would take something like that to set off the Yankees or any other team, we would have practiced it in spring training."

Hinch's intention was to address 2019 exclusively, to say the Astros were not doing anything wrong at the present. But the comment wouldn't look good for Hinch a few weeks later.

The ALCS ended in six games, the last at Minute Maid Park. Altuve hit a walk-off home run to send the Astros to the World Series, ending the Yankees' season. As Altuve crossed home plate, he did something odd. He overtly signaled to his teammates that he did not want them to tear or pull off his jersey in celebration.

Champagne flowed as Houston celebrated moving on to a second World Series in three years.

○

Taubman had watched Game 6 of the ALCS from the GM's box, as he normally does. Ownership was in and out all night. In 2019, Taubman would sometimes drink in the GM's box during the playoff games, and he told friends he had at least a couple that night before the game ended, maybe more. Postseason celebrations are jubilant, if not over-the-top bacchanals. Players spray one another and staff. Bottles and corks line the floor, and the lockers get taped down with plastic to keep people's belongings safe from the spray. Taubman headed down to the clubhouse, where, he told others, he continued to drink.

Roberto Osuna, the reliever the Astros traded for a year earlier, had nearly blown the game. One of the Astros' staffers mentioned to Taubman that Alex Bregman was encouraging everyone to try to keep Osuna's confidence up, that the pitcher was feeling dejected. Another team staffer is said to have mentioned a tweet that had been sent out by a reporter that same night when Osuna was pitching poorly: "suboptimal."

There was nothing about that tweet that should have been alarming to anyone working for the team. But the front office had been unreasonably irked by the reporter's tweets before.

Sometimes, right after the Astros got Osuna, the reporter would tweet out a domestic violence hotline when Osuna pitched. The reporter would often get attacked for those tweets by the ugliest corners of Twitter. But those hotline tweets, it turned out, annoyed more than just the dregs of the internet.

"I remember Jeff bitching in the GM's box one night," one employee said. Luhnow didn't think that the reporter's so-called political views, as he considered the tweets to represent, were relevant.

By this day, a full year had passed since the reporter had last sent out a tweet with the hotline number—not that it should have made a difference. Yet the "suboptimal" tweet caught Taubman's attention. When Taubman saw the reporter standing in clubhouse, waiting on players to speak with for a story during the celebration, he lashed out.

"I'm so fucking glad we got Osuna!" Taubman yelled. "I'm so fucking happy. Thank God we fucking have Osuna!"

There's a lot of noise during a champagne celebration, but the reporter Taubman was targeting eventually took notice and, horrified, asked Taubman, "Oh, is that for me?" He kept going briefly.

Taubman was about ten feet away from the reporter, who, like two others standing near, was a woman.

The media was often considered the enemy in Houston, with Luhnow's and Crane's own views toward the press in many ways tone setting. The staff usually kept the media at a distance, a chilly mentality, if not an outright display of us versus them. Taubman and the reporter he was yelling at had no preexisting relationship.

"None of them have ever bothered to try to understand, learn, or respect the media's role in baseball's coverage and in Major League Baseball," a Houston reporter said.

Taubman's general aggression had been tacitly condoned by Luhnow and Crane for years, and so Taubman did not consider that yelling at a reporter, just as a generality, might be a mistake. He seemingly did not care, in the moment, about Osuna's arrest for domestic violence, nor did he have any consideration—not at this time, anyway—for what Osuna's presence on the team might have made women in particular feel.

He seemed to be defending the core driver of his self-worth: the roster and player performance. What was a reporter who had tweeted out "suboptimal" about a player, if not a doubter and a naysayer of the roster he had built?

Certainly, Taubman did not consider what should have been obvious: that by yelling in support of a player accused of domestic violence, and doing so in the general direction of multiple women—never mind one woman—he would not only come off as a gigantic ass, but also grant room for people to question his own morals and values.

Taubman, in the time since the incident, has been adamant that he was not going after the reporter because she was a woman. That he was not trying to signal support for domestic violence, either. No one directly involved in the incident is known to doubt his sincerity about his intent. But it was he alone who put himself in a position where the world could wonder otherwise.

Even once Taubman made such a massive mistake, the Astros could have taken reasonable steps to keep the incident from growing into a wildfire. The old PR trick known as an apology, for example, might have helped. But Crane's Astros were not an organization of accountability—except when taking praise for winning games.

Stephanie Apstein of *Sports Illustrated* was one of the reporters standing near the one Taubman targeted, and began to get to work on a story the next day, October 20. Another outlet, too, was considering a piece.

October 21 was a workout day prior to the start of the World Series between the Astros and Nationals. Apstein gave the Astros ample chance to attempt to address what had happened, but the team only dug in.

Taubman was freaked out, and lied to Astros vice president of communications Gene Dias about what happened, saying he was just trying to pump up Osuna, and not yelling at anyone in particular. Dias, who was too easily convinced that a well-respected reporter at a prestigious national outlet like *Sports Illustrated* would simply lie, told Taubman not to speak to Apstein.

Anita Sehgal, the Astros' senior vice president of marketing and communications, told Taubman the rest of the organization was going to rally around him. The mistakes were multiple: Taubman was lying while the rest of management didn't bother to actually look deeper into what happened, and the communications bosses were also far too eager to assume Apstein would just make it up.

Apstein wrote what she saw: Taubman was yelling in the direction of a group of reporters, of three women. "The outburst was offensive and frightening enough that another Houston staffer apologized," Apstein wrote. "The Astros declined to comment. They also declined to make Taubman available for an interview."

Apstein was out to dinner near Minute Maid Park when the Astros did, actually, decide to comment. Sehgal and General Counsel Giles Kibbe had put together a statement that Luhnow and Crane reviewed.

"The story posted by *Sports Illustrated* is misleading and completely irresponsible," the Astros' statement began. It ended: "We are extremely disappointed in *Sports Illustrated*'s attempt to fabricate a story where one does not exist."

The Astros were trying to obliterate Apstein's credibility.

The next day was the start of the World Series, and the outcry over the Astros' errant statement was a massive distraction from what MLB cares about most, its championship round. The commissioner's office, fed up with the Astros' constant bungling of public relations during the postseason, began its own investigation into the clubhouse incident. Very quickly, MLB realized Taubman was lying.

Dias stopped talking to Taubman, and Kibbe, the lawyer, took over. Prior to Game 1 in Houston, Luhnow sent Taubman away from Minute Maid Park. It was a good idea, Luhnow said, for Taubman to watch the game from home.

Taubman knew he was finished. He had lied on top of screwing up. After the first two games in Houston, the teams had a travel day, on October 24. Luhnow met with Taubman for coffee and told his protégé he would be fired.

Luhnow flew to Washington, DC, where he and the rest of the brain trust continued to bungle everything. Luhnow took to the podium in the evening, and gave no clarity on how the original statement had been allowed to come out, the one where the Astros had tried to brand Apstein as a liar herself—a major accusation in any setting, but one particularly damning and significant for a reporter.

Luhnow said the Astros' initial statement was indeed wrong, but he also waffled.

"There are some varying degrees of detail recollection of who was where and all of that, as you would imagine after a long night," Luhnow said. "So it's not a hundred percent clear what the truth is, but what we do know is the truth is that those comments weren't appropriate."

Luhnow also tried to shoo attention away from the culture he had fostered, and suggested that the incident was out of the blue for Taubman.

"This was an employee that I hired, and that's worked for us for five years who did something that was out of character for him, not consistent with his behavior in the past," Luhnow said. "That is not something that we condone or not reflective of what the Astros' culture is all about or what we believe in. . . . This is not something that's endemic. This is not a cultural issue."

Before Game 3 on October 25, Luhnow met with Apstein in the dugout, but Luhnow would not commit to retracting the original statement. Finally, a day later, Crane sent Apstein a letter with a retraction and a promise that the Astros would learn from their mistakes.

Newly villains to some, the Astros lost the World Series in seven games. The Nationals had been leery of the Astros' sign-stealing rumors and took precautions.

Hinch had been a hair away from his second title in three years, yet he was fed up. Every time the front office did something controversial, he had to deal with it as the first face at the podium: The initial Osuna trade in 2018. Kyle McLaughlin's counterespionage missions later that year. Now, the assistant GM losing control, and the rest of the staff screwing it up further.

Hinch had a lot of good things in Houston: a handsome salary, wins on his record, and above all, comfort for his family, with his two daughters in school. But the trade-off was starting to become harder and harder to dismiss, and he knew it.

Crane, shortly after the season, made one major change: president of business operations Reid Ryan was out. Ryan's credibility had been valuable to the owner for a time, and then he was disposable. (The elder Ryan, Nolan, was already out of the organization.)

Crane's decision to give Ryan the boot was preplanned, unrelated to everything that transpired during the World Series. "Reid knew things weren't great," a colleague said, but "he didn't see it coming the day it happened."

In the same November 7 press release announcing Ryan's departure, Crane announced that his son Jared, then thirty-six years old, was joining the leadership team, although not in the role of president. Nonetheless, the press release read like nepotism: out with the veteran, in with the owner's son.

After the season, Sehgal, an architect of the initial statement about Taubman's incident, now only had more power, a colleague said: she previously reported to Ryan, and now reported directly to Crane.

Early in the offseason, at least one Astros employee directly told Crane what he had allowed his baseball team to become. That the Astros were run on fear and paranoia, and that no one wanted to tell Crane as much precisely because of that fear. At some point, Crane was told, the Astros have to be better than this, and if not, the whole place needed to be cleaned out. Cleansed.

Unbeknownst to the owner or his canary in the coal mine, the start of that process was mere days away. On November 12, 2019, The Athletic published an investigation Ken Rosenthal and I authored.

○

Once Ken and I paired up, there was an obvious choice to make. In instances where we thought we might have only one chance to get someone to pick up the phone, I wanted Ken to be the one to make that call. His cachet in the industry is unmatched.

Thirteen months after I had started to investigate the Astros' cheating, the endgame of our reporting was intense. Ken spoke to Danny Farquhar, the pitcher who had heard the banging while on the mound in September 2017, and Farquhar went on the record. The chances of finding someone who had been on the Astros who would also go on the record were slim, and we knew that the whole time. But we were going to keep trying.

Mike Fiers's name had come up in 2018 and did so again in 2019. Just three days before we wound up publishing—and within just a few hours of his conversation with Farquhar—Ken got Fiers on the phone.

"We are writing about sign-stealing in 2017," Ken told Fiers, then started to explain.

"I don't even know where to start. I don't understand," Fiers said. "What are you guys doing?"

Ken read him part of an early version of the story, with the details of the scheme.

"That's pretty much what I know," Fiers said. "I never read the rulebook fully. I don't know if that was in there or what the rule actually was. But they were advanced and willing to go above and beyond to win. As a pitcher, you have no say in it. It's not helping you at all. The pitching staff isn't using that to help them. And it's tough. Also, there were guys who didn't like it. There are guys who don't like to know and guys who do."

Ken asked Fiers if he was comfortable being quoted.

"Well, that's the whole thing about this. I don't want to be put out there like that. But they already know, so honestly, I don't really care anymore," Fiers said, referring to the fact the Astros already knew he had spoken up to the A's and Tigers. "I just want the game to be cleaned up a little bit because there are guys who are losing their jobs because they're going in, they're not knowing. Young guys getting hit around in the first couple of innings starting a game, and then they get sent down. It's bullshit on that end. It's ruining jobs for younger guys. The guys who know are more prepared. But most of the people don't. That's why I told my team. We had a lot of young guys with Detroit trying to make a name and establish themselves. I wanted to help them out and say, 'Hey, this stuff really does go on. Just be prepared.'"

Fiers, to his immense credit, stood by his words and never tried to back out before the investigation ran. He helped change the sport, and the toll ostensibly has been heavy for him.

At the time Ken spoke to Fiers, we were preparing to publish our findings without his account. It's impossible to say exactly how the world would have reacted to the story had Ken not spoken to him—if all the sources had been unnamed. But the facts of the story had already been ascertained, and we had Farquhar's account.

Within hours of the story being published on November 12, the internet was brimming with not only our explanation of how the 2017 Astros had broken the rules but also footage compiled by Jomboy, a Yankees fan named Jimmy O'Brien who was already known in baseball circles for his savvy in reviewing video and sound from games. Jomboy put together a clip where the bangs on the trash can could be heard.

Whether Fiers was quoted or not, it seems unlikely to me that MLB would have been able to ignore the general outcry. But our investigation was still in a much better position with Fiers on the record. His name helped validate everything instantly, making it harder for anyone to try to shove the story aside.

Ultimately, Ken and I were conservative in what we published on November 12. For example: Although we had been given an account of the Astros' road sign-stealing system, the baserunner system, we didn't have the same level of confirmation of that as we did for the home system and so figured it was safer to wait. We simply noted, "The Astros did not use the same system in away games."

Ken and I felt strongly that it was important to try to address the context, the sense in Houston and elsewhere that the Astros had not been the only ones to engage in at least some form of wrongdoing. We went down that road in the top portion of the story, and in the headline: "The Astros Stole Signs Electronically in 2017—Part of a Much Broader Issue for Major League Baseball."

We also knew that we had more reporting to do. We didn't yet have firsthand accounts of any other team behaving improperly, but we were going to continue to look. In January 2020, we published an investigation into the Red Sox' improper use of their video room in 2018, the year they won the World Series. But it remains the case that no team has been shown, through firm reporting or accounts, to have done something as blatant as Houston. (Ultimately, whether severity matters in cheating, I believe, is up to the reader. Is a little cheating better than a lot of cheating?)

During our investigations, not everyone answered their phone eagerly. "I'll go till the end to crush you people," one person told us. "Trust me."

○

The shine around the Astros had disappeared, and according to an investigative letter Rob Manfred sent to Jeff Luhnow, data on Luhnow's cell phone disappeared as well, erased by Luhnow.

Following our story, Major League Baseball's investigators sprang into action with full force. MLB isn't always eager to send in its detectives, but this time, they descended immediately. The furor over the scandal was just as rapid, as star players and average fans alike took their shock to Twitter.

Speaking at the winter meetings in mid-December, Manfred called the review of the Astros "probably the most thorough investigation that the commissioner's office has ever undertaken."

In a span of two months, the league's Department of Investigations would interview 68 people in all, including 23 Astros players, and collect more than 76,000 emails. MLB's forensic capability extended to Slack messages and cell phones, as well.

In any investigation, the league notifies people of interest in writing that they need to preserve their cell phones. Luhnow, investigators learned, had instructed one of his lieutenants, Bill Firkus, to give a personal heads-up to others with the team that MLB might collect their devices, a person with direct knowledge of the league's investigation said.

That source said that MLB interviewed several Astros employees in an attempt to figure out what message Luhnow delivered to Firkus and what Firkus subsequently relayed to others. The following bullet points are that source's recounting of the league's interviews.

- Speaking to investigators, Firkus's initial recollection of Luhnow's request is said to have been that Luhnow had called in a quick and hurried manner, and that Luhnow had asked him to tell others to delete information from their phone. Firkus, however, is said to have later clarified to the league he didn't think Luhnow had used the word "delete"; it was more that Luhnow had told him to contact a bunch of individuals and let them know their phones might be confiscated, and that they should be comfortable with what was on there. (Another source with knowledge of the matter said Firkus had only one conversation about this topic and did not change his story or provide two different versions.) Investigators ultimately did not consider Firkus to have changed his story.

- Derek Vigoa is said to have told investigators he remembered Firkus saying that Luhnow wanted him to know his phone might be confiscated, and that he should tell the truth. Two things struck Vigoa as odd, he's said to have told investigators: one, that Luhnow would ask that he tell the truth—because Vigoa felt it should have been obvious he would. And two, that Luhnow would funnel the message through Firkus in the first place, because Vigoa had a direct relationship with the Astros' GM.

- The source said that Matt Hogan described Firkus's message differently: that MLB is coming, and that there's a chance they can take your phone, so if you have things you don't want anyone to see, I would get rid of them.

- Tom Koch-Weser, meanwhile, is said to have told investigators he couldn't remember the exact message Firkus delivered, but had taken it to be a hint to do what was necessary, although Koch-Weser told the league Firkus had not used those words.

"I cooperated fully in the investigation and never discouraged anyone from doing the same," Luhnow said in a statement.

The exact message Luhnow told Firkus to deliver, and the message delivered, remain unknown. But in the end, MLB believes it found only one person who had deleted material from their phone after the league told the Astros not to, a person with knowledge of the investigation said: Luhnow himself.

In a letter dated January 2, 2020, Manfred outlined evidence the league had compiled against Luhnow. Many, but not all, of the specific allegations included in the letter were first published in the *Wall Street Journal*. Luhnow's phone deletion was not among those previously published.

"Your credibility is further impacted by the fact that you permanently deleted information from your phone and its backups in anticipation that my investigators would seek to search your phone," Manfred wrote to Luhnow. "You did not tell my investigators that you had done this until they confronted you about it in your second interview. While you explained that you were simply deleting sensitive personal photographs, I have no way to confirm that you did not delete incriminating evidence."

According to people with knowledge of the league's investigation, the GM of the Astros had wiped every backup from his phone, besides one, and other data was missing as well.

When Luhnow went for his interview with MLB in November 2019, he is said to have handed over his phone to be imaged. Investigators determined that at about 10:15 central time on the morning of his interview he had backed up the phone. His Apple iCloud account had no other backups.

But backups are snapshots of data—they don't affect what's currently on the device. Yet, MLB found Luhnow had deleted source data on the phone as well, people with knowledge of the investigation said. Investigators found that Luhnow's phone had no standard call logs, even though Luhnow had known phone calls with A.J. Hinch that should have been there. MLB also could not locate known email exchanges that should have been on his phone that were found on others' devices. But as MLB's investigators saw it, if Luhnow had been trying to delete a large amount of information, he didn't do a perfect job: the phone had Skype and WhatsApp call logs dating back to 2009.

MLB confronted Luhnow about the deletions in his second interview. According to sources with knowledge of the league's investigation, Luhnow admitted to MLB that he deleted photos of his wife the night before his interview, and acknowledged he backed up the device the next morning. He then deleted prior backups, he is said to have told MLB investigators, so that MLB would not get those photos.

Luhnow is said to have told MLB he did this despite correctly understanding the league's requirement that he preserve his phone for the investigation. Luhnow told MLB he deleted the data because he didn't trust MLB, a person with knowledge of the investigation said.

"I had pictures on my phone of my wife giving birth to our son, and I deleted those at her request prior to handing over my phone," Luhnow said in a statement. "When asked by the investigators, I told them about this. Not one work-related item was deleted and every email and text I ever sent was available to MLB and the Astros through my work computer."

Luhnow is not known to have asked for permission to delete the backups and he likely wouldn't have received it, a person with knowledge of the investigation said. But, it was at least possible MLB could have offered to have a third party process the phone to keep MLB from viewing the photos, had Luhnow raised the issue.

"In addition to submitting to two interviews by the Commissioner's Office, the Astros and MLB had completely unfettered access to every text message I sent or received during the relevant time period," Luhnow said. "MLB never identified a single text that suggested I had any involvement in the matter—and the league had plenty of texts to make its case. In fact, the investigation uncovered 22,000 text messages from the alleged actual participants in the sign-stealing. The alleged participants openly texted in real time about sign stealing activity—and not a single communication implicated me, directly or indirectly, in any way, shape, or form. I was not mentioned in these contemporaneous texts because I was not party to sign-stealing activities."

A person with knowledge of the investigation said that Luhnow told MLB he hadn't deleted anything else on the phone. Yet, when the league looked at the hex of the SMS database, MLB also found traces of nine messages between Luhnow and Koch-Weser, from March and August 2019, a person with knowledge of the investigation said. MLB couldn't recover those texts on either device, however.

"I never deleted any messages between myself and Tom," Luhnow said. "I have them all and the Astros and MLB had access to all of them from my work computer."

To the league's determination, the photos accounted for only a very small percentage of the data that was removed when Luhnow deleted the backups.

# 18

# WHY IS IT ALL ON ME?

"WHAT I THINK WAS GOOD ABOUT THE ASTROS CULTURE," AN ASTROS EXEC-utive said in 2020, "is that it was very much driven around innovation, around pushing the envelope, about moving the ball forward on a lot of things. I have spent a lot of time thinking about, could the Astros have done everything they did well, without the big implosion at the end? The front office being shaken up. The sign-stealing, I can see how the culture of the Astros enabled that to happen: the obsession with secrecy, the empowering of people in a weird way.

"There were definitely a lot of throats cut. It doesn't happen on accident. Like, do I think that Jeff wanted it to be cutthroat? Not necessarily.

"There's a double-edged sword when you empower people and you tell them, 'You can shake things up, you can take risks.' Sometimes you get Mark Appel being brought to Minute Maid to be looked at by your best pitching coach. And that blows up in your face, and you're like, 'Well, nobody did anything wrong there, it was worth a shot.' And sometimes you encourage people to experiment and take risks and MLB comes in and investigates and finds that you cheated in 2017. And that didn't work out, and you can also say, 'Well, that was a bad idea to begin with.'"

O

Two weeks into the new year, it was over. After going to Game 7 of the World Series in the prior season, A.J. Hinch and Jeff Luhnow were fired.

Hinch ended the 2019 season with 481 regular season wins in his five years with the Astros, second-most in franchise history. He already carried the highest win percentage of any Houston manager. Luhnow, meanwhile, had done what he said he would: turn the Astros into a winner.

Everything else along the way had been Luhnow's undoing, and by extension, Hinch's. For a team that could be so high-tech, to be caught with a cheating system that concluded with a hitter simply banging on a garbage can—something audible on game footage—was an ironic error.

Major League Baseball's investigators found exactly what Ken Rosenthal and I had reported for The Athletic, and more. The commissioner's office concluded that not only had the Astros cheated through the 2017 World Series, but they also continued their lesser scheme, the baserunner method, into 2018.

On January 13, 2020, MLB issued a report summarizing its findings and suspended Hinch and Luhnow for the 2020 season. Within a couple of hours of the report's release, Crane went a step further in a televised press conference: the GM and manager were fired.

The league suspended Brandon Taubman for the season as well, although not on the basis of electronic sign-stealing. The league did not find that Taubman knew of the cheating while it was happening in 2017, despite his involvement in counterespionage efforts the next year. Manfred wrote that he believed a punishment for Taubman's clubhouse incident, the Roberto Osuna outburst, was enough.

MLB waited to hand down judgment on Alex Cora, because at the time it punished the Astros, the league was still investigating the 2018–19 Boston Red Sox for using the baserunner method with the help of video. Cora's team, the Red Sox, did not wait. He was out a day later, in a decision the team aggressively tried to bill as mutual.

After two more days passed, Carlos Beltrán, who in November 2019 had become the field manager of the New York Mets, was fired as well. Beltrán never managed a game for the Mets.

In four days, three major league managers and one GM had all lost their jobs, a moment with little comparison in the sport, save perhaps for the banishment of eight White Sox players following a scheme to fix games in the 1919 World Series, in what's known as the Black Sox scandal.

Manfred also fined the Astros the maximum amount allowable under the major league constitution, $5 million. Houston lost its first two amateur draft picks in both the 2020 and 2021 seasons, too, a significant hit—although those picks aren't nearly as valuable for a team coming off a winning season, because, as the Astros well knew, the best draft picks go to losing teams.

For plenty of other reasons, MLB's punishments left people unsatisfied. Many wondered why Manfred had not stripped the Astros of their title.

"We thought about it," Manfred said. "It was high in terms of the minutes that we spent talking about it. My thinking involved several points. It had never happened in baseball. And I do believe—I'm a precedent guy. I'm not saying you always follow precedent, but I think you ought to start by looking back at the way things have been done. I think you have to have a really good reason to depart from that precedent, I think. Number two, I believe that the most fundamental obligation, I said this before, was to get the facts and put them out there and let the people make their own judgment as to what happened in the 2017 season, the 2017 World Series.

"Once you have a situation in which the 2017 World Series will always be looked at as something different, whether or not you put an asterisk or ask for the trophy back, I don't think it makes that much difference. . . . Once you go down that road of changing what happens on the field, I just don't know how you decide where you stop."

Manfred, who has often come off publicly as a steely suit, put his foot in his mouth on another occasion when he explained this thinking, by referring to the World Series trophy as a "piece of metal." The point he was trying to make was that taking away that alleged piece of metal would not actually change history. Yet such a callous reference to the trophy, which teams work so hard to achieve, angered players and fans alike. Manfred apologized quickly afterward.

The outcry was the loudest, however, around another of Manfred's choices. He did not suspend a single Astros player. He struck a deal with the players' union at the start of the investigation, granting players immunity.

"I'm more than prepared to tolerate and listen to the debate and criticism about whether or not the punishments that have been levied in this case are sufficient," Manfred said. "The one thing I do take issue with is the notion that anybody in the Houston organization escaped without punishment. And I think if you look at the faces of the Houston players, as they've been out there publicly addressing this issue, they have been hurt by this. They will live with questions about what went on in 2017 and 2018 for the rest of their lives. And frankly, it's rare that for any offense, you have a punishment that you will live with for the rest of your life."

Not everyone saw it his way. By February, a month after the league's investigative report on the Astros, players across the league arrived at spring training, and sign-stealing was top of mind.

"I don't agree with the punishments, the players not getting anything," the game's best player, the Angels' Mike Trout, told reporters.

"I thought the apologies were whatever," said Dodgers outfielder Cody Bellinger, a member of the team that lost to the Astros in the 2017 World Series. "I thought Jim Crane's was weak. I thought Manfred's punishment was weak, giving them immunity. I mean, these guys were cheating for three years. I think what people don't realize is [Jose] Altuve stole an MVP from [Aaron] Judge in 2017. Everyone knows they stole the ring from us.

"I know, personally, I lost respect for those guys. I would say everyone in the big leagues lost respect for those guys."

Manfred had agreed to grant the players immunity in exchange for truthful testimony. In part, that was because Manfred wanted players to be willing to speak openly about what happened.

"If I was in a world where I could have found all the facts without granting immunity, I would have done that," Manfred said in spring training of 2020.

But that premise is questionable. Even before the league investigation began, Manfred had a huge amount of information to work with. The report Ken Rosenthal and I published in The Athletic was detailed, and included an Astros player on the record. Video and audio from 2017 reinforced the allegations. The notion that Manfred could not have effectively found out the truth without proffering immunity seems tenuous. The core facts were out.

What was probably more compelling for Manfred was a fear that, had he tried to discipline players, he would have failed. Back in 2017, in his response to the Apple Watch scandal, Manfred had made clear that he was going to hold the field manager and the GM accountable for future electronic sign-stealing violations. He doubled down on that in the 2018 rules, and in the 2019 rules his office explicitly excluded players from discipline: "Clubs and Club Personnel (other than players) will be subject to progressive discipline by the Commissioner's Office for violation of these Regulations. . . ."

In labor relations, management is responsible for clearly laying out the rules of the workplace. The league has to give notice of the rules, as well as notice of what punishment follows if they're broken. The league cannot on a whim set a schedule of punishments for a type of behavior—or at least, it cannot do so without the expectation of a fight. Even after the Apple Watch scandal, Manfred had not established any understanding with the players' union about how players would be punished if an electronic sign-stealing violation took place.

So if Manfred had never granted immunity and tried to discipline the Astros' players, the players' union likely would have sprung to the players' side, as the union virtually always does when players face accusations. And the union might well have won, vacating any punishments or reducing them. One official tied into the sport's labor dynamics said that the commissioner's office would have been "smoked." Another said the league's case would have been "brutal" and the league would "look a fool."

As it played out, one of Manfred's key findings was that Jeff Luhnow did not pass on the league's September 2017 memo—the memo after the Apple Watch scandal that was supposed to draw a line in the sand—to others with the team. Assuming the league would have come to that same conclusion had players been eligible for punishment, the players would just have argued their bosses had not properly informed them of the rules.

"The memorandum went to the general manager and then nothing was done from the GM down," Manfred told ESPN. "So we knew if we had disciplined the players, in all likelihood we were going to have grievances, and grievances that we were going to lose on the basis that we never properly informed them of the rules.

"Given the fact that we didn't think we could make discipline stick with the players, we made the decision we made. Having said that, I understand the reaction."

Nonetheless, Manfred could have refused immunity and issued punishments. Then, if the punishments were overturned, he could have painted the players and their union as the bogeymen—"Look, I tried," could have been the message.

Now, would trying and failing to punish players have assuaged everyone, or anyone? It might have made Manfred look even worse.

Manfred's primary mistake, then, was not his decision to let the players go unpunished in 2020. The error was in the preceding years, by not seeing ahead of time how important it would be to make sure he could confidently punish players, and by not pursuing the topic with the union in advance. Even with his experience with the steroids issue, he didn't fully grasp how players could try to gain an edge through technology, nor what the reaction would be if he ever had to let players off the hook.

Fay Vincent, a former occupant of Manfred's office, decried the union's role in the lack of discipline.

"The real bad players in the cheating were the players, and yet the players never were punished," said Vincent, commissioner from 1989 to 1992. "I realize that what the commissioner did was to duck away because he didn't want to have major grievances, he didn't want to spend a lot of money, there were a whole bunch of political and some economic reasons. But from my point of view, and this is a much bigger point, the real mistake in baseball is to think that the players and the owners don't have to come together on major issues. . . . The union should have been taking a leadership role and saying, 'We can't have the game hurt by this kind of cheating.'

"I'm very critical of both sides. I think the commissioner punted. He didn't want to take the union on. He's a labor lawyer. He knows the union is almost, it's the Rocky Marciano of unions. It doesn't lose. And I understand what he was doing, but he was taking his eye off what the overall consequences are to the sport."

Yet the union would never proactively work to get its membership in trouble, to offer them up at the stake.

"He doesn't understand what a union does," said a former top lawyer at the union, Gene Orza, who retired in 2010 and was a contemporary of Vincent's. "I have great respect for Fay, but he is simply wrong. The union does not have a higher calling for the quote-unquote good of the game. He's suffering from what [White Sox owner] Jerry Reinsdorf would call 'commissioner-itis.'

"You cloak yourself with this mantle of authority that weighs so heavily upon your shoulders: 'But gee I have a responsibility for the game, you know, and so that transcends everything else.' That's a form of self-flagellation and masturbation. It makes you feel good to think you have this heavy, heavy weight on your shoulders. But the union is not about, first and foremost, the health of the game. It is about defending the players that are its constituency."

○

As players on other teams bashed Manfred and the Astros in spring training, the Astros themselves were livid. Top officials at the players' union annually visit every team during spring training, and in their stop at Houston's camp, anger poured out in all directions. The players felt abandoned, singled out, left out to dry by the league, by the union—you name the entity, they had a gripe. They were scared for their families, too. Josh Reddick said after the meeting that some players had been receiving death threats.

Rumors had been swirling in the offseason that the Astros had done even more than the commissioner had found: that when Jose Altuve hit a walk-off home run to win the 2019 American League Championship Series against the Yankees, he had been wearing some sort of buzzer or device under his shirt, something that could be pinged to let him know what pitch was coming. A whole other level of subterfuge.

Altuve had done two things to raise suspicion. First, he gestured to teammates as he arrived at home plate not to touch his jersey. Why was that top of mind at such a joyous moment, when he had just sent the Astros to the World Series? He also very quickly ran into the clubhouse afterward and emerged in the celebration wearing a different shirt.

MLB did not find any evidence Altuve or anyone else on the Astros had in fact used buzzers.

"We were aware of the file film well before we commenced the investigation," Manfred said in February 2020. "So it was in fact part of the investigation. Here's where I came down on it: The players were candid about 2017 and the fact that they violated in 2017. They were candid chapter and verse, consistent about the fact that the rules were violated in 2018. And they were equally consistent in the denials, and everybody, every single witness in the denials about this buzzer allegation.

"In my own mind, it was hard for me to figure out, why they would tell us, given they were immune, why they would be truthful, admit they did the wrong thing in '17, admit they did the wrong thing in '18, and then lie about what was going on in '19? Now, can I tell you I'm one hundred percent sure about that? You're never one hundred percent sure in any of these things. But that was my best judgment."

"Any of that would have been the best-kept secret in the clubhouse," one member of the 2017 team said of buzzers. "I never saw a trace of any of that." People with the Astros were also adamant that Altuve, of all people, would be unlikely to do such a thing, because he was not a large user of the trash-can system.

But all the suspicion served to make Altuve something of the poster child for the Astros' overall sign-stealing, which didn't sit well among his teammates and those who lived it. "Jose being the face of this is fucked-up if you were on that team," a longtime member of the Astros said. Tony Kemp, the same person said, didn't use the system, either, which was born out in Tony Adams's study of audio from the 2017 season.

Altuve heard bangs on 24 pitches, per the count of Adams, well fewer than Marwin Gonzalez, the leader at 147.

A couple of Astros employees nonetheless wondered about Altuve, after the fact—not in the context of buzzers, but his usage of the trash-can system.

With their high-speed cameras, the Astros tracked their hitters' hand movements. An analyst determined that in 2017, with an apparent accuracy of 70 to 80 percent, they could predict whether Altuve would swing at a pitch or not based on how he moved his hands prior to the pitcher delivering the ball. "So that was interesting because in the prior year, it was some much lower number," an Astros employee said. It suggested that in 2017, Altuve was newly guessing more—or at least, that he had seemed to become more predetermined in his swing decisions, which didn't fit his profile. Unbelievably talented as a hitter, Altuve had the ability to make contact with most anything, and adjust, rather than committing to swing ahead of time.

"What I'm trying to get at here is that Altuve was one of the players along with [Carlos] Correa and Marwin [Gonzalez] that seemed especially more aggressive and guess-centric—or 'predetermined' is probably a better word, because maybe it wasn't guessing at all," the employee said. But that was just speculation.

In a broad sense, the fact that anyone, internally or externally, could reasonably doubt what lengths the Astros would go to is among the worst self-inflicted wounds of the Astros' 2017–18 cheating. Even the rise of sign-stealing behavior more broadly, the baserunner schemes that the Astros and other teams employed, opened the door to a twisted imagination for anyone watching the game. Everyone—players, coaches, front-office members, fans—had new reason to doubt the veracity of what happened on the field.

One Astros employee, after the fact, came to an interesting but unsupported conclusion.

"I think the buzzer thing now is real," the employee said in 2020, "but if you asked me eight months ago when I was participating in the investigation, I did say, and would say, it's horseshit. It makes no sense."

Why the switch? Because the employee said they learned other things about clubhouse operations—how staff aided the purchase of sticky stuff to enhance pitcher grip, for example—during the investigation that made them question their overall judgment. They felt they had been naive in the past, that their sense of reality had already been proven wrong, so why couldn't the buzzer theory be true?

"I didn't really know about all this crazy shit that happens in the clubhouse until MLB brought it to my attention," said the employee, who spent time in the clubhouse. "And you feel like an idiot when you're like, 'No, that can't be,' and then they're like, 'What about that email between this person and this person?' And you're like, holy shit, there it is, it's real, this person knew."

Altuve himself has always denied using a buzzer.

"I didn't wear a buzzer," he said in February 2020. "I feel bad for 2017 but I did not do the buzzer thing. Nobody on this team wore a buzzer."

Carlos Correa jumped to Altuve's defense, too.

"Jose Altuve was the one guy that didn't use the trash can," Correa told Ken Rosenthal. "Nobody wore buzzers. That's a lie. The reason Jose Altuve didn't want to get his shirt ripped off, I'm going to tell you.

"Earlier in the year, he hit a walk-off at Minute Maid Park; I ripped off his shirt with Tony Kemp. There are pictures of that. There are videos of that. You can go look at it. I ripped off his shirt, and his wife told my wife, 'Why is Carlos ripping Altuve's shirt? I don't like that.'

"So when he's running from third base to home plate, I'm the guy up front. The first one waiting for him. He's like, 'Don't take my shirt off.' The second reason—he doesn't want me to talk about this, but I'm going to say it, is because he's got an unfinished tattoo on his collarbone that honestly looked terrible. It was a bad tattoo, and he didn't want nobody to see it. He didn't want to show it at all."

Funny enough, the Astros did at one point actually attempt to use an electric shock to their advantage, in their sport science endeavors. Tensiomyography, or TMG, is a technology that helps measure the attributes of muscle fibers.

The idea had a lot of pushback. One executive wanted to use it for scouting—they could correlate on-field performance if enough TMG measurements were gathered throughout the year.

"Basically we compromised on it and what we decided to do is, in spring training, we would use it on every player at the minor league level as part of their preseason physical," the employee said. "Players did not want us to fucking shock them all the time. It's not bad, it's like a doorknob shock, it's not like we're electrocuting them.

"The concern was about the data being used against players in arbitration, so the reaction to that was like, you're like a High-A player, you're probably not getting to arbitration, just take our test. But that was clearly not the right attitude and eventually where we went with it is, we created a waiver that was like a release form and it basically said, 'Hereby the club promises not to use any of this data against you at any point in time.' And also this data will be readily available to you and you'll have full access to it as long as you're an Astro."

○

But what about all the other teams?

Evan Gattis, in a 2021 appearance on the *'Stros Across the Globe* podcast, pointed to the Astros' suspicions of the Dodgers—and said Astros players had reached out to some of the Dodgers when Dodgers players were publicly critical of Houston's cheating.

"There's people in our clubhouse who have had to call other people from the Dodgers clubhouse and say, 'Hey you need to clean up your shit, because, yo, we know, bro. Why you gotta be like that?'" Gattis said. "Everybody has a system. Everybody knows a buddy that has a buddy that's on the Dodgers in the baseball world. It's like, 'Yo, we know, so you guys got to kind of chill out with that shit.'"

"I think a lot of fans are misinformed, because it wasn't just the Astros doing things," said Dallas Keuchel in 2021. "We were kind of keeping up with the times. And it's kind of sad that it is what it is at this point in time."

Joey Votto of the Cincinnati Reds said in 2021 that "the idea that they were the only ones doing something wrong just baffles me."

It is a fact that other teams, at varying points, had engaged in electronic sign-stealing through some means. The 2017 Apple Watch scandal involving the Red Sox and Yankees was proof of that, even before Ken and I reported on the Astros and 2018 Red Sox.

It is a fact, too, that no team has been shown to have done something as egregious as what the Astros did: relay, from a position off the field, what pitch was coming in real time to the hitter with the help of technology, a center field camera and a TV monitor. Could another team have done something equally as egregious? No one can rule that out. It's impossible to say what, exactly, all thirty teams were up to, or not up to.

Yet it also seems quite a stretch to say every team was cheating.

"I think the big market teams with it all on the line were all really good [at using video to steal signs]," said one member of the Red Sox. "Competitive edges are going to be the difference. And that was kind of the justification is that we're all so good here at the end, that it's the competitive edges that are going to make the difference. Whoever's better at cheating. Because everybody's coaches are good, everybody's players are good, that's all going to even out."

What has been rampant through so much of the sign-stealing saga is allegation: in the media, among players, executives, most everyone. Much rarer is actual evidence or firsthand, firm accounts. It's pretty easy to say, "Everyone is doing it," and walk away.

O

Everything in Houston sprang from the planning of two men: Jim Crane and Jeff Luhnow. Neither, in the aftermath of scandal, showed any interest in taking personal accountability for what had unfurled under their watch.

Luhnow went on the offensive. The day he was fired, he put out a statement saying he accepted responsibility. Yet, in the same statement, he pointed a finger at others inside the organization, to the 2017 bench coach, Alex Cora, and to Tom Koch-Weser and the advance staff.

"I am not a cheater," Luhnow said. "Anybody who has worked closely with me during my thirty-two-year career inside and outside baseball can attest to my integrity. I did not know rules were being broken. . . . The sign-stealing initiative was not planned or directed by baseball management; the trash-can banging was driven and executed by players, and the video decoding of signs originated and was executed by lower-level employees working with the bench coach."

Cora has batted back against Luhnow publicly on multiple occasions since.

"Out of this whole process, if there is one thing that I completely reject and disagree with is people within the Astros organization singling me out, particularly Jeff Luhnow, as if I were the sole mastermind," Cora told ESPN.

Luhnow's argument was that he was not directing any of the wrongdoing or aware of it. MLB did not find that Luhnow had direct knowledge of the Astros' trash-can scheme. Luhnow's alleged knowledge of the team's efforts to decipher signs was part of the league's case. Wrote Manfred in his letter: "[T]here is more than sufficient evidence that you knew—and overwhelming evidence that you should have known—that the Astros maintained a sign-stealing program."

Luhnow began to plan a lawsuit against the Astros for breach of contract, an attempt to recoup more than $22 million he said he was still owed on the contract he signed in 2018, plus his "profit interests" in the team. In advance of that lawsuit, which he filed in November 2020, Luhnow undertook what appeared to be a calculated publicity campaign. He spoke with two outlets: he turned again to Ben Reiter, who had written a book about Luhnow's championship season and was now putting together a podcast that was allegedly about everything his book missed; and he spoke to a reporter at a local Houston television station as well, Vanessa Richardson of KPRC.

Luhnow was looking for a way to get his side of the story out, and he tried to take down a lot of people along the way. Namely, he went after Koch-Weser, who had provided a substantial amount of the testimony to MLB suggesting that Luhnow knew about the Astros' cheating, although Koch-Weser was not the only one to do so.

The commissioner's office had decided not to punish the Astros' lower-level staffers, including Koch-Weser, at least in part because MLB didn't think the responsibility should lie with low-paid, low-ranking employees. MLB, instead, left a question of their punishment up to Crane and the Astros, who are not known to have subsequently disciplined anyone.

"These are kids essentially," a person with knowledge of the commissioner's thinking said. "They got the players on one side, they got the field manager, they got Captain Queeg up above [in Luhnow]. . . . Come on."

A more skeptical inference is that neither MLB nor the Astros wanted Koch-Weser or other staffers to be immediately cut loose and feel compelled to speak publicly about everything they knew.

Luhnow, though, went after Koch-Weser, went after Manfred, and went after his owner in a quest to exonerate himself.

"Getting fired for the first time in my life, I mean I've been working since I was sixteen years old, either working or going to school," Luhnow told KPRC. "So to get fired at this point in my career was a little bit stunning, but I never took vacation days so it was nice to have some time at home."

The irony was everywhere. Luhnow had fired so many people in Houston, some of whom felt stunned as well. But, to Luhnow, the usefulness of those people had expired. Why should his job be any different, when Crane and the commissioner's office no longer had use for him? Luhnow knew whom he was working for, and what Crane's MO was. He knew it might not end well, telling friends as much from the get-go. He saw Crane go through not one, but two team presidents in his time: George Postolos and Reid Ryan.

Luhnow's trips to Mexico at key moments in his tenure, including after the Roberto Osuna trade and at Brady Aiken's signing deadline, would also suggest Luhnow did, in fact, take vacation days. He also wasn't always the one to turn on the lights in his own office.

Regarding the PR failures after Brandon Taubman's outburst in 2019, Luhnow pointed the finger at Anita Sehgal and Giles Kibbe. "I don't write press releases," he told KPRC. "This particular response was crafted, edited, and written by the person that runs the legal operation for the Astros, and the person that runs the marketing and PR for the Astros. Those two wrote it, edited it, and sent it out. . . . And they botched this one big-time."

It was reasonable to place blame on Sehgal and Kibbe, but Luhnow acknowledged the statement had his and others' eyes on it. "Nobody said, 'Don't send this out.' I should've said that."

Luhnow also knew Taubman's behavior, what he was capable of.

Unsurprisingly, Luhnow's scorched-earth mission didn't sit well with folks inside the organization. Many people already hated him, but friends were also disheartened.

"I think he is very much in denial, and that's left me disappointed at times," a friend said. "He was like, 'Fuck these guys. They're fucking me, I'm going to fight 'em.' . . . All this shit."

That friend thought Luhnow would have been wisest to stay quiet and move on with his life. "Don't fuck with Jim [Crane] now; don't fuck with Rob Manfred now. Accept that you made mistakes and move on with that. But he's in denial, and he's angry. . . . There's just some people that see all this for what it is, which is a combination of successes and failures. And people that see things strictly on one side or the other, and I think Jeff sees that he's been horribly wronged by the world."

On sign-stealing, Luhnow's shrapnel touched people in the organization who were far removed from the heart of the operation.

"Think about for a second, all of the people who are with the organization that . . . no one questions why they didn't know," Luhnow told KPRC. "My special assistants, [Craig] Biggio, Enos Cabell, Reid Ryan, Jim Crane, all the marketing people, they're all around the clubhouse, they're all around the players. None of them knew. Why is it all on me?"

The answer would appear obvious: because he was the general manager. None of the people Luhnow named were centrally involved in the day-to-day of baseball operations. Naming the marketing team is comical.

Luhnow's attitude ruffled feathers inside the commissioner's office, too: How could the GM be so eager to take credit for everything that went right, and none of the blame for something that had gone wrong?

"Jim let Jeff run it," said Cabell. "Jeff became the man. He was almost untouchable until he became touchable. He ran it, and that's the way it was going to be. Jeff was never a people's person, sit there and have a conversation. . . . It got to where some people were afraid to tell the truth, and me, I've never been afraid to tell the truth, and I think that's where he got into trouble, not being able to communicate with his own people."

Ultimately, the question of whether Luhnow knew exactly how the

Astros had cheated, and when he learned of it, is almost irrelevant in evaluating his leadership and job performance.

"Whether he exactly knew what was going on or not is really beside the point," Manfred said in a radio interview. "I wrote to all the GMs [in 2017]. I put them on notice that it was their obligation to make sure that their organizations were not violating any of the sign-stealing rules.

"I think it's pretty clear from the facts that Mr. Luhnow failed to discharge that obligation. He damaged the game, and as a result, he was disciplined."

Even if one chooses to believe that Koch-Weser was lying to league investigators, or that Antonio Padilla and Matt Hogan misremembered that they had made no effort to hide their sign-decoding efforts in Luhnow's presence; even if one believes that Luhnow truly glossed over or missed the references to electronic sign-stealing in emails from Koch-Weser he responded to in 2017; even if one believes that Luhnow in 2018 never actually admitted to a colleague that by that point he knew the 2017 garbage-can scheme had been real, as reporting for this book revealed; and even if one believes Luhnow erased some of his phone for innocent reasons, a lack of knowledge is still both a terrible look and a dereliction of duty, particularly when framed around two questions: Why wouldn't he know, and why wouldn't mechanisms have been in place to both bring cheating to his attention and stop it?

The cheating is a poor reflection of the environment Luhnow fostered. Communication was "by far his biggest weakness," a member of the inner circle said. "Horrible. Tough to track down. Tough to maybe get a real reaction from. Send him a super long email, detailed. Lots of thoughts. 'Great stuff, thanks.' I get it, he's busy, whatever.

"There's no question he should have known. I don't know how relevant it is if he knew or not. More important thing is it happened on his watch."

In another organization, perhaps one where McKinsey & Company was not dropped into the clubhouse in the middle of the season, would the field manager have felt more comfortable coming to the general manager to discuss a growing problem?

The bottom line was emphasized at the expense of other concerns. It wasn't so much about what Luhnow and Crane focused on in Houston, but what they did not. What was never written on that blank piece of paper.

Luhnow, of course, generally disagrees.

"Everybody likes to boil things down to sound bites, or Twitter, or tweets. 'Luhnow's the mastermind,' 'Luhnow was behind this,' 'this is Luhnow's culture,'" Luhnow told KPRC. "It's not. It couldn't be further from the truth. And I have to let people know that."

Multiple Astros executives see it differently.

"I think that's wrong," one said. "I do think there is a cultural component, and I do think people also made choices that they knew or should have known was wrong. I think both things are true. I don't think that there was necessarily a culture of breaking the rules. I didn't see that there. I did see just this urgency to win, and whatever you did yesterday wasn't good enough, you had to do better tomorrow. And I think that was everywhere in the clubhouse, including in the clubhouse with the coaching staff. There was just like: we've always got to be finding an edge somewhere. And the edge we found yesterday isn't good enough, we've got to be finding a better one. And if the Yankees are doing some of this, we've got to figure out how to do it better. And that was definitely the culture.

"It's not good enough to be World Series–quality players, we've got to be doing something more. . . . I don't think it was ever a goal of the organization to say, we're going break rules, we're going to run over people."

What there was in Houston, the executive said, was pride in upsetting the establishment. The Astros front office didn't want to be true villains. But the message from the top was always to "try twenty percent harder than everybody else if we're going to keep up with things. And that that was more important than taking care of people, following the rules, etc. Taking care of people, and following the rules, being good citizens and all that was important, but when push came to shove, what was more important was being better."

In the wake of all that happened, a different Astros member of the inner circle said "everything needs to be questioned."

"Something went terribly wrong here for this to happen," they said. "There's no way that everyone in that clubhouse was comfortable with what was happening. Like, every staff member. There were people who were really concerned, right? How that didn't make its way to Taubman, Jeff, like, is kind of unfathomable to me. And I would like to think if that happened in other organizations, it would be brought to a senior person's attention very quickly, and it would then be brought to the president of baseball ops very quickly."

Opinions from top executives in Houston and with rival teams varied as to whether a general manager would, without question, always know of a cheating scheme. "To say you can completely know what's happening from A to Z? That's not true," one rival GM said.

Not everyone agrees.

"If we were doing something like that, I believe I would know," said another. "You know why? Because the people who are involved are helping us win games, which is what the general manager wants to do. And those people would go up and pat themselves on the back, to try to curry more favor, get promotions, make more money. There's just no fucking way that wouldn't happen. They weren't doing it in a selfless way. They were still doing it for their own selfish outcomes, and the only way for those selfish outcomes to be rewarded is to tell the general manager."

The industry was not surprised the Astros were the team that had crossed the line.

"It's kind of a logical extension of the pressure and the cultures that existed there," said one of Luhnow's Cardinals colleagues.

"There's no fucking way. If he didn't know, he put himself intentionally in a position to be able to say he didn't directly know. But he absolutely knew," suggested another rival GM. "Who are you fucking kidding? He absolutely knew. Look at their performance with runners in scoring position. That doesn't just fucking happen. The Red Sox and Astros, and the Yankees, again, standard deviations above the rest of the league. They had the best systems. And he knew that the front office was there to like provide competitive advantages to the players. . . . It was a whole pyramid scheme of who knew what, and Jeff knew everything and very few people knew much else."

Plenty of people were happy to see Luhnow go down, too.

"Part of it is Jeff just being so condescendingly dispassionate and sort of not willing to invest in people," a rival executive said. "He was just so fucking smug, thought he had all the answers, thought the answers rested in like basic business efficiency and value-engineering principles and not in, like, people who have given their lives to the game. And he was not just smug, but unworthy of any modicum of trust. He was very slimy from the get-go. So yeah, I couldn't fucking stand him. And some of it was competitive, he was obviously getting results, and not doing it in a way that I respected, so I had lots of reasons not to like him."

Luhnow was right that change is not easy. But he eliminated most any guardrails along the way. He had pressed forward in the face of pushback for so long, dating to his time in St. Louis as the maligned outsider. Eventually he was rewarded with the results he sought. But he didn't do enough to ensure the wrong boundary was never tested—not just in sign-stealing, but in, say, the trade for Roberto Osuna.

"You need humans to do that, right?" one Astros employee said. "I think you need wisdom in the room that's maybe seen something pushed, and has the ability to push back. And that wisdom was often kicked out of the organization. At all levels, whether it's coaches, scouts, front office, leadership in the senior leadership in the organization. It wasn't strictly about firing scouts, or firing coaches, or the manager. But you lost a lot of wisdom along the way."

Manfred did something extraordinary in his nine-page report: he skewered the culture Luhnow had built. The sitting commissioner publicly ripped the environment of one of the best-performing baseball teams in his sport.

"But while no one can dispute that Luhnow's baseball operations department is an industry leader in its analytics, it is very clear to me that the culture of the baseball operations department, manifesting itself in the way its employees are treated, its relations with other Clubs, and its relations with the media and external stakeholders, has been very problematic," Manfred wrote. "At least in my view, the baseball operations department's insular culture—one that valued and rewarded results over other considerations, combined with a staff of individuals who often lacked direction or sufficient oversight, led, at least in part, to the Brandon Taubman incident, the Club's admittedly inappropriate and inaccurate response to that incident, and finally, to an environment that allowed the conduct described in this report to have occurred."

A person with knowledge of the league's investigation called the Astros' culture "a disaster."

"People have a lot of kind of misimpressions about how that club was run," they said. "Everybody thinks it's just like this well-oiled kind of machine. When you look in, it looked like a disorganized mess."

One of Luhnow's close friends in Houston shared with him directly what they thought the fundamental error was.

"He would talk about how baseball was a zero-sum game, one team is winning and one team is losing," they said. But MLB is not actually a zero-sum business. There are thirty franchises in one business that make up Major League Baseball, with measures in place to keep all teams afloat.

"Good coaches and executives will go to other teams. Draft picks [help struggling teams], revenue sharing, there's unwritten rules," they said. "We're all living in this thing together. If you get out of that a little too far, it's ultimately not good for the enterprise for the whole. I don't think he and Jim appreciated the degree to which they really weren't running their own company."

# 19

# LOGISTICS

WHEN SPRING TRAINING BEGAN IN FEBRUARY 2020, THE ASTROS STILL hadn't come close to figuring out the right tack to take in public relations, even though Crane had brought on an outside crisis specialist.

The Astros held a press conference at their spring training home in Florida, where a couple of players were awkwardly trotted out for some opening remarks before a question-and-answer session with reporters. Crane said the Astros were sorry. Yet he had apparently done no wrong.

"No, I don't think I should be held accountable," Crane said in Florida. "I'm here to correct it. And I'm here to take this team forward."

Crane, at one point, said that sign-stealing "didn't impact the game." Pressed on that shortly afterward, he contradicted himself: "I didn't say it didn't impact the game."

The press conference was a disaster and only stirred more critiques. "He handled the post-article period of time worse than any crisis issue I've ever seen in my eighteen years in baseball," said former Marlins president David Samson. "And that's saying something, given that we've had some serious PR crises."

Although it didn't garner as much attention, Crane was also outwardly defiant toward one key portion of Commissioner Rob Manfred's report: the excoriation of the baseball ops culture.

On the day the report came out, Crane had also held a press conference, the one to announce Hinch and Luhnow's firing. The owner said in his opening statement that he accepted Manfred's findings. But apparently, that was a limited acceptance, because that same day, he said he disagreed with the assessment of the team's culture.

"I don't agree with that. I think we've got a lot of people here; we've got a lot of great people," Crane said. "We have over four hundred people working here, and they work hard, and I think there was some isolated situations that led to that. We have one of the best business operations in baseball. And you know, I think if we did have any problems, we'll quickly define those problems and move forward in a very positive way. I don't think there's anything difficult. We had one of the best baseball operations in the business and got a lot of great results."

He doubled down as 2020 proceeded.

"People say we had a culture problem," Crane told *USA Today*. "We didn't have a culture problem. They're isolated incidents that are unrelated."

In the summer of 2020, I spoke with Manfred for thirty-five minutes about his first five-plus years as a commissioner. In that conversation, he answered every question I asked but one: Had he found it troubling that Crane kept implying he got a piece of his investigation wrong?

Manfred's silence was not surprising. It was a reflection of what the job of commissioner has become, or has almost always been. Manfred is not an impartial arbitrator who does everything for the good of the game. He is a highly trained labor negotiator and the lead lawyer representing the interests of a group of thirty owners.

O

Wearing a Detroit Red Wings T-shirt in a video dated January 17, 2001, Mark Fierek said that he was told by his manager at Eagle Global Logistics that he should not advertise job openings in a Detroit newspaper.

"Mr. Horn said that if you do that, you know, then you're going to have basically every n****r in Detroit applying for those jobs, and you don't want to have that," Fierek said in deposition footage aired by ABC.

Jim Crane founded Eagle Global Logistics in 1984. In 1997, the company's in-house counsel, Judith Robertson, was fired, and shortly afterward, she filed discrimination charges with the Equal Employment Opportunity Commission. A lawyer for Eagle subsequently described Robertson as a "sad and unhappy" lawyer, according to a 1998 story by the *Houston Chronicle*'s L. M. Sixel, who led the reporting on the case.

Robertson later recanted most of her claims, but she wasn't alone. The EEOC alleged that Eagle, a company of more than two thousand employees, refused to hire Blacks, Hispanics, Asians, and women for various positions and maintained a hostile working environment for those groups.

"Eagle USA's workforce is primarily white and male, a profile that is known as 'The Program' inside the company, according to an affidavit by Rosa De La Cruz, senior investigator for the EEOC in Houston," Sixel reported in 1998. "The EEOC also alleged that Eagle USA has failed to properly investigate allegations of sexual harassment, failed to discipline wrongdoers, and failed to protect employees from sexual harassment, according to the commissioner's charge. Witnesses alleged that high-level managers of Eagle USA used corporate money to entertain male clients with female prostitutes and nude female dancers and wrote the expenses off as business expenses, according to the EEOC affidavit."

Crane and EGL denied everything, and the legal wrangling that followed took years and multiple jurisdictions, with a complicated play-by-play. The allegations, though, were serious and grim.

"Eagle's chief executive Jim Crane's 'Program' is to rarely hire African Americans and not hire women 'unless they are attractive,'" Jim Smith of the *Philadelphia Daily News* reported of a lawsuit filed in federal court in that city. "Another white woman, Kshanti Morris, 45, of Houston, was manager of the Human Resources Department. She alleges she was busted to secretary for refusing to implement discriminatory policies.

"The white male who replaced her 'was paid five times' her salary, the suit contends."

A plaintiff's lawyer, Reuben Guttman, told industry magazine *Traffic World* in 2000 that the EGL case was "one of the worst cases of discrimination I've ever seen." Crane, on the other hand, told the same publication, "We've done nothing wrong."

"If we treated our employees as they claim we have, we wouldn't have been this successful," Mike Slaughter, then Eagle's director of investor relations, told *Traffic World*. Slaughter joined the Astros as chief financial officer in 2015.

Eagle wanted the case to be heard in Houston rather than Philadelphia, and that's what wound up happening. Judge Lynn Hughes—who was later involved with both the CSN Houston debacle proceedings and Chris Correa's hacking case—sealed the original case in 1998 at the request of Eagle USA.

(Hughes has become a controversial figure himself because of how he has addressed matters of gender and race. In 2022, when plaintiffs in civil rights cases asked Hughes to recuse himself, the *Houston Chronicle* reported: "Hughes' past indiscretions include the time he attributed errors made by the government in a fraud case to a female federal official's sex, saying, 'We didn't let girls do it in the old days.' The 5th U.S. Circuit Court of Appeals reversed Hughes' ruling in that case in 2018. He was criticized by the appellate court in 2013 for his 'apparent failure to appreciate racist implications' in a case . . . involving an official who said that 'if Barack Obama were to be elected president, the Statue of Liberty would have its torch replaced by a piece of fried chicken.'")

When a $9 million settlement was reached in the Eagle case in 2001, Crane said, "While we continue to deny the EEOC's allegations, we feel that it is in the best interest of our Company and its future to resolve this matter at this time in a productive, forward-looking manner." Once claims were filed, about $6 million wound up returned to Eagle.

The discrimination suits weren't EGL's only high-profile trouble. The federal government brought war profiteering charges against the company—hiking up prices in Iraq illegally—which led to fines for the company and prison time for EGL employees.

How did someone with such a past wind up a Major League Baseball owner?

When Crane was attempting to buy the Astros, he met with MLB's ownership committee, chaired by Larry Dolan, Cleveland's owner, with Bill DeWitt Jr. of the Cardinals leading the questioning. Dolan was a former prosecutor and reprised that role. "They were really skeptical. They asked him a lot of tough questions," a witness said. "It was, I don't want to say touch-and-go, but it wasn't a foregone conclusion that he would be accepted. They really gave him a grilling."

A lot of the heavy lifting at baseball's owners' meetings, held quarterly, was done outside of the actual meetings themselves, over dinners. "During big ownership meetings, there are very few questions asked because that's not the forum that is appreciated by the commissioner's office," said Samson, the former Marlins president. "It's all done off the record. It's all done in small groups. And word circulated quickly around ownership meetings that there was trouble with votes for Jim because of how it may look."

Selig, an avuncular man who knew well how to wax poetic and lay on the saccharine, had often talked about baseball's position as a social institution. He was concerned with diversity, establishing Jackie Robinson Day in the sport, but an expression of public concern for diversity doesn't mean he always served that goal as he could or should have.

While the actual league investigation into Crane itself may have been thorough, the weight it was given was cursory to Samson. It was CYA: cover your ass. "If you can get the money and you can cobble the group together, the biggest price wins," he said.

Ultimately, what Selig and the owners had over Crane was leverage, reasonable grounds to try to hold up the sale—and a few incentives to do so. One was PR. They had a means to achieve something else they wanted, too: to switch the Astros from the National League, where they had always played, to the American League. That happened when Crane took over.

In November 2011, Selig's office sent out a formal letter to all thirty teams notifying them of the ownership transfer. The fourth section of the letter explained some of Crane's time at EGL, including the discrimination.

"Mr. Crane denied and continues to deny each of the findings made by the EEOC and has explained that EGL was a very high growth company, which put a strain on both capital and human resources, leading to a situation where not enough attention was paid to who was being hired and to keeping proper records," someone in the commissioner's office wrote.

The tune was the same on the war profiteering allegations.

"Mr. Crane was never accused of having any involvement in these matters and the background investigation did not reveal Mr. Crane had any personal knowledge of the filing of the false claims during the period in any question," read the letter, which is not attributed to any one individual.

Nine years later, in the very first paragraph of his nine-page report on the Astros sign-stealing in January 2020, Manfred went out of his way to say that his investigators found "absolutely no evidence that Jim Crane, the owner of the Astros, was aware of any of the conduct described in this report."

When Manfred took the Astros' culture under Luhnow to task later in the report, he again excused the owner: "Like many Clubs with very experienced individuals running their baseball operations departments, Astros owner Jim Crane and his senior executive team spent their energies focused on running the business side of the Club while delegating control and discretion on the baseball side to Luhnow. And it is difficult to question that division of responsibilities in light of the fact that Luhnow is widely considered to be one of the most successful baseball executives of his generation."

Three massive scandals—discrimination, war profiteering, and cheating—have, somehow, befallen Jim Crane's companies. Publicly, he appears to have taken personal responsibility for none, and MLB has condoned that stance at every turn.

Crane was sensitive to his own past, insomuch as he instructed his employees to do what they could to be sure he could avoid reliving it. "He didn't want to get sued again, and so he made a real request to us to hire," an Astros employee said. "We should try to hire Black people so that he won't get written up."

An employee also remembered a discussion about the competency of a Black employee at the organization in which Crane said, "We can't fire Black people."

○

The Astros' sign-stealing scandal dominated the talk of spring training 2020, in ways that perhaps no one saw coming. A congressman even suggested an oversight hearing. But the fervor was interrupted when COVID-19 arrived, shutting down every training camp. Eventually, a sixty-game season was played, with no fans allowed in the stands anywhere until a limited number were let in toward the end of the postseason, in October.

Without fannies in the seats, club revenues dropped severely around the league. The owners started cutting costs via furloughs and layoffs, despite soaring franchise values and revenues in all years prior—and despite the reasonable expectation the spigot would turn back on once the pandemic ended. By late October 2020, the Chicago Cubs, owned by the Ricketts family, had laid off more than one hundred people. The Orioles, owned by the Angelos family, let go of about fifty, and other teams acted similarly.

The layoffs affected business and baseball operations alike, but scouts found themselves on the chopping block ahead of most, including in Chicago.

"What the Cubs did, which was just ridiculously dramatic—they had not undergone that sort of scouting reconfiguration that Houston, I believe, was the first team to do kind of famously. Not that you have to do that or go that far," one GM said. "You're seeing a simultaneous thing of teams needing to reduce expenses, and also, there's this new world based on technology. They know the model's out there, they know other people are doing it. It's not that much worse, and it's arguably maybe better in some ways and so like, let's do that now."

Even before the pandemic, some teams had started to follow the Astros' model, to reach the conclusion the Astros did during the 2017 season: Why are we spending so much to send scouts on the road when video and data capture methods can be more reliable and comprehensive? The Milwaukee Brewers, run by David Stearns, had already largely pivoted to video prior to the pandemic. So, too, had Elias's Orioles, and the Cubs were now doing the same.

Owners were ripping off the Band-Aid across departments. Whether the owners, predominantly billionaires, truly needed to make cuts lies in the eye of the beholder. But the incentive, or the cover, to do so came with the dip in income during COVID-19. Teams were no longer interested in carrying skill sets that could be deemed excess, and now they had an entrée to rock the boat in ways they otherwise might have tried to avoid.

Luhnow and Taubman were, in many ways, correct about where the industry would go. The same push for efficiency that owners and GMs had applied to the evaluations of players in the Moneyball era almost twenty years earlier was now taking hold across every part of team operations, not just player decisions.

"I think twenty years ago, there probably was a little bit more of: 'That guy can't hit anymore, but he's a good dude, and he got a big hit for us in the playoffs last year, let's sign him up again,'" a GM said. "And then that went totally out the window in the last eight years, ten years, and then the competition has now shifted in other areas, and there's a year-to-year vibe with baseball, and everyone signs these one-year contracts, basically.

"It's capitalism, but the worst teams don't go out of business. Right?" the GM continued. "Like the Yankees have not bought the Orioles yet. Like, it's not going to happen. So there's a certain amount of handholding that needs to go on that has kind of softened the edges over the years, but I think the technology shift has been so funda-mental that if your skills—it used to be like if you were a bad pitching coach, how much worse would you typically be than the next guy? Ten percent worse? Twenty percent worse? But you can be like one hun-dred percent worse if you just don't use TrackMan as a pitching coach. You're just destroying value. So people need to swap all those guys out now. It just has to happen. I think that's why this has been so frenetic. Because the technology just changed everything.

"If you're always hanging on to everybody because they've been there forever, you get a mess on your hands eventually, and then some-body comes in and cleans up the mess."

Not all executives in the sport seemed quite as comfortable with that fatalism, however.

"The closer I get to the world of the thirty owners, many of them are among the worst people in the world," one said. "You'll never go broke betting on their desire to act in pure self-interest, with pure shortsightedness, to protect their power, their wealth at the expense of the good of others in the industry."

In a loaded comparison, one Astros executive invoked Amazon.

"One of the interesting data points is to see what the rest of the industry has done," they said. "Amazon has done the same thing, but they've handled the change management piece a lot better, where they've eliminated jobs in favor of better technology, more efficient and more cost-effective technology, and a lot of people hated Amazon for that. But they have a good product at an effective price and that makes them a great company, to their shareholders at least."

Houston wasn't the only team moving in this general direction. Were the Astros indeed ahead of everyone else? Or were they just the loudest in broadcasting or boasting about their methods?

"Sport science, Dodgers were doing more on that front. I think the Yankees were," one Astros executive said. "I think that we were ahead in player development. I think the evidence for that is there were a few years where our minor league win percentage and strikeout rates were just blasting people out of the water. And the other evidence for that is, other teams were trying to hire from us, certainly wanted to look under the hood. I think we were loud about it, and were certainly in the top five of everything, but it would be foolish to think that it was smarter. Who can do everything optimally? We were erring very hard into dynamism, and it was erring into radicalism."

○

In 2021, MLB began cracking down on another form of cheating, one that was more out in the open than electronic sign-stealing and had proliferated to the point that it was negatively impacting the entertainment value of the sport. Pitchers have always wanted to put foreign substances on the ball, because better grip could enhance both a pitch's accuracy and movement. Although it was technically outlawed, umpires and the league had always allowed some usage of foreign substances except for the most obvious and blatant. A pitcher couldn't have pine tar slathered dramatically across his arm, for example.

By 2021, pitchers were taking the practice to new extremes, greatly and artificially increasing the spin rate on their pitches. More spin means more effectiveness, which means more strikeouts, which means less action on the field, because fewer hitters make contact. And less action usually means less entertainment. The fun of baseball is usually when a ball is put in play, when a hitter succeeds, or perhaps is robbed by a fielder making an astounding catch while running at full speed. All of that happens less when pitchers are engineering their pitches with sticky substances.

The Astros, based on multiple firsthand accounts, were using sticky stuff as much as any team. Pitching coach Brent Strom, who has since left the organization, made no bones about asking new pitchers if they were using foreign substances.

"Strommy, he would like, in spring training, he'll meet a young guy, a pitcher, 'Hey, how are you doing, where you from?'" one member of the Astros recalled. "'Oh good, oh hey, I want to ask you, are you familiar with sticky stuff?'"

Craig Bjornson, the bullpen coach through 2017, was said to be involved as well.

"CB, he had like five, six different things: pine tar, sunblock . . . a light cream, a mid-light cream, a hard one," a member of the team said.

Said Strom via email: "I plead the fifth, as does every other pitching coach in baseball. Nothing to be gained by even talking about it. Over [and] done with . . . game moves on."

Justin Verlander and Gerrit Cole, multiple members of the Astros with firsthand knowledge said, were prime users of sticky stuff. The fact that Astros players were using sticky stuff was a reason that one member of the team suggested he felt he had to stay quiet about what he believed other teams were up to with electronic sign-stealing. Cheating, his point was, was everywhere. No one's hands were clean, literally and figuratively.

"It's cheating, but they fucking engineered their own shit, and it worked incredibly well," one GM said of the Astros. "I mean like Justin Verlander was on the downside [of his career], he fucking was. Until he went there. And then as players left the Astros is when it started to proliferate around the league."

Verlander and Cole were among players named in court proceedings by Bubba Harkins, a clubhouse attendant whom the Angels fired over providing players substances.

"Hey Bubba, it's Gerrit Cole. I was wondering if you could help me out with this sticky situation," the pitcher wrote in a text message that was part of the court file, adding a wink emoji. "We don't see you until May, but we have some road games in April that are in cold-weather places. The stuff I had last year seizes up when it gets cold."

In 2021, Cole, who had signed with the New York Yankees after the 2019 season for $324 million, was asked directly in a press conference whether he had used a foreign substance.

"I don't quite know how to answer that, to be honest," he said after stumbling to find words. "There are customs and practices that have been passed down from older players to younger players, from the last generation of players to this generation of players, and I think there are some things that are certainly out of bounds in that regard. I've stood pretty firm in terms of that, in terms of the communication between our peers and whatnot. This is important to a lot of people who love the game, including the players in this room, including fans, including teams, so if MLB wants to legislate some more stuff, that's a conversation that we can have. Because ultimately we should all be pulling in the same direction on this."

Were the Astros doing more than other teams?

"Probably yes, more advanced, because it was part of a pitching culture. It was just, like, known," one Astros employee said. "I've heard a thousand conversations with Strommy, CB [Bjornson], and the guys where they're joking around. They have some concoction. Whether it was actually superior to the tack used by other clubs, I have no fucking idea. I just know that like Strommy had some crazy concoction of stuff.

"That is not a front-office project. No one as far as I know ever tested the efficacy of chemical composition of tack. That'd be a pretty cool project, though."

When MLB started to crack down, the Astros got rid of what some referred to as "cheat bags," even in the minor leagues as well. "When all that shit went down, all the cheat bags disappeared," an Astros employee said.

In general, pitchers applied sticky stuff to their hands once on the mound. A pitcher would put the substance somewhere on his body, perhaps the hat, glove, or belt, and would reach for it before a pitch. MLB, in 2021, started to have umpires regularly check pitchers for such substances, asking them to show their belt or cap or glove.

But baseballs are not distributed to the field of play straight out of a box. Clubhouse staff always put some mud on them to achieve the appropriate texture, as they are supposed to do. Over time, some teams developed different habits than others, and MLB at one point, around 2017–18, studied how teams muddied the balls prior to them entering the field of play, multiple people with knowledge of the study said.

"This guy at MLB, his people did this study that was basically looking at how muddied up the balls up are by team," an Astros employee said. "And apparently Houston muddied their balls the least. Which is better for hitters, and worse for pitchers, all else equal. And that ended up being an issue because what the league discovered is that we were the most extreme with not rubbing up the ball, or keeping them the cleanest, the whitest.

"The Dodgers I believe were on the other extreme side of the spectrum where they like muddied up the balls the most. And one of the other things that they learned is that the Astros loved scuff balls. Like Strommy would always have players scuff up their balls or use scuff balls. That's like a pine-tar thing. I remember CB had some crazy concoction. . . . Everyone is greasing. But Strommy and CB were most into that stuff."

MLB was interested in standardizing the rub color and sent out a poster to all thirty clubhouses. A person with knowledge of the league's effort said that there were times, particularly before postseason games, where teams were asked to add or reduce the mud on the balls.

The league has also attempted to tighten up the custody of the baseballs from storage to umpire, as well. Another theory cropped up about Astros wrongdoing that remains a case of finger-pointing. That, at home games, the Astros would try to time the release of baseballs to the umpire, such that their pitchers would receive more favorable baseballs. Ball boys bring the baseballs to the umpire, and ball boys are typically clubhouse employees of the home team.

"They were using different balls at home. He [Bjornson] would rub up the balls with this special like stick, to where it was enough to where it helped guys when they added the other stuff on their hands to that concoction," a major league player said, relaying a conversation they said they had with Bjornson. "That made it really sticky and so then he said they had two separate bags. So when the Astros' pitchers were on the mound, every time the umpire needed new balls, they would pull it from this bag. But they would only pull two or three at a time. Hopefully, by the time that the opposing team goes out, there might be only one or two in the bag, so they wouldn't notice that big of a difference."

Multiple rival teams had heard this theory or a variant, and the Dodgers in particular had a suspicion of it.

The distribution scheme is still only an allegation. What is known, via firsthand accounts, is that at least some pitchers in Houston were, once on the mound, using foreign substances.

Unlike sign-stealing, however, there is good reason to believe that over time, pitchers truly everywhere were doing the same thing, to varying degrees.

"Well, the sticky stuff got everywhere," one GM said. "It was sort of carried everywhere by players. The sign-stealing I thought was Houston, Boston, New York. I didn't see that anywhere else. Milwaukee, we thought they had a scoreboard system [where some activity on the scoreboard indicated to hitters what pitch was coming]."

How much of the Astros' pitching success should go to foreign substances is, naturally, hard to determine.

"Definitely improving spin rate," a rival GM said of what they were most jealous of about the Astros. "But naively I thought they were doing something different than, like, crazy foreign substances.

"That was the thing that caught our eye the most and was the thing that we dove in on the most."

Another GM echoed the same thing. "I've had players tell me, their entire pitching model, was based on, get a new pitcher, give 'em the shit. And you know they laugh, it wasn't like, hey, we had a front office, or Brent Strom presentation, where I was misutilizing my [pitches], and change grips and change my pitch mix. No, it was: Brent Strom would come in, my first side [session] there, bring out a can of the shit, rub it on my fingers and show me how much better it made my stuff. That was it."

An Astros executive, while acknowledging the team's use of sticky stuff, disagreed as to its impact.

"Everything is about the cheating stuff and how else the Astros might have cheated, but I would offer a completely different theory on it, which is that we were religious about teaching pitchers proper finger and wrist positioning and release," the executive said. "We had done all this work in the field where we would correlate the spin rate on TrackMan to the finger and wrist positioning at release from video took during bullpens. So basically what I'm saying is, we worked with pitchers, and asked them to change your grip. 'Do this, oh, look at this video, do you see how right at the moment of release, your thumb is imparting a little bit of side spin on the ball that's reducing the overall spin rate.' We had that feedback loop religiously with the players.

"TrackMan will show that we have been able to help pitchers improve how much they can make the ball move, and people very quickly assume, 'Oh, that's because of the tack that they're using.' But you look at that and all throughout our organization and then also what's interesting, when our pitchers leave our organization to go to others—the increased break that they added at the Astros, they take with them when they go to other teams. So all of that is suggestive that it's actually like credible player development. We made pitchers better. And not that we're using tack. And that's where the suspicion came from that we were like messing with TrackMan data. I don't really know. I never understood that one, that we were polluting the TrackMan data that the rest of the league was getting or something.

"But I thought it was like, OK, it's probably part the tack, maybe like fifteen percent that if I had to guess, and it's like eighty-five percent what we're teaching our players to be better versions of themselves."

The early returns in 2021, when MLB started to crack down around the league, were positive. Numbers compiled by one team showed that the Dodgers' pitchers, by far, had the highest spin rate at the time the crackdown began, as well as the largest subsequent drop, suggesting their pitchers had been the heaviest users.

"They're like eight standard deviations above everyone else before enforcement, and still higher than anybody else," one executive said of the 2021 Dodgers. "So like, yeah I think that's a shame, right? We all have like psychotic levels of competitive drive, but there are limits. And there are things that you don't do and lines you don't cross, and it's probably not a coincidence that when the Wall Street, McKinsey guys got involved, those lines were like blown past. They've always been danced over, there's always been, from the '51 Giants, to myriad historical examples, but it's not institutionalized."

In 2022, spin rates climbed again. Wrote The Athletic's Eno Sarris: "It looks like pitchers have found something clear and wipeable that gives them more of a boost than sunscreen and rosin, because spin rate is back up in baseball. Almost back to where it was before enforcement started." That year, MLB was newly testing its own sticky substances in the minor leagues, including one developed by Dow Chemical, with the intent of finding something that enhanced grip, but not so much so that it significantly improved performance. The experiment was a disaster.

# EPILOGUE

CARLOS BELTRÁN STAYED OUT OF THE PUBLIC EYE UNTIL EARLY 2022, when he was hired by the Yankees' television network, YES, as an analyst. He gave an interview to that same station in the spring in which he admitted the 2017 Astros were wrong, and had crossed the line.

Beltrán resurfaced just as he was nearing eligibility for the Baseball Hall of Fame. He suggested that players would have stopped had they been asked to stop—yet, that it didn't make sense for players to stop cheating on their own.

"A lot of people always ask me why you didn't stop it," Beltrán told interviewer and coworker Michael Kay. "And my answer is, I didn't stop it the same way no one stopped it. This is working for us. Why you gonna stop something that is working for you? So, if the organization would've said something to us, we would've stopped it for sure."

Added Beltrán: "I wish I would've asked more questions about what we were doing." Beltrán was as powerful a clubhouse presence as there was on the 2017 Astros, begging the question, what was stopping him from asking those questions?

A.J. Hinch and Alex Cora both quickly found work once their suspensions ended following the 2020 season, Hinch as manager of the Detroit Tigers, and Cora once again as manager of the Boston Red Sox.

Both managers have continued to publicly acknowledge their role in the Astros' scandal, although neither has provided detailed, public explanations of exactly what happened behind the scenes, and why they felt it happened. It's likely that the finger-pointing nature of any such discussion makes it difficult to go down that road while they still hope to work in baseball.

Hinch has long been remorseful, both in conversation with the commissioner's office and publicly. "I wish I would have done more," Hinch told MLB Network in 2020. "Right is right and wrong is wrong, and we were wrong."

Hinch was asked whether the championship was tainted.

"I understand the question. It's a fair question. People are going to have to draw their own conclusions. Unfortunately, we opened that door as a group. And that question . . . we may never know. We're going to have to live and move forward and be better in the sport. But unfortunately, no one can really answer that question. I can't pinpoint what advantages or what happened or what exactly would have happened otherwise. But we did it to ourselves."

Not everyone in the sport was happy that Hinch and Cora received coveted opportunities to manage again so quickly when other candidates hadn't been part of a major scandal. Yet, at the same time, the duo also remain regarded as two of the most talented managers in the game.

The second electronic sign-stealing investigation MLB undertook, into Cora's Red Sox, produced a much tamer response than Houston's.

Although the Red Sox had promised in 2017 that they would stop their sign-stealing behavior following the Apple Watch scandal, they had again used the baserunner scheme the very next year. MLB found that during the regular season in 2018, a year the Red Sox won the World Series, J. T. Watkins, a member of their advance staff, had decoded signs in-game using video as part of a baserunner system.

Ken Rosenthal and I reported that the Red Sox were able to occasionally do so in 2019 as well, because the security personnel assigned to watch the video rooms were young Red Sox fans who could be lenient.

MLB did not formally come to that conclusion, even though Manfred wrote that "four witnesses said that Watkins used gestures or notes to communicate to them sign sequence information when a Video Room Monitor was present in the replay room, which led them to believe that he was engaged in prohibited conduct because he was attempting to conceal his communications." As a member of the Red Sox put it: "The dude [the monitor] was always sitting on the chair on his damn phone anyways and he wasn't there all the time. He'd get up and move around, it's really not that hard." The Sox also effectively had two video rooms.

On one hand, the Red Sox did not seem to deserve to be punished to the same scale the Astros did. Only Watkins, who denied all wrongdoing, was suspended. The Red Sox lost one draft pick, compared to the Astros' four, and the Red Sox were not fined. But the way the league framed its findings and punishments was a flip-flop. Even though MLB had said it would hold field managers and GMs accountable for sign-stealing, a point Manfred harped on with the Astros, MLB positioned Watkins as a rogue employee. MLB said that the Red Sox, unlike the Astros, had taken many steps to ensure compliance.

"I do not find that Cora or any member of the Red Sox staff either knew or should have known that Watkins was utilizing in-game video to update the information that he had learned from his pregame analysis," Manfred wrote in his report about the Red Sox in April 2020.

Yet, Manfred also wrote "that Cora did not effectively communicate to Red Sox players the sign-stealing rules that were in place for the 2018 season."

Cora, like Hinch, Luhnow, and Taubman, was suspended for the 2020 season—not on the basis of what the 2018 Red Sox had done, but exclusively for his role in the Astros cheating in 2017.

All around, MLB's findings in Boston appeared convenient. Just one employee had done something wrong? Cora, and the rest of the Red Sox, have done little to address their collective willingness to allow a lower-level staffer to take all the blame for their 2018 cheating. Typically, strong leadership is not associated with allowing a junior member of the staff to be suspended for a season for actions that benefited many others, including the manager himself.

Watkins, who remained with the Red Sox as a scout, was said to have some money come his way, even though he was supposed to be on an unpaid suspension. On a phone call with Red Sox staff and players, "One player spoke up and was like, 'Guys, we gotta take care of J.T. financially,'" a person with knowledge of the call said. "'We know what he did for us, so it's on us to take care of him.'

"He made more money than ever that year with the players helping him out."

The episode also left lingering division between members of the 2018 Red Sox. During the investigation, the commissioner's office was said to have told Watkins which players told investigators he was guilty.

"There's still some guys in this league that are hated by other Red Sox people," a Sox source said. "It created some problems in the clubhouse. Because J.T. fucking confronted people about it."

Astros outfielder George Springer became a free agent after the 2020 season, at a time when the market was shaky because of the pandemic. He would have hit free agency a year earlier—and a year younger—had the Astros promoted him to the majors in 2013, or to begin the 2014 season. The Toronto Blue Jays signed him for six years and $150 million.

Starting pitcher Dallas Keuchel left Houston after the 2018 season, never able to work out a long-term extension with the team as he wanted. When he returned to Houston in 2021 as a member of the Chicago White Sox, Keuchel made a reference to Jeff Luhnow.

"Luhnow's not there anymore, so I don't have anybody to dislike," Keuchel told reporters prior to arrival in Houston. "We never got along, no bones about it."

"There was no communication. I said that in '17, when I made my thoughts known about the trade deadline. And that's pretty much it," Keuchel told reporters once back in Houston. "When there's no communication . . . no personal relationship in the slightest, that rubbed me the wrong way.

"I played this game very hard and just wanted a little bit of respect, and I don't think that was given for a lot of the guys. So I spoke up, and I'm still speaking up."

In 2022, Crane extended one of the Astros' best young players, Yordan Alvarez—whom Luhnow had acquired in a shrewd trade with the Dodgers—on a team-friendly deal, for six years and $115 million.

Top pick Mark Appel retired without making the major leagues, but eventually he got the itch to play again. He made his big-league debut in 2022 with the Phillies, nine years after he signed with the Astros.

Alex Jacobs and Aaron Tassano, the former Astros pro scouts who had roamed back fields in Florida and Arizona respectively, were no longer working full-time in Major League Baseball at the time of publication. Jacobs moved on to the Diamondbacks and then to a job outside baseball, holding a part-time scouting role with the Phillies on the side. Tassano is with a Korean team, the Samsung Lions.

When Jacobs meets people and tells them he worked for the Astros, "Oh, of course, they laugh: 'Oh you're a cheater,'" he said. "And then I just show 'em a ring. Do I look at that ring any differently? I'm proud of that ring. Because I know I didn't do anything wrong."

Jacobs saw many flaws in the Astros' culture, but he didn't think everything was off. He decided to get an MBA, and he made a point of telling Luhnow over the phone that Luhnow was the reason he was doing so.

"He's an alpha, in a way," Jacobs said. "He's an extremely brilliant person who did things that I would have done differently, especially knowing some of the business school terms that he used.

"Value of human equity. That's number one. Culture. Creating a culture, and it's funny, in one of my classes, which is about the same thing—everything is like, 'If you win, you're going to have a great culture.' I'm like, 'Woah woah woah, just one second, I worked for a team that just won a World Series, and the culture was absolute shit.' And no one believed me."

Chris Correa was released from federal prison on December 31, 2018, the forty-six-month sentence he received for hacking into the Astros reduced. He spent close to three years working for the Bail Project, which has a mission to end cash bail and combat mass incarceration, before moving on to other opportunities in criminal legal reform and civic data.

Mike Fast hooked on with the Atlanta Braves after he left the Astros. "It's not by accident that the Braves are the second-biggest investor in Edgertronics after the Astros," one of his former Astros colleagues said. Colin Wyers eventually made his way to Atlanta as well. The Braves won the 2021 World Series over the Astros, clinching the title at Minute Maid Park.

Kevin Goldstein was let go by the Astros in 2020, amid all the layoffs across the sport during the pandemic.

"I think this industry as a whole treats people like shit," Goldstein said. "I think the Astros were especially good at it at times. It's not like they're sole proprietors or anything like that."

Goldstein returned to the media world at FanGraphs before joining the Minnesota Twins' front office for the 2022 season.

Running the Orioles, Mike Elias and Sig Mejdal embarked on a massive tanking project with parallels to the Astros: a low payroll and terrible baseball for years. The team finally showed signs of life in 2022.

Brandon Taubman sought counseling and volunteered at the Houston-based organization Aid to Victims of Domestic Abuse, or AVDA, and found work with a real estate investment company. He became thankful that he finally saw how skewed his priorities had become. He also tried to make amends in the sport, including with the reporter whom he yelled at the night the Astros won the 2019 American League Championship Series. They coincidentally wound up in a yoga class together, went out for coffee, and have stayed in touch. MLB has technically reinstated Taubman, allowing him to work for a team again, if an opportunity arises. He's kept a toe in the sport, helping third-party companies with player valuations and projections.

With his bridges burned, Jeff Luhnow remains out of baseball. His lawsuit against Crane was settled, presumably for an undisclosed sum of money. (Of all the things that make a return to baseball unlikely for Luhnow, suing an owner might be the leading item.) In 2020, he advised former player Alex Rodriguez—a controversial figure himself because of performance-enhancing drug use—when Rodriguez was interested in buying the New York Mets. Many opportunists that year rushed into a craze around SPACs, or special-purpose acquisition companies. For Luhnow, then, it would be another fast follow. He cofounded a company in early 2021 called SportsTek, which sought a

$125 million initial public offering. SPACs raised a record $78 billion on US exchanges in 2020, according to Bloomberg. In 2022, Luhnow became part owner of a pair of soccer teams, one in Mexico, Cancún F.C., and another in Spain, C.D. Leganés.

Commissioner Rob Manfred made bold changes for 2023: he banned the defensive shift and instituted a pitch clock. The rise of analytics, and outgrowths such as the defensive shift, had affected game play, and to many, made for a lesser product: the rise in home runs and strikeouts, and less overall action.

"Optimizations come at a cost," one GM in the sport said. "I think the real tragedy for the game started when these analytical optimizations started to push their way onto the field. To me there's a big difference in letting it dictate your draft behavior, or how you allocate your payroll. . . . But the fans have suffered and the game has suffered when this shit started creeping directly onto the field. Whether it was sticky stuff, or sign-stealing, or just three true outcomes [strikeouts, walks, and home runs], and just everything else that we're trying to fucking clean up right now."

As for tanking, and service-time manipulation? Those issues were front and center when baseball's players and owners confronted one another in the sport's first work stoppage in more than a quarter century.

"I think MLB has benefited a lot from the sort of Wall Street–ization and McKinseyization of front offices and of player personnel decision-making," the GM said. "But it's also cost them in certain ways. But a lot of it, they like, for sure."

In December 2021, the owners locked out the players. Regular-season games were on the brink of being missed when the sides reached a deal in March 2022 that maintained a full 162-game season, albeit one that pushed back Opening Day.

Behaviors of teams like the Astros were at the heart of the fight. The new deal included incentives for teams to promote young players straightaway, without playing service-time games to hold them down, à la Springer. The new CBA also instituted a draft lottery to help disincentivize tanking, as the worst record would no longer promise the best pick in the draft. But that measure didn't stop the Oakland

A's from selling off every decent player they had right as the lockout ended, nor was it, frankly, expected to, when tanking is so much a cost-saving measure for owners.

The labor issues didn't disappear when the lockout ended. Fed up with poor pay, minor league baseball players formed a union in 2022, under the umbrella of the Major League Baseball Players Association. MLB also settled a class-action lawsuit minor leaguers brought over wage-law violations for $185 million.

Manfred after the Astros scandal put in stricter rules for electronic sign-stealing, although players and staff are still allowed to watch the games on TV on a delay—a right Manfred returned to players in 2020 after briefly removing it. In 2022, for the first time, players had the choice to use a headset system that would allow a catcher to call pitches electronically, without giving a traditional hand sign. Catchers told pitchers what to throw by pushing a button on a device they wore on their wrist.

In another technological pursuit, MLB is looking into an automated strike zone, to have balls and strikes called with at least the help of electronics. "If you think for one minute that there's not going to be some funny business with the strike zone, some hacking, like, you're crazy," one major league manager said. The same fear, even if extreme, applies to the new pitch-calling system.

Manfred and the owners in 2020 permitted the sale of the Mets to billionaire Steve Cohen, who had once tried to buy the Dodgers, and whose company, SAC Capital Advisors, was ordered to pay $1.8 billion for insider trading—the largest insider trading penalty in history. Employees went to prison, but Cohen was not charged. Cohen stands as the richest owner in the sport.

Jim Crane remains owner of the Astros. To replace Luhnow, he hired a general manager with an R&D background, James Click, away from the small-market Tampa Bay Rays. The Rays are the franchise that executive Andrew Friedman, whom Crane targeted before hiring Luhnow, first made famous for building cheap, successful teams.

Under veteran field manager Dusty Baker, the Astros remained a powerhouse on the field. In 2022, they won their second World Series title, in six games over the upstart Phillies. Only five players from the

2017 team remained. When fan-favorite Carlos Correa became a free agent the prior offseason, Crane let him walk. A talented, younger, and cheaper shortstop, Jeremy Peña, awaited in the minors. He was named MVP of the '22 World Series.

Despite the success, Crane and Click that season clashed over "disagreements about the size of the baseball operations staff and concern from Click about other voices in the organization influencing the owner," Ken Rosenthal reported. In a development that would have been stunning had it involved any other baseball franchise, Click left the Astros six days after the '22 World Series ended. He reportedly declined a one-year offer from Crane to return. Many in the industry felt the contract was an insult, not only because the Astros had gone to the World Series for two straight years and won a title, but because Click had steadied the ship after arriving in the wake of the scandal. Earlier in the year, Forbes estimated the Astros were worth $1.98 billion, about triple what Crane paid a decade earlier for the team and its share of the TV network.

Jay Edmiston, whom they used to call the Mayor of Kissimmee, helped the Astros move the team's spring training complex from Kissimmee to West Palm Beach. The transition over, he was cut loose in September 2019, just a few months before Luhnow would be fired. Luhnow, still GM at the time, did not fire Edmiston himself, but had an underling deliver the message.

"I did everything they asked and got let go because of it," Edmiston said. "I want people to know how it used to be. How good it was. When I met my wife, I told her, I said, 'You have no idea how unbelievable my job is.' And then after Jeff took over it's like, 'I don't like this anymore. They don't do the right things. They don't take care of their people.'"

After thirty-four years with the Astros, Edmiston was making $80,000. Today, he sells Ford cars and trucks in Florida.

# ACKNOWLEDGMENTS

THE DAY THAT KEN ROSENTHAL AND I BROKE THE ASTROS STORY, WE WERE coincidentally on site together at baseball's annual general managers' meetings in Arizona. Off to the side, I told him I thought we probably would never have a bigger story in our lives. He wasn't sure of that at first, but it didn't take long for him to come around.

Besides his skill as a reporter, Ken is a fount of perpetual energy and kindness. His motor is unlike any other I've seen, and yet he still finds time to guide so many at The Athletic and across the industry. I'm forever indebted to him—for his encouragement to join The Athletic in the first place, for our eventual collaboration on the Astros' investigation, and for all the talks we've had about everything other than the story du jour. Although he couldn't take on this project with me, Ken is present throughout these pages.

Harper editor Eric Nelson showed great patience in a long process. Like all great relationships, ours started when he slid into my DMs on Twitter. He suggested there could be a book in my reporting on the Astros, and after way too long a wait, it seems he was right about at least that one thing. Harper's Beth Silfin and James Neidhardt guided me as well.

David Black, who runs an eponymous literary agency, kept me on track and steady when that seemed impossible.

As a book can destroy both one's time and sanity, and as those are key components to being a good employee, I owe a special thank-you to the management team at The Athletic, including David Perpich, Adam Hansmann, Alex Mather, Paul Fichtenbaum, Sarah Goldstein, and Lauren Comitor. Maury Gostfrand of The Montag Group helped navigate everything.

The original story had the fingerprints of many at The Athletic, including the excellent editors Emma Span, George Dohrmann, Claire Noland, and Kaci Borowski.

Many people spent time answering my questions during the reporting process, both once the book was underway and in the many years beforehand. I'm grateful for everyone who spoke with me: your experiences and thoughts made this project. Vince Lee, archivist at the University of Houston, assisted with research. Newspapers.com was a particularly valuable resource.

The *Houston Chronicle*—both the work of others at the paper and my own time there—played a central role. David Barron and L.M. Sixel produced key reporting, as did former Astros beat writer Zachary Levine. Reid Laymance and Nick Mathews were marvelous editors in my time in Houston, the same for Nancy Barnes and Vernon Loeb. Jose de Jesus Ortiz was a terrific beat partner. Thanks to Randy Harvey, Greg Rajan, Matt Young, and Steve Schaeffer as well. There isn't a better sports photographer in the world than Karen Warren.

The first allegation of the Astros misusing a garbage can was reported by Jeff Passan, now of ESPN, and long a friend. He was on to something, and, superstar that he is, I'm glad he left some scraps for me, if just this one time.

A collection of friends in the industry were supportive throughout this process. The non-exhaustive list includes Nicole Auerbach, Dan Barbarisi, Rob Bradford, Maury Brown, Ian and Amy Browne, Marc Carig, Sarah Cordeiro, Chris Cotillo, Jared Diamond, Rustin Dodd, Mark Feinsand, Steve Hewitt, Emily Kaplan, Laura Keeley, Casey Keen, Hannah Keyser, Jason Mastrodonato, Jen McCaffrey, Tania Ganguli, Kristie Rieken, Chandler Rome, Brian Rosenthal, Michael Silverman, Chris Smith, Alex Speier, Lauren Spencer, John Tomase, and James Wagner. Tim Britton, Saheli Sadanand, Jake Kaplan, Andy

McCullough, Chris Mason, Meghan Ottolini, and Heather Sullivan were particularly tolerant of my antics.

I wish I could share this book with Nick Cafardo and Art Martone, both kind and thoughtful New England sports media fixtures gone too soon.

When I agreed to this project, the pandemic was just beginning. "You'll have plenty of time at home to report and write!" folks kept telling me. In the end, it was immensely difficult working on the book with few avenues for distraction or separation. Alex Coffey's encouragement was a bright light amidst the chaos.

For many years, I've had the benefit of a supportive circle. A heartfelt thank-you to Vlad Alexandre and Tiffany Marie Corpuz, Rose Lazarre, Sofia Barbaresco, Nicoletta and Maria Bumbac, Jeannie Fischman, Jason Geiseinheimer and Amanda Manfredo, Dan and Marlaina Wing Hunter, Susan and Jeffrey Hunter, Drs. Jonah Mandell and Sara Soshnick, Alan Mandell and Vicky Shick, Josh Mirsky, and Tim Yeo.

My family is small but formidable. My love to Dave, Hal and Elizabeth Drellich, Deborah Berry and Susan Mayer, Ali Thom, James and Phil Maslow, Curry Glassell, and Dave, Emma, and Rebecca Piscia.

Lindsey and Fisher Adler provided unrelenting kindness, the best cheering section one could have. To my mother, Linda Ekstrand, my grandmother Mary Ekstrand, and my father, Steve Drellich, thank you for everything, and I love you.

Last but not least, the music of the Killers was the soundtrack of this book.

# INDEX

# ABOUT THE AUTHOR

EVAN DRELLICH, a senior writer for The Athletic, broke the story of the Houston Astros' cheating scandal. He covered the franchise for the *Houston Chronicle* from 2013 to 2016. He now lives in Queens.